The Management of Tourism

BY PROFESSOR S. MEDLIK

Published by Pitman:
The British Hotel and Catering Industry

Published by Heinemann:
A Manual of Hotel Reception (with J. R. S. Beavis)
Profile of the Hotel and Catering Industry
The Business of Hotels

BY A. J. BURKART AND PROFESSOR S. MEDLIK

Tourism: Past, Present, and Future

The Management of Tourism

A Selection of Readings

compiled and edited by

A. J. BURKART

M.A. (Oxon), F.T.S.
Reader in Tourism
Department of Hotel, Catering and Tourism Management
University of Surrey

and

S. MEDLIK

M.A., B.Com., F.H.C.I.M.A., F.T.S.
Formerly Professor and Head of Department
of Hotel, Catering and Tourism Management
University of Surrey
Currently Visiting Professor and
Director Horwath & Horwath (UK) Ltd.

HEINEMANN : LONDON

William Heinemann Ltd
10 Upper Grosvenor Street, London W1X 9PA

LONDON   MELBOURNE   TORONTO
JOHANNESBURG   AUCKLAND

First published 1975
Reprinted 1981
SBN 434 90194 6

Printed in Great Britain by
Richard Clay (The Chaucer Press) Ltd,
Bungay, Suffolk

Preface

The manuscript of our earlier book *Tourism: Past, Present, and Future* was completed in the autumn of 1972, and wherever possible included revisions up to the summer of 1973. It thus recorded tourism up to but excluding the 1973 Middle East War, the so-called energy crisis, the collapse of some of the world's largest tour operators, and the events in Cyprus, all of which are having their effect on the pattern of tourism.

Nevertheless, the phenomenon of tourism remains a part of contemporary life, and we are convinced that the story put forward by us in the earlier book and by our contributors in this book remains valid in a changing world. We hope that both books will be of use to those who study or manage tourism.

Tourism, both domestic and international, will continue to affect the economic and social well-being of most countries of the world. As it grows in volume and diversity and in its impact, it calls for systematic analysis, planning, and co-ordination. This need remains as important in a difficult climate as in a balmy one.

Our basic text *Tourism: Past, Present, and Future* appeared in the summer of 1974 and the response to it of students and teachers as well as of practitioners of tourism exceeded our expectations. Our modest aims in writing it were to provide a systematic framework in which tourism may be explained and examined in its various manifestations, and to establish a set of benchmarks which tourism reached on the threshold of the 1970s and from which the future may be contemplated. Our approach was to provide a simple and reasonably comprehensive outline, rather than a detailed and exhaustive treatment of all or even some aspects of tourism in depth.

However, the serious student of tourism needs more than an outline. For him we made suggestions in our first work for further reading on particular aspects at the beginning of each of the ten main parts and listed over two hundred sources in the bibliography. These were confined in the main to publications in the English language and published in the United Kingdom; articles in journals, papers presented at conferences, publications in languages other than English or published outside the United Kingdom were, with a few exceptions, excluded.

This book of readings is seen as a companion volume to *Tourism: Past, Present, and Future* and as an extension of that basic text, although it may be read on its own, without assuming that the basic text has been covered first, or indeed without any prior study of tourism. The readings bring together twenty quality contributions of long-term value and interest, otherwise only available in scattered publications or not published at all, often not known even to the serious student of tourism, and sometimes not easily accessible. Their arrangement follows the same ten-part structure as the basic text, and brief notes at the beginning of each Part are intended to serve as an introduction to what follows.

The sources of our twenty contributions are of three main kinds: books, journals, and talks and papers at conferences, courses, seminars, and similar occasions; each of the three provides about a third of the contents of this volume, although in several cases there is an overlap between the last two, when what was spoken might have also appeared in print subsequently. Their authors represent a wide spectrum of interests involved in tourism in four broad groups, each providing about a quarter of the contents: academics, practitioners, tourist organizations, and other public bodies. The designation of authors is that which obtained when their contributions were originally written. This was in the 1970s for thirteen of our contributions and the 1960s or earlier for seven of them. The information given and the views expressed inevitably relate to the time the contributions were written although they retain their relevance. Although three-quarters of our contributors are British, at least one-half of this volume draws on the experience of other countries and on international comparisons, and most of it is of relevance to readers wherever they may be.

This volume would not have been possible without the willing co-operation of the authors, publishers, and organizers of events in which our contributions first featured, all of whom readily agreed to their publication here. Their part is gratefully acknowledged and details of each source are shown in the heading of each chapter. We are also indebted to Mrs Linda Marshall and Miss Elizabeth Westley, secretaries in the Department of Hotel, Catering, and Tourism Management at the University of Surrey, for their work in typing the manuscript.

We hope that the readings will appeal to all who found our first book of interest: students and teachers in higher and further education; men and women in international, national, regional and local tourist organizations; in transportation, accommodation, catering and entertainment, tour operation and travel agencies; in central and local government; as well as in other walks of life, where an understanding of tourism is important. For few human activities can be of such absorbing interest and have so much significance for the lives of so many.

University of Surrey   A. J. BURKART
Guildford, Surrey   S. MEDLIK
1975

Contents

		Page
Preface		v

PART I   HISTORICAL DEVELOPMENT
1   Tourism Before 1840   3
    by L. J. Lickorish and A. G. Kershaw, British Travel Association
2   Tourism Between 1840–1940   11
    by L. J. Lickorish and A. G. Kershaw, British Travel Association

PART II   ECONOMIC ASPECTS OF TOURISM
3   The Growth of Tourism   27
    by International Union of Official Travel Organizations
4   The Economics of the Tourist Boom   34
    by J. Harrop, University of Hull

PART III   DIMENSIONS OF TOURISM
5   Travel Propensity and Travel Frequency   53
    by H. Schmidhauser, University of St Gall, Switzerland
6   Self-catering Holidays   61
    by Research Department, British Tourist Authority

PART IV   PASSENGER TRANSPORTATION
7   Transport and Tourism   71
    by S. F. Wheatcroft, British European Airways
8   Trends in Car Ownership and Leisure   80
    by Dr M. Abrams, Social Science Research Council

PART V   ACCOMMODATION AND CATERING
9   Catering for the Tourist   89
    by J. P. Longden, Forte's Limited
10 Co-operation and the Small Business   99
    by Dr J. F. Pickering, University of Sussex

PART VI   TOUR OPERATION
11 The Contribution of Civil Aviation to the Economic Strength and
    Well-being of the UK   111
    by Lord Boyd-Carpenter, Civil Aviation Authority

12 The Role of the Large Tour Operator in the Development and
   Promotion of Tourism   120
   by A. J. Burkart, University of Surrey

PART VII   MARKETING IN TOURISM
13 The Tourist Product and its Marketing Implications   131
   by Professor S. Medlik and V. T. C. Middleton, University of Surrey
14 Design as an Instrument of Competition   140
   by A. J. Burkart, British European Airways

PART VIII   PLANNING AND DEVELOPMENT
15 Conservation of Historic Areas – Management Techniques for
   Tourism in the USA   151
   by T. G. McCaskey, Colonial Williamsburg Foundation, USA
16 Planning for Conservation and Development – an Exercise in the
   Process of Decision-making   160
   by P. E. McCarthy and M. Dower, United Nations

PART IX   TOURISM POLICIES
17 Tourism and the Government   177
   Sir John Eden, Department of Trade and Industry, London
18 International Tourism in Four European Countries   182
   by P. Maison, Greater London Council

PART X   THE FUTURE OF TOURISM
19 Tourism and Developing Countries   205
   by World Bank
20 Forecasting at Pan Am   215
   by G. Newman, Pan American World Airways

   Index   231

Part I
Historical Development

Introduction

G. M. Trevelyan wrote in the Introduction to the complete edition of his *Illustrated English History* as follows (Vol. 1, Penguin, London, 1964, pp. 11–12):

> 'Social history might be defined negatively as the history of a people with the politics left out. It is perhaps difficult to leave out the politics from the history of any people, particularly the English people. But so many history books have consisted of political annals with little reference to their social environment, a reversal of that method may have its uses to redress the balance. During my own lifetime a third flourishing sort of history has come into existence, the economic, which greatly assists the serious study of social history. For the social science grows out of economic conditions, to much the same extent that political events in their turn grow out of social conditions. Without social history, economic history is barren and political history is unintelligible.
>
> But social history does not merely provide the required link between economic and political history. It has also its own positive value and peculiar concern. Its scope may be defined as the daily life of the inhabitants of the land in past ages; this includes the human as well as the economic relation of different classes to one another, the character of family and household life, the conditions of labour *and of leisure, the attitude of man to nature,* the culture of each age as it arose out of these general conditions of life, and took ever-changing forms in religion, literature and music, architecture, learning and thought.'

In its pure sense, tourism is a leisure activity, which involves a discretionary use of freely disposable incomes and of free time. In that sense a history of tourism is, therefore, a part of social history which, as Trevelyan points out, grows out of economic conditions. It may be also conceived as part of economic history, although we are not aware of any books on economic history which do more than touch on tourism.

In their outline history of tourism, Lickorish and Kershaw provide a most comprehensive account of how tourism came to play such an important part in our lives and what have been the main landmarks from the early days to the Second World War. The two chapters reprinted here deal with two distinct phases: the first to the early days of the railway age, the second with the hundred years which followed, when the railway, bus and coach, and the steamship dominated the movement of tourists, before the private car and the aircraft took over. The two chapters also differentiate clearly between tourism as a small minority pursuit and the first mass tourism, which has given rise to the need for its management.

1 Tourism Before 1840

BY L. J. LICKORISH AND A. G. KERSHAW

From *The Travel Trade* (Practical Press Ltd., London, 1958)

It is necessary to go as far back as the Roman Empire to find a precedent to tourism, properly so called, as it began to develop in the middle of the nineteenth century. Lines of communication at the height of Roman civilization are said to have been more efficient than those in eighteenth-century England. During the greatest period in Roman history travelling was more extensive than it was in Europe up to the nineteenth century.

Prosperity, leisure, and the quest for pleasure and recreation, which were indispensable to the development of tourism, gave rise to annual movements of large numbers of people from Rome to the country, or to the seaside during the summer. Romans visited temples, shrines, festivals, and baths for health or for amusement.

With the decay of the Roman Empire came a sharp decline in commerce and disuse of lines of communication. In the absence of a prosperous community with the incentive to travel for pleasure, travelling for its own sake ceased to exist.

In the feudal society of the Middle Ages, the essence of which was the individual's fixed place in the community, there was little opportunity for a man to travel away from his home except in cases of extreme necessity. It is true, however, that thousands of pilgrims made journeys across Christendom under incredibly difficult conditions. The 'Wyfe of Bath', one of Chaucer's companions on the road to Canterbury, was highly esteemed for having travelled to the famous shrine of St James in Northern Spain.

The Crusades gave a renewed impetus to trade and commerce during the eleventh century and onwards, and to the movement of soldiers, merchants, clergy, and pilgrims along the high roads of medieval Europe. Yet in numerical terms the traffic must have been small; society was predominantly agricultural and necessarily immobile. According to Mr A. J. Norval, travel beyond the movement of Christian pilgrims remained in a dormant state up to the sixteenth century. At this time there was some travel other than for the purpose of trade or administration which was 'aimed rather at utility than enjoyment. Only the quest for knowledge could under existing conditions be a sufficient inducement to make people undertake costly and dangerous journeys.' Fynes Morison, who travelled very extensively on the Continent during the years 1591–5, gave his motive for travel as 'his innate desire to gain experience by travelling into foreign parts, as well as the ornament of his profession'.[1] However, at this late date it

[1] Quoted by A. J. Norval in *The Tourist Industry* (Sir Isaac Pitman & Sons Ltd, London, 1936).

was nothing new for the scholar to travel abroad to improve his learning, for there had been an̦extensive exchange of students and professors between the European universities from the eleventh century onwards. The sixteenth century, nevertheless, had seen an increasing secularization of learning: as a part of learning in itself, travel was recommended for the training of young men who were to take up careers as lawyers, soldiers, and secular administrators as a valuable contribution to their experience of the ways of the world. Travel constituted an initiation, intended to improve and develop a sense of responsibility and achievement. At the end of the sixteenth century odds of 5 to 1 were laid against the return of these young travellers.[2] Their stay on the Continent was about three years. There exists, in consequence, an extensive literature of travel of this kind during the sixteenth and seventeenth centuries. John Milton as a young man, accompanied by a manservant through Italy, had letters of introduction to important people in the cities he visited. In 1575 J. Turler's *The Traveller, divided into two Bookes, the first containing a notable discourse of the manner and order of travelling oversea* was published. In 1600 we had Sir R. Dallington's *Method of Travell* and T. Palmer's *Essay of Means how to make our travailes into foraine countries the more profitable and honourable* in 1606; then, in 1617, J. Hall's *Quo Vadis? A just censure of Travell as it is commonly undertaken by the gentlemen of our Nation.* Young men far from home too often pursued pleasure rather than learning and returned much the worse for their three years' absence. There were repeated arguments up to the beginning of the nineteenth century for and against this type of educational travel, which came eventually to be called the 'Grand Tour' (the earliest-known mention of the term was in 1670).[2] One of the most interesting of these arguments was Bishop Hurd's[3] reported conversation between Lord Shaftesbury and the philosopher Locke, published in 1764. The two adversaries discussed the 'uses of foreign travel – considered as a part of modern breeding and education'. '*For by the knowledge of the world*', Lord Shaftesbury says, 'I mean that which results from the observation of men and things; from an acquaintance with the customs and usages of other nations: for some insight into their policies, government, religion; in a word, for the study and contemplation of men; as they present themselves in the greater stage of the world in various forms and under different appearances. This is the master science which a gentleman should comprehend and which our schools and colleges never heard of.' Young men should acquire on the Continent an increased appreciation of the arts and of civilized society, and return, so Lord Shaftesbury believed, to enrich their own country. 'Or to take policy in the vulgar sense,' he continued, 'where would be the harm, if Britain were the seat of Arts and Letters as well as of Trade and Liberty? Then might we be travelled to, in our turn, as our neighbours are at present; and our country amidst its other acquisitions, be enriched (I use the word in its proper, not metaphorical sense) with a new species of commerce.'

[2] Quoted by J. A. R. Pimlott in *The Englishman's Holiday: A Social History* (Faber & Faber, London, 1947).
[3] Quoted by Bishop Hurd in *Dialogues on the Uses of Foreign Travel . . . Between Lord Shaftesbury and Mr Locke.*

The last comment is an early mention in English literature of the great potential commercial as well as cultural value of the tourist movement.

Education was at first the strongest motive for travel, and remained afterwards not the least important of motives of tourists in the nineteenth century and twentieth century, for whom travel was a means of self-improvement and education in its broadest sense. Cook's tourists who 'did' the great cities of Europe from the 1850s onwards were moved by a spirit and eagerness akin to that of the 'Grand Tourists'. Today the great numbers of tourists of all nationalities who move about Europe, and, indeed, the Far East, India, and South America, visiting monuments, museums and places of historic interest, are in the same tradition. It is true too that the sense of adventure which the early 'Grand Tourist' felt is still experienced in a milder form by the traveller abroad. Even now there surely remains to the returning tourist a vestige of that prestige, even if only among his close social circle, which was the 'Grand Tourist's' reward for his experience.

As young men sought intellectual improvement and adventure in travel abroad, the sick sought a remedy for their ailments in places nearer home. These travellers were soon enough followed by those in pursuit only of pleasure, recreation, and society. This stage, nevertheless, was reached after an extremely gradual process. Only twelve spas on the Continent are mentioned in a treatise on bathing cures at the end of the sixteenth century.[4] According to Mr J. A. R. Pimlott, Bath and Buxton were mentioned in the Poor Law Act of 1572 as places of great resort by poor and diseased people, but were the only relatively important centres of this kind. 'The provision,' says Mr J. A. R. Pimlott, 'which was beginning to be made for the amusement of the patients is, however, significant in retrospect'. The modest entertainment provided for visitors prepared the way for the transformation of these centres into pleasure resorts. By the middle of the seventeenth century pleasure-seekers were mingling with the sick. In the last half of the seventeenth century there was a tremendous increase in the popularity of spas. The discovery of a hundred new springs was recorded in England during this period.[5] There was a similar trend on the Continent.

Royal patronage set the seal on Bath; society and its entourage of entertainers and providers of creature comforts were sure to follow. At the end of this century, according to a contemporary, the Cross Bath at Bath was 'more fam'd for pleasure than for cures'. Yet the clientele must have been small by modern standards; in 1700 the population of Bath was still only 2,000.

The first half of the following century, however, marked a tremendous development in Bath and in some other resorts. The brilliant organization of its social life by Beau Nash (the first resort publicity officer) attracted to it the wealthy and fashionable of all England. Other resorts, sometimes close imitations, were to follow – Tunbridge Wells, Harrogate, Cheltenham, and many lesser spas.

Their heyday was not long-lived for, though inland resorts continued to be popular, they were seriously challenged by the new fashion for cold-bathing and

[4] R. Lennard, *Englishmen at Rest and Play* (Clarendon Press, Oxford, 1931).
[5] R. Lennard, *Englishmen at Rest and Play*.

subsequently sea-water bathing. Medical confidence in the efficacy of such bathing dates from late in the seventeenth century. Dr Richard Russell, who published his *Dissertation on the use of Sea Water* in 1752 and in so doing turned the attention of the sick from the inland spas to the seaside, began a vogue which was to create the pattern of the English seaside holiday up to our own time. Of the 23 million British people who go away for a holiday each year, over 70 per cent still go to the seaside. There was sea bathing in Scarborough in the first half of the eighteenth century. The first great seaside resort in England, however, was to be Brighton. Only a fishing village in 1760, it became in the latter half of the century, according to one writer, 'the gayest, most fashionable place not only in England, but in all Europe'. As in the case of Bath, pleasure-seekers had soon arrived in the wake of the sick; royal and fashionable patronage transformed Brighton, and soon many other seaside resorts, into great centres of recreation and entertainment which were beginning to eclipse the older inland spas in the late 1700s.

Many resorts owe their present-day popularity to their original 'discovery' by wealthy minorities – by royalty and the aristocracy as well as, in later days, by millionaires and perhaps even by film stars. Weymouth dates as a seaside resort from the visit of King George III in 1788. The Duke of York and the Duke of Gloucester were among the very earliest visitors to Nice in the last half of the eighteenth century. Some English and Continental resorts show very clearly traces of the tastes and characters of the particular minorities which originally brought them into fashion. They were deserted by their original patrons when their exclusiveness was invaded by the middle classes, who were again superseded by the working classes. This is a common travel pattern. Certain minorities popularized the South of France, Switzerland, and gambling resorts in Europe in the nineteenth century. In the twentieth century wealthy Americans who travelled to Europe in luxurious liners in the 1920s and '30s have been followed by an ever-broadening section of the American community.

Almost all of the older English resorts show a similar pattern. There were perhaps variations on the same theme; some resorts have always been the preserve of the middle classes; no two resorts, however, appear to have an exactly similar history. Each has its own atmosphere, its own associations, and its own type of clientele. How often do we hear a reference to this resort as 'high-class' and that as 'quiet' and another as 'international'? The character of a resort may not only depend on its climate, its geography, and its proximity, say, to industrial towns, but also to its original patrons and its subsequent social evolution. Up to recent years there had been no innovation without the sponsorship of the 'leaders' of society. It should be remembered however that in the twentieth century new forms of holidays as well as new places of holiday resort have been found without the patronage of a well-to-do minority; for example, camping, caravanning and youth hostelling.

In the last quarter of the eighteenth century, according to Mr J. A. R. Pimlott,[6]

[6] In the following section the authors are greatly indebted to J. A. R. Pimlott for data on transport and the development of resorts in the eighteenth and nineteenth centuries. Readers

the traffic to the seaside or to inland resorts was still small by modern standards. Bath, by far the most important resort, still could number only 12,000 visitors in a season, and though many other resorts existed, none could have shown an equal number of visitors. In the 1780s Cheltenham was said to have received 1,000 visitors in a season, and visitors to seaside resorts, with the exception perhaps of Brighton and Scarborough, were counted in hundreds rather than in thousands. Yet signs of an impending change are unmistakable in the latter half of the eighteenth century; with the great increase of wealth consequent upon the Industrial Revolution and the creation of a large and prosperous middle class with new needs and tastes, increasing numbers of people began to travel for pleasure. In the second half of the eighteenth century and first quarter of the nineteenth century improvements in transport were as rapid as the transformation of the country's economic and industrial life as a whole. By 1833, 480 passengers were carried to Brighton in one day, and in 1837 the number of travellers by coach in the whole year was 50,000. The same writer states that 18,000 people travelled to Margate in 1800 in the famous 'hoys', or sailing boats, from London. When steamers were introduced, the passengers dealt with by the Margate Pier and Harbour Company rose from 17,000 in 1812–13 to 21,931 in 1815–16, 43,947 in 1820–1, 98,128 in 1830–1, and to the record total of 105,625 in 1835–6.

All this points, of course, to the existence of a relatively large proportion of the community having the money, the time, and above all the incentive to travel for pleasure. For such developments to have taken place, a revolution in social habits equal in momentum to that which had taken place in commerce and industry, and which was indeed caused by this material revolution, had been necessary. Nevertheless, apart from the special excursion traffic down the Thames to such places as Margate and Ramsgate, travel was still available only to the well-to-do. According to Mr J. A. R. Pimlott, 'in 1840 it cost as much to travel post from St Leonards to Tunbridge Wells, a distance of less than 30 miles, but involving the payment of three postmasters and post-boys and twelve turnpike men, as to stay a fortnight at the former'.

Travel abroad was the prerogative of the very wealthy, and was even then fraught with discomfort and danger. Frontier restrictions, Customs examinations, and heavy tolls at frequent intervals made the prospect of travel uninviting.

'On arrival at Dover,' says Nugent's famous *Grand Tour*, 'you are conducted by a soldier upon the guard, which is always mounted upon the quay, to a searching office just by, where you must give in your name and quality, the purpose in your coming over and the intended tour; thence you are shown into a small inner room and very civilly searched by the proper officer, who only just presses upon your coat pockets or outer garments; afterwards the soldier conducts you to the governor's house, where you are shown to the governor. When this farce is over, you are at liberty to proceed to your inn . . .'

Yet the wealthy English were to be found everywhere in Europe, spurred by

wishing to know more about the growth of the holiday movement in this country are advised to read his detailed study, *The Englishman's Holiday: A Social History*.

a sense of adventure and curiosity, which has characterized English tourism in Europe for two and a half centuries. In Sir Gavin de Beer's interesting list of itineraries in Switzerland[7] we have this curious account of a journey in 1794: 'On the St Gotthard Pass the monks told Miss Williams that the day before her arrival, "a numerous retinue of horses, oxen, mules, and other cattle had passed in the suite of a great man, whose carriage they had dragged, by his order, from the bottom of the mountain, that he might have the fame of crossing the St Gotthard in a vehicle with wheels". As our countrymen are known to be the only travelling philosophers who make experiments of this kind, the monks had no difficulty in conjecturing on the approach of this long procession, that if it was not the Emperor, or the Burgomaster of Berne, the two greatest personages they had heard of, it must be an English Lord.' It is not perhaps to his discredit that today's tourist retains a touch of the same summer madness.

In the latter half of the eighteenth century daring innovators in an extreme minority had taken an interest in mountain-climbing. One Thomas Brand in 1786 described Packard's achievement of the 'long wish'd for adventure of gaining the highest summit of Mont Blanc'. William Coxe stayed at St Moritz, Switzerland, in 1779, where he was lodged in 'one of the boarding houses, which abound in this place, for the accommodation of persons who drink the waters'. In 1787 we hear of someone who 'slept at Chamonix where there was only one inn', though he goes on to say that 'the company was a mixed one of men and women from every country in Europe'. A glance through Sir Gavin de Beer's admirable list of itineraries in Switzerland is sufficient to find a reflection of changing attitudes and tastes which transformed Switzerland into the first play-ground of Europe. The Romantics, it is said, taught people to look at nature and mountains with a new kind of pleasure and awe. When medical opinion drew the public's attention to the healing and invigorating effect of mountain air, new health resorts in high positions as well as in valleys grew up to cater for the sick as well as for the adventurers and pleasure-seekers.

Before the beginnings of the Romantic Movement, few saw in the Alps an object of beauty. Horace Walpole in 1739 said of the Alps: 'I hope I shall never see them again'. What an argument he would have struck up with Wordsworth or Byron or the millions of tourists who have followed them!

In 1766, said Hirschfield, 'What struck me most in Switzerland among the curiosities of nature were those horrid structures the Alps . . . one is awe-stricken at the view, and longs to impart this pleasant sense of horror to all one's friends'. Goethe declared: 'Switzerland at first made so deep an impression on me that I was bewildered and restless'.

Leonard Meister exclaimed in 1782: 'Inspired, I raised my face to the sun; my eyes drank in the infinite space; I was shaken by a divine shudder, and in deep reverence I sank down before God', and Wordsworth in 1790: 'Ten thousand times in the course of this tour have I regretted the inability of my memory to retain a more strong impression of the beautiful forms before me . . .' And so after the turn of the nineteenth century Switzerland's popularity was established.

[7] *Travellers in Switzerland* by Sir Gavin de Beer (Oxford University Press, London, 1949).

In 1812 one writer confirmed 'it has now become the custom for learned persons to visit the valleys and mountains of Switzerland, partly in order to gain health or to restore it, and partly to acquire useful knowledge and happiness . . . Englishmen, Frenchmen, Germans, Italians come every year. What do they look for, but pleasure and health?'

The English were predominant. Lady de Clifford, in 1816, says: 'On the day when we visited these icy wilds there were not less than thirty persons who came to indulge a similar curiosity. Almost all of these were English.' And a French writer: 'Les Anglais se reposent des heures entieres aux chalets que se trouvent sur ces pentes, et dans leur admiration, qui est aussi longue que profonde, souvent ils s'oublient jusqu'au soir'.

Beneath this change of attitude lies the great current of political and social thought of the late half of the eighteenth century. The real motive for travel was again education or the pursuit of experience, in however diluted or disguised form. The change in society and literary fashions tended to turn men away from the great seats of government and places of historic interest (the principal object of the Elizabethan travellers) to the wonderful spectacles of nature.

By the 1800s, then, the way was already prepared for mass tourism. So far, however, one important factor in the later growth of tourism was barely discernible: the Industrial Revolution threw up great factory towns and a populace burdened by long working hours and poor living conditions. As a result of the disintegration of agricultural and village life, opportunities for sport and recreation were much diminished. For the great mass of the people there was little relief from narrow industrial routine and bad social conditions created by the sudden concentration of population in the cities. There was a marked tendency for holidays to be cut shorter and shorter. According to Mr J. A. R. Pimlott, the Bank of England, for example, closed on 47 days in 1761, on 44 in 1808, on 40 in 1825, on 18 in 1830, and only 4 days in 1834. Small wonder that 'the imprisoned millions' seized the first opportunity within their narrow means to escape from such conditions on the few days that were left to them. Industrial momentum gathered and cities and their populations increased at an enormous rate, making the need for escape even more acute. London families with relatively little money might seek a change of atmosphere and environment, if only for a day, on a trip to Margate in a 'hoy' or steamer. The well-to-do proceeded to resorts and smaller numbers to the Continent. Milton's 'tomorrow to fresh woods and pastures new' is a cry of the times.

The introduction of railways vastly increased the opportunities for escape from oppressive urbanization, and in the nineteenth and twentieth centuries it has been not the least powerful of all tourist motives. It is perhaps significant that even today a high proportion of the world's tourists are from large cities – London, New York, Chicago, Los Angeles.

To say that cities provide the greatest number of tourists because the population is concentrated there is an over-simplification; a survey of people travelling on Cross-Channel routes between Britain and France in 1957 showed that 24 per cent of all British travellers came from the London postal area, whereas only

11 per cent of the British population live there; 43 per cent of all French traffic came from Seine (including Paris), whereas only 12·2 per cent of the French population live there; more startling still – whereas only 2½ per cent of the Italian population live in Milan 24 per cent of Italian visitors to Britain came from that city. A study of US passport statistics will show that about 26 per cent of applications for passports come from the New York area, whereas only 9·8 per cent of the US population live there. It is true now that nearly everyone in Britain travels away from home, even if only for day trips, but the fact that so many *international travellers* come from cities shows the importance which travel generally has assumed over a long period in the lives of city dwellers.

The concentration of population is, of course, essential to the development of mass tourism, but there are many instances shown in this short history of increases in the volume of tourist traffic which were much greater than corresponding increases in total population.

Thus by the early nineteenth century all the main characteristics of modern tourism were evident in embryo. Changes in mental attitude towards pleasure-seeking, an increase of material wealth and improvements in transport, the recognized value of travel for education, social prestige, and pleasure, and of resorts and spas for health and relaxation, the increasing need to find relief from workaday routine, and the city dweller's yearning for physical exhilaration and adventure – all these factors produced fertile ground for the development of pleasure traffic on a large scale, and are indeed factors upon which the maintenance of tourism today is dependent.

Tourism, still largely latent and unrealized, was to receive the greatest impetus of all from the railways. Strangely, few people at the time realized that railways would do more than attract away the clientele of the already flourishing, though comparatively small, coaching trade. There was considerable opposition to the lowering of fares, for it was thought that such action would merely reduce the revenue of the railway companies without actually increasing appreciably the number of passengers. Few understood that whereas a train might run at a moderate profit by carrying fifty persons first-class at high prices, it could run at considerably greater profit by carrying 1,000 at greatly reduced prices. The simple fact was, however, that there was demand of this kind; the tendency to think in terms of coaching days and of travel as the exclusive need of the rich was understandable. Later, Parliamentary measures were taken to ensure that a certain number of trains were run at a maximum fare of 1*d.* per mile.

The Liverpool and Manchester Railway, opened on 15 September 1830, was the first passenger railway to be built with a view to the conveyance of passengers. From then onwards enormous numbers began to use the railways which were being built all over the country. In just over a decade the number of passengers had risen to the astonishing figure of 23 millions – or well over one journey per head of the population. This was in 1842; however, the most memorable year was 1841.

2 Tourism Between 1840–1940

BY L. J. LICKORISH AND A. G. KERSHAW

From *The Travel Trade* (Practical Press Ltd., London, 1958)

On 9 June 1841 Thomas Cook[1] walked fifteen miles to a temperance meeting in Leicester. On this journey he conceived the idea of hiring a train to take fellow members of a temperance society to Loughborough. He put his idea to his friends, and accordingly organized a trip to Loughborough shortly afterwards: 570 passengers were carried on this famous excursion. The experiment was unique in that, for the first time, tickets had been bought by an agent from the railways for re-sale and arrangements had been provided by the organizer; it was so successful that it was soon followed by another trip – one to Glasgow of some 800 persons. Before Cook had begun to operate, passenger traffic was already enormous. 'On the occasion of Derby Day in 1838,' said Kemball Cook, 'eight trains were advertised to run from the Nine Elms terminus. The authorities were confounded when they found that 5,000 were clamouring to get into the station.' In the 1840s a train to see Queen Victoria on a visit to Edinburgh carried more than 1,500 people. Thomas Cook, however, was a remarkable innovator; he bought tickets from the railway companies for re-sale, he personally conducted his excursions, published guide-books (the first for a Leicester to Liverpool excursion in 1845) and invented a coupon scheme to provide hotel facilities. He was to the new traveller and tourist what the courier had been to the 'Grand Tourist'.

Cook brought 165,000 excursionists from Yorkshire alone to the Great Exhibition of 1851 and it was in 1856 that he organized the first tour to the Continent. Thereafter more numerous 'excursions' were extended further and further afield.

Many years later Gladstone said 'Among the humanizing contrivances of the age I think notice is due to the system founded by Mr Cook, and now largely in use, under which numbers of persons, and indeed whole classes have for the first time found easy access to foreign countries and have acquired some of that familiarity with them which breeds not contempt but kindness'.

But Cook by no means possessed the monopoly of normal passenger or excursion traffic. In 1851, 774,910 passengers to and from London were carried by excursion trains of the London and North Western railway. In other parts of Great Britain traffic was growing at an astounding pace. About a thousand passengers were carried on the first excursion train run by the Great Western in

[1] Information on Thomas Cook obtained from *The Business of Travel* by W. Fraser Rae (Thomas Cook & Son, London, 1891).

1844. In the second half of the same year 360,000 passengers travelled from London to Brighton yet only seven years earlier the annual coach traffic of 50,000 was surely regarded as unsurpassable.

In 1851 a total of approximately 79 million passengers were carried on railways in Britain; the figure rose from 160 million in 1860 to 604 million in 1880, 817 million in 1890, and 1,455 million in 1913.[2]

The great bulk of the population in 1851, when 51 million passengers were carried (which is two passenger journeys per head of the population), found itself in an era in which travel was rare to one in which travelling, if only on day excursions, was accessible to all. It is difficult now to imagine the extent of the social and economic repercussions of this change.

This mass movement of people brought into being a flourishing holiday industry. In the 50 years up to 1851 it was the watering places, not the manufacturing towns, which had registered the greatest expansion in population. In this period the annual rate of growth of resorts was 2·56 per cent as compared with 2·38 per cent for manufacturing towns. Brighton's 7,000 inhabitants in 1800 increased to 65,000 in 50 years. Eleven seaside towns were included in the 1851 census report. By 1871 the list had extended to 48 towns. The population of these amounting to over 430,000 in 1861 increased by nearly 100,000 in ten years. The increase was to continue during the latter half of the century during which time the population of these resorts was more than doubled. Enormous trade was brought to relatively obscure towns by the very first excursions. An acute problem arose: the accommodation of tremendous numbers of visitors. For the benefit of excursionists on one occasion in the early 1840s a list of boarding houses was kept at the railway refreshment rooms in Scarborough. But such makeshift arrangements could not hold for long. Capital was poured into the building of hotels, promenades, public amenities, meeting places, and piers to attract more and more visitors. A hotel and lodging list giving lodgings, 'private' hotels (including Claridges) and hotels in London was published in February 1851 for the benefit of visitors to the Great Exhibition. *The Royal Hotel Guide* issued in 1854 lists no fewer than 8,000 hotels in Great Britain of which many were certainly old coaching inns, but a great number were new hotels in the full sense, many in the rapidly expanding seaside resorts. A number of railway termini hotels had made their appearance, the first major one at Euston in 1838. The railways had quickly realized that good hotels and a guarantee of service were indispensable to an increase in traffic.

We must now describe the development of Continental travel after the 1840s. At first the railways were developed to some extent in the United Kingdom and America, but tended to be eyed with misgivings on the Continent. The enormous prosperity they brought, however, soon encouraged their widespread construction on the Continent.

By now, the English were not the only tourists, but because England enjoyed a high degree of prosperity and the English already enjoyed a long tradition of

    [2] Quoted by J. A. R. Pimlott in *The Englishman's Holiday: A Social History* (Faber & Faber, London, 1947).

Table 2.1

Miles of Railway Track Built[3]

	1835	1845	1855	1865	1875	1885
Great Britain and Ireland	471	3,277	13,411	21,382	26,803	30,843
France	176	883	5,535	13,562	21,547	32,491
Germany	6	2,315	8,352	14,762	28,087	37,572
Austria–Hungary	—	728	2,145	5,858	16,860	22,789
Russia and Finland	—	144	1,048	3,940	19,584	26,847
Italy	—	157	1,211	4,347	7,709	10,484
Belgium	20	576	1,349	2,254	3,499	4,409
Holland and Luxembourg	—	153	314	865	1,407	2,804
Switzerland	—	2	210	1,322	1,948	2,850
Europe, including Great Britain and Ireland	673	8,235	35,185	75,882	142,494	195,833

travel, they were by far in the majority, and they influenced the development of Continental resorts to emulate those in Great Britain.

Defert[4] points out that England had its industrial revolution well before the rest of Europe; the development of a large comfortable middle class provided an enormous reservoir of clients. It was due to their patronage that between 1870 and 1900 the hotels 'D'Angleterre', 'Britannic', 'Londres', 'Windsor', and 'Prince de Galles' appeared everywhere. English words became part of the international tourist vocabulary – 'express', 'comfort', 'sleeping', 'liner', etc. The wealthy tended to desert the most important resorts at home – Bath and Brighton – for the Continent. Great Continental resorts, such as Wiesbaden and Homburg in the first half of the century, were superseded by Monaco, Cannes, and Nice in the second half. Small townships and villages became places of international fame in a few decades as a result of the arrival of railways and the resorts' particular suitability to the needs of the classes they catered for. Though the English were followed by the Germans, and in some areas outnumbered by them towards the end of the century – particularly in Switzerland – they continued on the whole to be the most numerous.

They also continued to take the lead in opening up new forms of holiday-making. Celebrating the centenary of the foundation of the Alpine Club of Great Britain, the *Swiss Hotel Review* made this comment:

'Nous ne devons en effet point oublier que le 31 juillet 1855, les Anglais James-Greenville Smith, Christophe Smith, Charles Hudson, John Dirbeck, E. W. Stephenson, conduits par les guides Jean et Pierre Taugwalder, de Zermatt, et Ulrich Lauener, de Lauterbrunnen, accomplissaient la première

[3] Table quoted by A. J. Norval in *The Tourist Industry* (Sir Isaac Pitman & Sons Ltd, London, 1936).
[4] *See* 'Quelques Repères Historiques du Tourisme Moderne' by Pierre-P. Defert in the magazine *The Tourist Review*, January/March 1958 (Berne).

ascension de la plus haute cime suisse qui devait être baptisee plus tard la –
Pointe Dufour –.

Ce furent ces passionnés de la montagne, ainsi que tous les autres Anglais qui
partirent à la conquête des alpes suisses, qui donnerènt à l'alpinisme l'essor
qu'il a connu et qu'il doit connâitre encore, malgré l'évolution des techniques
et les téléphériques ou les avions qui amènent maintenant les alpinistes à pied
d'oeuvre.

Si nos stations de montagnes connaissent aujourd'hui des saisons d'hiver qui
sont plus importantes que les saisons d'été, c'est aussi grâce à ces pionniers qui
rechèrcherent inlassablement des moyens de vaincre les difficultés crées par la
neige pour se déplacer et s'évader, transformant ainsi des villages autrefois
replies sur eux-mêmes pendant les premiers mois de l'année en des ruches
bourdonnantes où l'on défie le froid pour ne profiter que des lumineux rayons
de soleil qui sont les meilleurs régénérateurs du corps humain.'

British travel to the Continent is revealed in the increase in cross-Channel
traffic. The first steamer passage of the Channel was in 1816, and the first regular
steamer service in 1820. The cross-Channel traffic of some 100,000 in the 1830s
had increased to 500,000 in 1882. Thomas Cook alone took 75,000 visitors to the
Paris Exhibition in 1878.

In the meantime, a tourist movement apart from that within Europe was
beginning to stir. The first regular steamship service of the North Atlantic was
begun by the *Great Western*, and on its first eastbound journey in 1838 it carried
68 passengers from New York to England. According to the United States
Department of Commerce, the number of returning American-born citizens in
1820 was 1,926, which had risen to 6,245 in 1838. In the two great decades of the
railway age, 1840–60, the number of Americans travelling abroad rose from just
over 8,000 to 26,000 in 1860. The figure quickly rose again, and stayed at
approximately 50,000 annually until the early 1880s, when another great increase
occurred.

Transatlantic shipping lines achieved much-improved standards in comfort
and speed for this increasing traffic. The 'Grand Tour' pattern set by the English
was to be followed. The same causes – increasing wealth, improved transport –
are discernible and so too are the same motives, but in this case education,
experience, and curiosity played a greater part than the pursuit of health and
recreation, largely because the latter could be found by Americans in their own
country.

'The beginnings of oversea travel between the United States and foreign
countries by "tourists", or travellers for pleasure, may be dated safely from the
1860s. As early as 1850, Thomas Cook planned a trip to the United States for
the purpose of arranging excursion parties to America from England and from
America to Europe; but the journey was postponed until 1865.

The five months' voyage of the *Quaker City* to the Mediterranean and the
Holy Land in 1867 with sixty passengers (including Mark Twain, who recorded
the journey in *The Innocents Abroad*) was probably the first ocean cruise

conceived and advertised for "tourists". The cost of the passage was $1,200 for each adult passenger, and it was estimated that $5 in gold a day would cover shore expenses. A few years later a conducted tour of Europe was taken by a group of fifty-five members of an American fraternal order.

Two excursions from England to the United States were organized in 1866, the first and larger of which included thirty-five persons. The parties visited, among other points, Richmond and the battlefields of Virginia and Mammoth Cave in Kentucky.'[5]

Tourism for the newly developed parts of the world was by no means exactly in the pattern of that established in Europe. An American, Price Collier, wrote in 1909: 'This is the England, I take it, that makes one feel his duty to be his religion, and the England that every American comes to as a shrine'. Though this was probably not true of all American visitors to Europe at the time, it was the reflection of an attitude. Obviously the same could be said to a far lesser extent of the English tourist to the Continent or the Continental visitor to Britain. The tourist movement from the New World bears closer resemblance to the pilgrimage than inter-European tourism. The movement of tourists to a country indeed reflects the nature of that country and its relations with others.

Up to the beginning of the twentieth century, tourists travelled almost exclusively by rail and steamship. The whole shape of the tourist industry was therefore to be transformed by the invention of a new transport medium: travel by private car and coach received its first great impetus in the ten boom travel years which preceded the First World War.[6] In 1904 there were already 8,465 private cars in use in Great Britain, but in only ten years this number increased to 132,015 – or 1,460 per cent! In the same period, the number of motor-propelled 'hackneys' in use increased from 5,345 to 51,167. Motor transport gave access to new places which could not be reached by railways, it increased the possibilities of new kinds of holidays and offered holiday-makers more freedom and independence, but for the moment the volume of travel by rail was not seriously affected. This was to happen early in the post-war period.

During the period of international tourism in the 1880s in which the middle classes predominated, still further developments were beginning to take place to increase the volume of tourists at home. It was in the last quarter of the nineteenth century that increasing attention was paid to the desirability of holidays with pay and, at least, of cheap holidays for working-class people, who had still largely failed to benefit from the new opportunities provided by cheaper travel. During this time a few factories gave paid holidays to their workers, but the idea was only accepted here and there, and paid holidays for workers were not established to any great extent even ten years after the First World War.[7] However, there were increased opportunities for cheap pleasure travel. In 1872 the Midland

[5] From *Overseas Travel and Travel Expenditure in the Balance of International Payments of the United States* by August Maffry (United States Government Printing Office, Washington, 1919–38).

[6] *Basic Road Statistics, 1957* (The British Road Federation, London, 1957).

[7] *Report of Conference on Workers' Holidays* (Industrial Welfare Society, London, 1938).

Railway Company decided to provide third-class accommodation at 1*d*. per mile on all trains, to abolish second-class and reduce first-class prices to the former second-class level. Other railways had to follow suit, and the decision marked a yet greater era in railway travel. At about the same time the August Bank Holiday was introduced. On the first such holiday in 1871, thousands freed from work hastened to the seaside and countryside: the capacity of the railways was strained to its utmost. The great mass of people, even if they did not have annual paid holidays as yet, were at least able to escape on the main public or religious holidays of the year – Easter, Whitsun, and the August Bank Holiday. 'The Great Eastern Railway must have been well satisfied,' said Kemball Cook[8] 'with having carried 300,000 excursionists on a Whit Monday in the 1880s'.

In the last two decades of the nineteenth century there were further developments in holiday-taking at home and abroad. During this period there existed in their early stages the Cyclists' Touring Club, the National Cyclists' Union, Polytechnic Touring Association, the Co-operative Holidays Association, Frame's, and Sir Henry Lunn's – all organizations which offered travel at reasonable prices.

Defert[9] has found evidence of travel by the residents of other European countries in the foundation of many tourist organizations on the Continent in the last half of the nineteenth century. The Duchemin Agencies opened in France in 1890, the Touring Club de France in 1890, the Alliance Internationale de Tourisme in 1898, and many others too numerous to mention here. 'Tourism,' says the writer, 'appeared all over Western Europe at the end of the nineteenth century as the fruit of a liberal expansionist economy based on technical and industrial progress'.

On the Continent, the introduction of ski-ing and tobogganing had added fresh attractions to the Swiss holiday trade. The operations of new tourist organizations in the UK were enabling working-class people to travel abroad for the first time and in any case fares to the Continent had become increasingly cheaper. The Board of Trade give the following figures of total passenger movement to Europe for the last decade of the nineteenth century:

1891: 418,003	1896: 479,913
1892: 405,998	1897: 569,150
1893: 395,362	1898: 590,226
1894: 477,318	1899: 609,570
1895: 493,946	1900: 669,292

Only a small proportion of this movement can have been migratory. Although by this time there were numbers of Continental visitors to Great Britain, not to mention American and Commonwealth visitors, most of the cross-Channel traffic must have represented British tourists.

In step with the increase in tourism by British people in the last decades of the

---

[8] From *Over the Hills and Far Away* by Hartley Kemball Cook (Allen & Unwin, London, 1947).
[9] See *The Tourist Review*, January/March 1958 (Berne).

nineteenth century, there were greater numbers of American travellers. The numbers of returning American citizens increased from 52,812 in 1882 to 120,477 in 1900. By the turn of the century, famous shipping lines, such as Cunard, Canadian Pacific, Holland-America and others, were operating luxury services between the USA and Canada and Europe.[10]

But there was yet another sharp rise in international tourism in the ten years preceding the First World War. The number of returning American citizens rose again from 177,488 in 1906 to 286,586 in 1914. The number of passengers to the United States grew from 998,323 in 1904 to 1,689,667 ten years later. In the same period, passenger movement from the UK increased from 669,292 to 853,636 in 1914. This, however, was a bad year, and in the years 1910, 1911, and 1913 the figure had exceeded 1 million annually. In these boom years tourism had at last taken on modern proportions, as Mr A. Norval confirms:

'At the close of the last century and up to the outbreak of the World War in 1914, the tourist movement had assumed considerable dimensions and sur-passed anything of its kind ever known in the history of the human race – it had developed from a purely local into a world phenomenon, from which countries such as Austria, France, Italy, Norway, Switzerland, and others were at that time deriving a very substantial income annually. The number of tourists who annually visited Switzerland before the war was estimated by Swiss experts to oscillate between 350,000 and 450,000, with an annual expenditure for hotel accommodation, purchases of travel mementoes, post-cards, and souvenir jewellery of 200,000,000 francs. On the basis of a careful investigation undertaken by the Austrian Ministry of Finance, the total number of tour-days which foreigners passed in Austria was estimated at 5,070,000, bringing in, at an average, daily expenditure of 15 kronen per tourist, 85,000,000 kronen in one year. In 1897 Italy is said to have derived 300,000,000 lire from her tourist traffic, while in 1908 this source of her national income is said to have produced 427,000,000 lire. The amount foreigners are estimated to have spent annually at the French Riviera before the First World War is 300,000,000 francs. The income France then derived from her tourist traffic was estimated at 350,000,000 francs. It was estimated by the shipping companies before the First World War that 150,000 Americans then annually crossed the Atlantic to Europe and the North of Africa, where they are said to have spent vast sums of money.'[11]

After the First World War, tourist travel quickly reached pre-war peak levels, and within three or four years greatly exceeded them. The war itself had forced on the development of motor and air transport and had increased the pace of economic life. Certain commercial civil air services were inaugurated and developed in this period.

After 1919 private companies and governments began to interest themselves

[10] From *North Atlantic Seaway* by N. R. P. Bonsor (T. Stephenson & Sons, Prescot, Lancs, 1955).

[11] *op. cit.*

seriously in civil aviation as a commercial proposition – a competitor with older forms of transport – for mail and passenger carrying. Even so, the early development of regular passenger services was frequently interrupted by economic causes. Some countries subsidized the infant of the transport world. Among the first to do so were Germany and France, which were said by Goldstrom[12] to be in the lead in the sphere of civil aviation in the 1920s. Air transport, however, was developed in many other European countries, as well as in the USA, Canada, Australia, and New Zealand, with a rapidity which is shown in Table 2.2.

Table 2.2

Route Mileages and Miles flown by Regular Services throughout the World[13]

	Route mileage (approx.)	Millions of miles flown
1919	3,200	1
1920	9,700	3
1921	12,400	6
1922	16,000	6
1923	16,100	7
1924	20,300	9
1925	34,000	13
1926	48,500	17
1927	54,700	22
1928	90,700	34
1929	125,800	53
1930	156,800	70
1931	185,100	84
1932	190,200	90
1933	200,300	101
1934	223,100	103
1935	278,200	149
1936	305,200	179
1937	333,500	199
1938	349,100	234

In 1919 the Air Ministry started a special 'regular' service to carry members of the Government to the Peace Conference in Paris. The service lasted till September, by which time 749 flights had been made and 924 passengers carried. In the same year two private companies started operations. Aircraft Transport and Travel Ltd ran services between London and Paris; Handley Page Ltd ran services London–Paris and London–Brussels. Within two years these services had ceased, due to competition from French companies subsidized by the French Government.

The British Government began a temporary scheme for subsidizing air companies in 1921, and by the time the scheme was revised in 1922 four com-

[12] *Narrative History of Aviation* by J. Goldstrom (Macmillan, New York, 1930).
[13] Source: *Aviation* by H. E. Wimperis, CB, CBE.

panies were in existence. These were absorbed by Imperial Airways on its formation in 1924.

Within two years Imperial Airways built up services over 2,500 miles. A daily service operated throughout the year between London and Paris, and during the summer season as many as three flights a day were made in each direction. A daily service was maintained beyond Paris to Zurich via Basle, and other daily services to Ostend and to Cologne via Brussels were operated. Weekly services operated between Southampton and Guernsey, and from London to the Middle East and India.

Table 2.3

Passengers carried by the Associated Companies of
Imperial Airways on Empire Routes[14]

1925: 11,000	1932: 48,200
1926: 16,000	1933: 79,100
1927: 19,000	1934: 135,000
1928: 27,300	1935: 200,000
1929: 28,500	1936: 236,300
1930: 24,000	1937: 244,400
1931: 23,800	1938: 222,000

Regular cross-Channel services were normal long before the outbreak of the Second World War, but it was not until 1939 that services UK–USA were inaugurated by Imperial Airways and Pan-American Airways simultaneously. Although cross-Channel services were established, only a tiny proportion of British tourists to the Continent used them.

In 1931 some 900,000 British holidaymakers went to the Continent, yet according to the *Board of Trade Journal*, the total number of air passengers (both British and non-British) travelling outwards from the United Kingdom to the Continent amounted only to 22,400. However, the rate of progress of civil aviation in the inter-war years was truly phenomenal, as Table 2.4 illustrates. It shows that air traffic United Kingdom–Continent in 1931 was 234 per cent higher than in 1923, and in 1937 it was 1,321 per cent higher.

Table 2.4

Passenger Traffic by Air, United Kingdom to the Continent 1923–37[15]

1923: 6,700	1931: 22,400
1924: 8,300	1932: 35,300
1925: 9,400	1933: 45,400
1926: 12,700	1934: 62,100
1927: 13,700	1935: 75,700
1928: 21,100	1936: 86,600
1929: 23,600	1937: 95,200
1930: 20,600	

[14] Source: *Aviation* by H. E. Wimperis, CB, CBE.
[15] Source: Board of Trade Journals.

The most important factor in tourist transport in the inter-war years was the growth in car and bus travel. The figures given in Table 2.5 will illustrate that growth.

Table 2.5

Vehicles in Use in Great Britain

	Private Cars	*Buses and Coaches*
1926	683,913[16]	40,118
1927	786,610	42,458
1928	884,645	46,298
1929	980,886	49,889
1930	1,056,214	52,648
1931	1,083,457	49,134
1932	1,127,681	47,656
1933	1,203,245	45,656
1934	1,308,425	45,689
1935	1,477,378	47,215
1936	1,642,850	49,116
1937	1,798,105	50,979
1938	1,944,394	53,005
1939	2,034,400	not available

One-third of Britain's holidaymakers now travel by coach. It was in the inter-war years that the motor coach gained its great popularity, as Mr E. L. Taylor has shown, though he points out that the motor-coach holiday was not unknown before the First World War. His remarks on the development of the motor coach for holiday purposes are of interest:

'With the return to peace in 1919, progress was greatly accelerated. The urge of war had stimulated mechanical improvement of the motor vehicle enormously, and thousands of surplus Army vehicles were converted for passenger carrying. In 1919 or 1920 British coaches ran six-day tours of the battlefields of France and Flanders – these were probably the first to extend their operations outside Great Britain. By 1921 they had reached the Côte d'Azur, followed in the next two or three years by tours to Holland, Germany, Italy, and Spain – the last taking 22 days and visiting Gibraltar. Meanwhile, two enterprising young Englishmen acquired from the American Army in France two trucks, on which they installed French bodies equipped with an opening roof, swivelling armchair seats, a buffet-kitchen and a toilet compartment, and in 1920 they started a regular service from Calais to Nice, which operated successfully through the period when the demand for seats in the Blue Train far exceeded the supply. Later, with the advantage of newly-fitted pneumatic tyres, they extended their touring range over most of Europe and even, in 1924, North Africa; and later still a thrust towards Istanbul was defeated by

[16] In 1914 the figure was 132,015 and in 1919, 109,715.

bad roads and finished in Belgrade. In 1935 they ran a tour to Leningrad and Moscow.

It is estimated that in 1939 37 million passengers were carried on regular long distance services and tours, paying fares totalling £4·7 million. Of these, some 10,000 were carried to continental Europe on holiday tours in British coaches.'[17]

The First World War brought about many changes which were to influence the volume of tourism. It had wrought great social changes: people returning from the war expected new opportunities, better living standards, more 'breadth' to their lives; the war had broken down international barriers, and it had resulted in the fostering of an ideal, an optimistic, peaceful internationalism – just the climate in which tourism was most likely to flourish.

The post-war era saw a rise in the standard of living of the working and middle classes in America and certain European countries. On the other hand, some countries – such as Germany and Italy – suffered severe devaluation of their currencies, and this was a further encouragement to travel to citizens of other countries which enjoyed greater economic stability. The war had brought nations together; after the war tourists began to appear in countries where tourism had been practically unknown a few years earlier. The major tourist countries enjoyed an unprecedented boom in the late 1920s. In 1929 there were nearly 1½ million visitors to Switzerland, 1¼ million visitors to Italy, approximately 1,950,000 visitors to Austria, and 331,000 visitors to Great Britain (excluding visitors from the Commonwealth).

Tourism for the first time received wide recognition as a factor of considerable economic importance to many countries, ranking sometimes in net value higher than the most important physical exports. Recognizing both its economic value and its contribution to international understanding, the League of Nations actively encouraged tourism by the recommendation of simplified frontier formalities, reduction or abolition of *visa* fees, issuance of international *carnets de passage en douanes* (Customs passes) for tourists' cars and international driving licences. Approximately thirty countries in 1929 authorized the American Automobile Association to issue these documents to American tourists. A list of the signatories will serve to show to what extent car travel had already assumed importance in international tourism: Algeria, Austria, Belgium, Bulgaria, Czechoslovakia, Denmark, Egypt, Finland, France, Germany, Great Britain, Greece, Netherlands, Hungary, Irish Free State, Isle of Man, Italy, Latvia, Liechtenstein, Luxembourg, Morocco, Northern Ireland, Norway, Poland, Portugal, Rumania, Spain, Sweden, Switzerland, and Tunisia. Indeed, the list also shows how wide the official interest in tourism had become.

Few figures exist to compare pre- and post-war tourist traffic. The number of American citizens returning from trips abroad, which reached the pre-war peak in 1913 of 286,604, was exceeded for the first time in 1923, when the number was

---

[17] *Tourist Review*, January/March 1956, 'Development of Motor Coach Touring' by E. L. Taylor, ACA, MInstT, Member of Board of BTHA (Berne).

308,471, and this progressed to a new peak of 477,260 in 1930, which was not to be bettered until after the Second World War. The number of British subjects travelling to Europe in 1924 was only 7 per cent higher than in 1913, but by 1927 it was 26 per cent higher, and by 1930 it was 47 per cent higher than in 1913.

Before the Second World War, world travel reached a peak, generally speaking, in 1929–30, receded, and was already showing an encouraging upward trend when the war intervened. Tourist traffic to Australia increased from 23,236 in 1925 to 26,721 in 1928 and dropped to 18,125 in 1933.[18] The total number of foreign visitors to Austria rose from 1,204,196 in 1925 to 1,849,463 in 1928 and fell to 602,573 in 1934.[18] The number of tourists to Canada rose from 9,452,379 in 1925 to 20,024,697 in 1930 and fell to 9,705,484 in 1933.[18] The number of foreign visitors to Britain (275,842 in 1924) reached a peak in 1930 (333,815) and thereafter fell to 253,374 in 1932.

From this pattern it will be seen that tourism is sensitive to world economic conditions. Tourism can only occur on a large scale where the great mass of people enjoy some prosperity and security.

Despite changing economic conditions, tourism had reached new proportions, not only in the traditional tourist countries – Switzerland and Italy – but also in many countries outside of Europe. A résumé given in the *Promotion of Tourist Travel by Foreign Countries*, published by the US Department of Commerce in 1931, indicates the very wide range of countries for which tourism had become such an important economic factor as to justify *substantial* expenditure on tourist publicity overseas. It shows that nineteen European countries, six countries on the American continent, and eight other countries spent large sums in maintaining tourist offices in the United States or in carrying out publicity to attract American tourists.

The International Union of Official Organizations for Tourist Propaganda was set up in 1924. Its first Congress, at The Hague in 1925, was attended by delegates from the National Tourist Offices of fourteen countries, all European. Its aims were to exchange information on tourist publicity, to obtain international Customs concessions for the export and import of tourist publicity material and to alleviate frontier formalities or other obstacles to free international tourist traffic.[19] It was the forerunner of the present International Union of Official Travel Organizations.

Tourism and holiday-making on a national scale is a manifestation of prosperity. As greater numbers of people in many countries have higher living standards, they can afford to set aside a proportion of incomes on holidays and other 'non-essentials'. Yet in the United States and in some European countries surely the most important single development in the years 1918–39 was the gradual acceptance of the idea of paid holidays as a *necessary* provision for the health and recreation of working people. Before the First World War paid holidays were received by a few privileged workers; immediately after the war

---

[18] A. J. Norval's figures from *The Tourist Industry*.
[19] *The Need of International Collaboration in Favour of Tourism* (Union Internationale des Organes Officiels de Propagande Touristique, The Hague, Holland, 1937).

a movement started to encourage the widespread recognition of the need of annual paid holidays for workers. It was suggested at the Manchester National Conference for the Leisure of the People that two weeks' paid holiday was a minimum requirement. The trade unions and the International Labour Organization played a major part in securing legislation to permit paid holidays. 'In 1925,' Miss Elizabeth Brunner says, 'the Ministry of Labour estimated that $1\frac{1}{4}$ million *manual* wage earners were in receipt of holidays with pay. But the movement from then on grew very slowly, and in April 1937 the Ministry estimated that there were still only $1\frac{1}{2}$–$1\frac{3}{4}$ million manual wage-earners covered by the agreements. The setting up of the Committee on Holidays with Pay in 1937, however, gave a new stimulus, and the number rose to 3 million during the year. Although of the $18\frac{1}{2}$ million workpeople earning under £250 per annum there were 4 million in receipt of holidays with pay in April 1937, by March 1938 there were $7\frac{3}{4}$ million, and by June 1939 over 11 million.'

In 1937 it was reported that holidays were enforced by legislation in over twenty countries, and in 1938 that many countries were taking State or municipal action with regard to workers' holidays. In Belgium there was a National Office for Workers' Vacations, in France an Under-Secretary for Leisure and Sports, in Germany a special vacation section of the 'Strength through Joy' organization, in Luxembourg a National Committee for Leisure, in Poland a Committee for Leisure, in the USSR the Central Council for Trade Unions, and in Italy rest-houses run by *Il Dopolavoro*. The result of this combined action and wider publicity was interesting. In Germany in 1934 the number taken on holidays was 2,000,000, and in 1937 9,000,000. In 1937 those going on cruises numbered 30,000, and in the following year 100,000. In Russia 800,000 went to rest-homes in 1930, and in 1938, 2,200,000.[20]

Partly as a result of new facilities for workers in Britain, new types of holiday found immense popularity. By far the most important new development was the camping and youth hostel holiday. Membership of the Youth Hostels Association increased from 6,439 in 1931 (its first active year) to 83,418 in 1939. Its objects were 'to help all, especially young people of limited means, to a greater knowledge, love, and care of the countryside, particularly by providing hostels or other simple accommodation for them in their travels; and thus promote their health, rest, and education.'[21] The membership of the Camping Club of Great Britain – 820 in 1910 – rose to 3,000 in 1933 and 7,000 in 1935. Mr Butlin pioneered the first large-scale holiday camp at Skegness in 1937. By 1939 there were about 200 permanent camps owned by various companies scattered around the coast of Britain, catering for some 30,000 per week.[22]

It must not be forgotten that 'all-in' group holidays for workers were organized long before the advent of the large-scale commercial holiday camp. Drummond Fraser, speaking for the Co-operative Holidays Association in 1929, said that

[20] Information given at the Conference on Workers' Holidays, Park Lane Hotel, London, 1938.

[21] Youth Hostels Association (England and Wales) *Annual Report* for 1957.

[22] Miss Elizabeth Brunner's figures quoting from PRP Planning No. 194 in *Holiday-making and the Holiday Trades* (Oxford University Press, London, 1945).

one of the unique features of its activities was the 'spirit of *camaraderie* expressed in terms of mutual service'. The Association's guest-houses contained in miniature some of the essential features of the mass holiday camp of a later date. Workers tend to favour the 'all-in' holiday, and this is not necessarily because they cannot seek out an individual holiday for themselves. The industrial town dweller with limited means lives among crowds and enjoys mass entertainments. Used to close contact with his fellows in the large factory, he seeks the same comradeship whilst on holiday. Even when travelling abroad, most workers wanted the group holiday. The Workers' Travel Association, whose annual bookings for workers' travel abroad grew from 700 in 1922 to nearly 24,000 in 1937, stated that from its inception the most popular holiday was the 'all-in' tour with its conducted party travel, full-time resident leader, included excursions and organized social life. It is interesting to note in passing the emphasis which organizations catering for workers placed on the educational value of tourism. Though new types of holiday were being introduced to people who were not used to holidays at all, the traditional theme – education, self-improvement – was as strong as ever. In 1919 the Co-operative Holidays Association claimed to provide a holiday which was 'spiritually and physically bracing'. And were there not many other famous travel organizations – Polytechnic Tours, Sir Henry Lunn's and others – which were founded long before the First World War by educational or religious bodies interested in the welfare of the less well-to-do? The Workers' Travel Association, in its *Annual Report* of 1924, claimed that travel was the best means of achieving mutual understanding between the workers of all countries: 'Such understanding is only possible by actual contact, by interchange of visits, by the study of languages, and by an interest in the history, literature, art, and social movements of other countries'. How well this recalls the words of Lord Shaftesbury speaking 160 years earlier!

Through the holidays with pay movement in the more advanced countries of the world in the late 1930s, tourism and holiday-taking ceased to be a special luxury for a small number of well-to-do people, and became a national habit: 15 million British people, it is estimated, went away for holidays annually during this period.[23] The transformation took place in the space of only thirty years, a relatively short time when one considers the immensity of the change and its effects upon the social and economic life of the community. In a little over a quarter of a century, a complex industry with a greater turnover than many of the more important manufacturing industries, operated by world-wide networks of agencies, transport companies, hotel groups, publicity organizations, and trade associations had been created.

[23] Figures given by Miss Elizabeth Brunner in *Holiday-making and the Holiday Trades*, and by Sir Ronald Davison in *Britain's Holiday Crisis*, (The Bureau of Current Affairs, London, 1946).

Part II
Economic Aspects of Tourism

Introduction

The analysis of the tourism phenomenon has most fruitfully been undertaken from an economic point of view. Historically governments have been interested in tourism as a factor in a country's balance of payments or as a means of developing regions or sites with little other economic potential. Both chapters in this Part are devoted to the economic aspects of tourism.

The first examines on the basis of available data the relationship between income levels and travel expenditure whilst recognizing the influence of other factors on the growth of tourism. Limited data on domestic travel expenditure, which is estimated to account for 75–80 per cent of world expenditure on tourism, makes it possible to attempt only a limited analysis in this field of activity; moreover, there is a wide variation in the relative significance of domestic tourism between countries. However, data on international travel expenditure lend themselves to a more substantial treatment and lead to the calculation of the income elasticity coefficient of foreign travel expenditures. Exceptions or digressions from the 'norm' are explained.

In the second chapter Jeffrey Harrop makes a wide-ranging review of the volume and value of international tourism in Western Europe and in developing countries, before examining the position and performance of the United Kingdom in international tourism. He concludes that international tourism merits support, provided that the problems to which it gives rise are recognized and tackled.

Both contributions bring together much of what is known about the economics of international tourism and provide a convenient summary supported by a statistical analysis.

3 The Growth of Tourism

BY INTERNATIONAL UNION OF OFFICIAL TRAVEL ORGANIZATIONS

From Study on the Economic Impact of Tourism on National Economies and International Trade, *Travel Research Journal*, Special Issue (IOUTO, Geneva, 1966).

The Economic Significance of Tourism

World tourist expenditures in 1963 – foreign and domestic travel together – are estimated to have been almost $40 billions. This figure excludes expenditure on transport which probably added another third; thus producing a total tourist expenditure of approximately $53 billions. Of these total tourist expenditures some 20–25 per cent was spent on foreign travel and 75–80 per cent spent by tourists in their own countries.

The foregoing figures are, of necessity, only broad estimates of the scale of world tourist expenditures. They are presented here to give a perspective to this economic review of world tourist development. They show that we are dealing with a major economic activity; a form of expenditure which now absorbs, on a world-wide basis, about 5 per cent of total consumer expenditure.

In view of its importance in the world economy surprisingly little attention has been paid to the fundamental economic factors which have controlled the past growth of tourism and which may be expected to shape its future development. Perhaps one reason for this is the persistent puritanical nature of the economic science: 'travel for pleasure' has a frivolous connotation which seems to have made it unattractive as a field for serious economic study. This is, of course, an absurd view. Recreational activities become increasingly important as the peoples of the world grow richer, and even the most austere economist could console himself by reflecting that these recreational activities are a desirable means for maintaining or increasing human efficiency.

Another reason why relatively little attention has been paid to the economic significance of tourism is the somewhat amorphous nature of this activity. There is no 'tourist industry' as such, however convenient this term may be to describe this activity. Many industries are involved in providing goods and services to meet the needs of tourists throughout the world. It is the collective needs of these consumers which gives a homogeneity to tourism, but the diversity of their needs makes this activity a more complex field for economic study than most agricultural, extractive or manufacturing industries.

Domestic Tourism

In the opening paragraph of this report it has been estimated that 75–80 per cent of world expenditure on tourism is spent by travellers within their own countries. This estimate has been based on very limited data: only eighteen countries were able, in their answers to a questionnaire circulated by IUOTO in 1965, to give estimates of domestic tourist expenditure. Even with this limited data, however, it is possible to establish an approximate 'consumption function' for tourism which relates total travel expenditure (domestic and foreign) to the level of income. Using this method it has been estimated that annual total tourist expenditure rises from an average of approximately $0·3 per capita when personal consumption expenditure is $100 per capita to approximately $120 per capita when personal consumption expenditure is $2,000 per capita. This relationship produces an estimate of $40 billion for total tourist expenditure of which foreign travel accounts for $9 billion and domestic tourism for the remaining $31 billion.

The proportion of total tourist expenditure which is devoted to domestic tourism, rather than foreign travel, varies a great deal from country to country. The geographical and social circumstances of each country have a large influence in determining this distribution. From the few figures which are available it appears that the distribution varies from European countries, like Belgium, where only about 21 per cent of total tourist expenditure is domestic, to countries like the United States, where about 90 per cent of total tourist expenditure is domestic. The proportion of domestic tourist expenditure was even higher in Japan (96 per cent) but currency restrictions on foreign travel influenced this distribution.

The most important conclusion to be drawn from this brief survey of domestic tourism is that this is a very large field of economic activity about which very little precise information is currently available. It is to be hoped that in future issues of this annual study it will be possible to present far more data on this major section of the world's tourist industry.

International Tourism

According to figures submitted to IUOTO world receipts from international tourism amounted to $8,885·2 million and world expenditures on tourism amounted to $7,666·1 million in 1963. The difference between these two figures can be reconciled by (*a*) the substantial expenditures of US servicemen overseas, which probably amount to $1,000 million a year and (*b*) unreported figures of more than twenty countries unable to estimate these expenditures.

World foreign travel expenditure has been increasing at an average rate of approximately 12 per cent for many years. This is a growth rate substantially larger than most other economic activities. In the period from 1958 to 1963, world tourist expenditure increased by 75 per cent: in the same period world industrial production increased by 44 per cent and world trade in manufactures by 45 per cent.

Figure 3.1 shows the growth of world tourist expenditures from 1950 to 1963 and compares this with the growth of world national incomes over the same period. It can be seen that tourist expenditures have increased at almost exactly twice the annual rate of increase in national incomes: tourism has increased at 12 per cent a year and national incomes at 6 per cent a year.

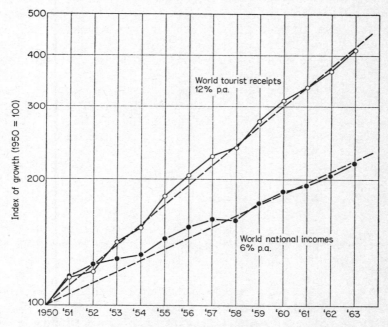

Figure 3.1 Growth of world tourism compared with national incomes

This relationship between growth of tourism and increased national incomes is extremely interesting, particularly from the point of view of forecasting future tourist developments. If the relationship continues to hold good, and if a continued growth of about 5 per cent a year is achieved in aggregate national incomes, it would be reasonable to expect a continuing growth of about 10 per cent a year in world tourism over the next decade.

An alternative approach to basically the same relationship between foreign travel expenditure and income level can be made by a 'cross-country' analysis, i.e. by comparing the experiences of different countries at the same point of time. It is, of course, self-evident that the level of expenditure on foreign travel in each country is directly related to the income level within each country. The precise statistical value of this relationship is, however, of considerable interest and importance.

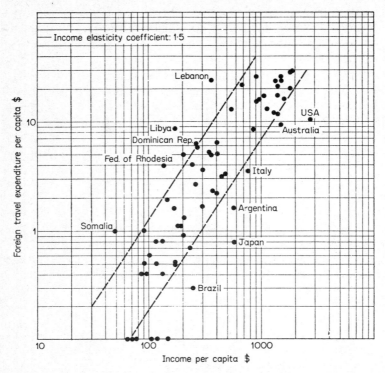

Figure 3.2 Relationship between foreign travel expenditure and income per capita
(1963 data)

In Figure 3.2 the foreign travel expenditures of 73 countries (as reported
to IUOTO for 1963) have been reduced to a per capita basis and plotted in
relation to the income per capita of the country concerned. In this presentation
both scales of the graph are logarithmic and an analysis of this kind produces
what economists commonly call a 'consumption function' for the product concerned. The slope of the regression line in this analysis gives an 'income elasticity
coefficient' which indicates the relationship between the percentage change in
the expenditure on the particular product and percentage change in income. In
Figure 3.2 there is quite a large spread amongst the 73 points plotted but,
nevertheless, all but 11 of the points fall within the two parallel regression lines
which have been fitted visually to the data.

It may be worthwhile to digress at this point to examine why certain countries
should be exceptions to the general relationship between travel expenditure and
income level. There are, as may be seen in Figure 3.2, eleven significant exceptions to the broad general pattern of this relationship: six where foreign travel
expenditure is lower than the generalized expectation and five where it is higher.
These exceptions can be explained by the particular geographical, social or
political circumstances of the countries concerned. Of the countries where

foreign travel expenditure is lower than might be expected, the most important is the United States. Because the United States is the largest foreign travel market in the world, it is common to think of Americans as having a high propensity to travel abroad. In fact, however, relative to the income level of the United States, foreign travel is a comparatively undeveloped industry in that country. The explanation for this is not difficult to find: apart from travel to the neighbouring countries Canada and Mexico, almost all other foreign travel by US nationals involves a long and comparatively expensive journey. Hence a much higher proportion of total US tourist expenditure is for domestic travel than is the case in, for example, many European countries where a short cross-frontier journey takes holidaymakers abroad.

The same sort of geographical explanation accounts for the relatively low development of foreign travel expenditure in Australia. Travel to Europe and North America both represent very long and expensive journeys for Australian travellers. It is for this reason that, like American residents, almost 90 per cent of Australians take their holidays within their own country.

Italian foreign travel expenditures are also lower than the generalized expectation. In this case, however, the explanation appears to be merely a time lag in the changing pattern of consumer expenditure as the country has grown richer. This is now changing: foreign travel expenditure has grown very rapidly in the past few years. In 1963 Italian foreign travel expenditure was 48 per cent higher than in the previous year and there was a further 25 per cent increase in 1964. It seems likely that Italian foreign travel expenditure per capita will soon reach the norm suggested by the regression lines in Figure 3.2.

Japanese foreign travel expenditure has, in the past, been low in relation to income. The explanation for this has undoubtedly been the limitations on foreign currency allowed for travel, as is evidenced by the very high proportion of total tourist expenditure devoted to domestic travel. The substantial relaxation of these limitations which became effective in 1964 will no doubt have a major effect on the growth of Japanese foreign travel in the next few years.

The other two countries where foreign travel expenditure is below the generalized expectation are Brazil and Argentina. The experiences of these two countries are difficult to interpret because of fluctuations in exchange rates, but in both the factor of geographical isolation from the major centres of tourism is significant.

Five countries, Libya, Lebanon, the former Federation of Rhodesia and Nyasaland, Dominican Republic, and Somalia, are shown in Figure 3.2 to have had a higher average foreign travel per capita in 1963 than the generalized expectation. In each of these countries, though for different reasons in each, the explanation appears to be connected with the distribution of income. In any country in which a relatively large part of total national income goes to a small percentage of the population it is reasonable to assume that there will be a much higher expenditure on foreign travel than the average income of the country would, by itself, suggest. This phenomena of uneven income distribution is commonly found in oil-producing countries, like Libya, and in African countries, like Rhodesia, which have a white settler population.

This digression to discuss the exceptional points plotted in Figure 3.2 serves to strengthen the general nature of the relationship between foreign travel expenditure and income level which is expressed by the regression lines in that chart. The slope of these lines indicates an 'income elasticity' of 1·5; that is to say, it may be expected that a 10 per cent increase in income per capita will be associated with a 15 per cent increase in foreign travel expenditure per capita. An average income elasticity of 1·5 would not, by itself, be enough to explain the growth of world tourism over the past thirteen years shown in Figure 3.1: other factors are involved. One explanation of the apparent discrepancy between the conclusions suggested by Figure 3.1 and Figure 3.2 may possibly be that the income elasticity coefficient for foreign travel expenditure tends to rise as income per capita increases. There is some evidence for this. An analysis of US foreign travel expenditure per capita relative to US income per capita over the period 1950 to 1963 indicates that the US income elasticity coefficient for foreign travel is substantially higher than the world figure suggested by Figure 3.2.

Other Factors Influencing the Growth of Tourism

In the foregoing sections of this report a great deal of stress has been laid on the relationship between the increase in incomes and the growth of tourism. There can be little doubt that this wealth factor is of primary importance in explaining the development of tourist travel. There are, however, a number of other factors which have considerable importance in determining the rate of growth and the pattern of distribution of tourist expenditures.

Of particular importance amongst the other factors are:

(a) *Demographic considerations.* The growth of populations, changes in age distribution, and increasing urbanization of population are each factors of importance. It has been noted in travel studies that variations in financial commitments at different stages in the life cycle of a family have a marked influence on the amount spent on travel.

(b) *Working conditions.* Reductions in hours of work and lengthening of paid holidays are factors of importance. Some data on the latter subject have been published in reports of the International Labour Office. Minimum figures of this kind may, however, obscure more significant changes in the average vacation periods actually enjoyed in some of the countries concerned.

(c) *Educational factors.* The marked trend throughout the world for more people to have the advantage of higher education is a significant factor in tourist development. Many travel surveys in recent years have pointed to the relationship between educational standards and the desire to travel.

(d) *Social habits.* The whole pattern of social organization in North America and Western Europe has increasingly changed in ways which create new desires for different kinds of leisure activities. An increasing proportion of the working population in sedentary occupations appears to be one explanation for this growing demand for active leisure; and travel gains from this particular recreational trend.

(*e*) *Car ownership*. The general level of car ownership has had considerable effects on the size and type of tourist flows.

In addition to these factors, we must not overlook the considerable effect which the promotional activities of the travel industry itself have had upon the demand for travel.

It is, however, extremely difficult to quantify the influence of these various social factors on the growth of tourism. From a statistical point of view there is a major problem which arises from the 'cross-correlation' of many social factors with increase in incomes. The cross-correlations make it very difficult to isolate the influence of individual factors. It is extremely important, however, that more data should be collected in order to establish more precisely the trends throughout the world in the social factors known to influence the growth of tourism.

A factor which has a considerable influence on the distribution of tourist traffic is the relative price levels of different countries which are, in effect, competing for a share of the total market. The available data show that over the past five years the prices of hotel and other facilities in most of the main centres of tourism have increased by approximately 20–30 per cent. Price increases of this order of magnitude are broadly in line with the increases in purchasing power enjoyed by residents of the main producing countries. There are, however, a few exceptional cases where price increases have been substantially greater than this general average, but in some of these the final price level remains, nevertheless, below that of most other countries. A good example of this is Spain, where, despite the fact that tourist prices appear to have risen by 84 per cent from 1961 to 1965, this country still remains one of the least expensive holiday areas in Europe. The price-movements recorded in the 43 countries taken into consideration are very likely due to (*a*) demand-pull inflationary tendencies, (*b*) cost-push inflationary pressures, or (*c*) a combination of both. This example illustrates the dangers of drawing simple conclusions from the available data. Nevertheless it is essential that the tourist industry should have regard to the general trends in the level of prices, and should note the effect which these may have on the distribution of traffic. This may be another field in which further research could be rewarding.

4 *The Economics of the Tourist Boom*

BY J. HARROP

From *Journal of World Trade Law*, Vol. No. 7, Issue No. 2, March/April 1973
(edited in Geneva, published in Twickenham, Middlesex)

It is intended in this article to examine some economic aspects of the tourist
boom during the last decade. The phenomenal growth of international tourism
during the 1960s still only represents the limited development of a sector whose
future growth potential is enormous. In the light of this it is worthwhile to assess
some of the most important features and implications of tourism's growth.
What, for example, have been its effects on the balance of payments' position of
Western European countries? How can the benefits from international tourism
be maximized for the developing countries to mitigate inherent balance of payments' problems, and to accelerate the rate of economic growth? Can the United
Kingdom's performance, and position in the international tourist market be
adequately explained?

Before considering these questions, however, it is necessary to clarify briefly
the terminology which will be used. By the term tourist, one means a temporary
visitor who stays in a country at least twenty-four hours. The purpose of most
travel journeys will be leisure activities like holidays and also business trips.
Those visitors who do not make an overnight stay in the country visited are
merely listed as 'excursionists'.

The Magnitude of the Tourist Boom

During the 1960s there was a phenomenal expansion of international tourism,
which grew at a faster rate than domestic tourism and became a larger proportion
of total tourist receipts each year. By 1970 gross world tourist receipts were
estimated at $17,400 million. In some areas like Asia and Africa tourist earnings
were rising even faster than the average, though this was from a relatively low
base, and it is Europe and North America which account for the bulk of world
tourism.

International travel for recreational, pleasure, and personal reasons is growing
at a faster rate than international business travel. International tourists are also
tending to travel longer distances and to visit a larger number of countries.[1] This
growth is mainly the outcome of both a high income elasticity of demand and a
high price elasticity. Estimates of income elasticity vary, but the world-wide

---

[1] International Union of Official Travel Organizations (IUOTO), *Economic Review of World Tourism* (1968), pp. 18–22.

average national income coefficient in recent years has been about 1·5.[2] Further-more for the major tourist generating countries it has been even higher.[3] The high price elasticity has been manifested by the sensitive response to the major reduction in the price of air fares and in the growth of air charter inclusive vacation travel; the latter now account for some 70 per cent of all air departures from Europe.[4]

The future growth potential of world tourism is considerable. Once countries pass a threshold per capita income level, foreign travel expenditure begins to increase quite rapidly. Meanwhile, unlike the consumption of most other goods, marginal utility diminishes only slowly since each purchase seems to whet the appetite for more travel.[5] In fact the main constraint on travel may well be time as much as income and greater prosperity in the future could be reflected more in longer paid holidays as in Scandinavia.[6] Other factors stimulating the growth of demand are perhaps demographic and sociological. For example, population growth is biased in age distribution towards the young. Thus it is the young age group between 16 and 24 which accounts for 31 per cent of total British holiday-makers abroad and for 41 per cent of Scandinavian visitors to Britain.[7] A better educated, but more industrialized and urbanized society also reinforces the need for a widening of horizons and the mass media have made people increasingly aware of this.[8] During the past five years world tourist spending has risen by about 8 per cent a year; and appreciably faster than the world's real economic output which has increased by less than 5 per cent a year. It has been estimated that world tourist arrivals could increase to 260 million in 1975 and 325 million in 1980, and that tourist expenditure in these years may reach $23 billion and $34 billion respectively at current prices.[9] Thus, the following sections will examine the effects of tourism and whether its further growth is likely to be beneficial.[10]

The Effects of Tourism in Western Europe

Since approximately three-quarters of foreign tourist arrivals and over two-thirds of international tourist receipts are in Europe the effects there are worth examin-ing.[11] In particular it seems appropriate to consider these in the context of the balance of payments, and the travel account position of eighteen Western European countries is shown in Table 4.1.

[2] G. Colley, 'International Tourism Today', *Lloyds Bank Review*, July 1967, p. 30.

[3] IUOTO, *Economic Review* (1968), *op. cit.*

[4] H. D. Davis, 'Potentials for Tourism in Developing Countries', *Finance and Develop-ment*, December 1968, p. 36.

[5] L. J. Lickorish and A. G. Kershaw, *The Travel Trade* (1958), p. 106.

[6] J. G. Hamilton, *International Tourism*, EIU, No. 7 (1970).

[7] *British Travel News*, No. 29, Spring 1970, pp. 35–6.

[8] Hamilton, *op. cit.*, p. 55 provides figures showing that British tour operators and travel agents spent £3m. on advertising in 1969. This compares with advertising expenditure on cars of £5·2m., and on washers and refrigerators of £1·2m. in the same year.

[9] *Ibid.*, pp. 23, 24.

[10] For an interesting account of the early historical growth of travel, *see* H. M. Paint, 'The Usage and Fashyon of Al Maner of Countres', *Lloyds Bank Review*, July 1968.

[11] Estimated to exclude USSR and Poland, but to include the rest of the Eastern bloc.

Table 4.1

Balance on the Travel Account of Eighteen West European Countries during the 1960s ($m.)

	1960	1961	1962	1963	1964	1965	1966	1967	1968	1969	1970*
Austria	+171	+216	+280	+313	+386	+420	+424	+396	+430	+489	+676
Belg-Lux	−1	−2	−2	−3	−68	−82	−90	−128	−124	−138	−144
Denmark	+33	+30	+21	+22	+30	+25	+15	−6	+3	+12	+41
Finland	−23	−30	−35	−31	−36	−34	−30	−26	−2	+1	+34
France	+234	+208	+194	+118	+33	−28	+11	−5	−133	+33	+135
W. Germany	−159	−316	−529	−479	−496	−637	−767	−682	−674	−985	−1,469
Greece	+30	+43	+53	+68	+52	+66	+103	+86	+78	+102	+139
Iceland	−2	−2	−2	−4	−6	−7	−9	−9	−3	−1	—
Ireland	+69	+76	+74	+76	+93	+111	+94	+107	+95	+97	—
Italy	+548	+647	+724	+749	+826	+1,011	+1,199	+1,126	+1,112	+1,139	+912
Netherlands	+5	+5	+6	−1	−24	−33	−97	−79	−116	−106	−177
Norway	−23	−10	+6	+47	+4	+6	+10	+2	−1	−2	+16
Portugal	+11	+13	+28	+43	+70	+88	+185	+196	+144	+93	+124
Spain	+247	+331	+466	+611	+852	+1,027	+1,202	+1,111	+1,110	+1,195	+1,568
Sweden	−20	−37	−52	−71	−80	−113	−143	−178	−199	−238	−338
Switzerland	+217	+249	+279	+298	+247	+365	+382	+395	+404	+368	+424
U.K.	−48	−67	−76	−148	−199	−272	−219	−112	+27	+84	+109
Yugoslavia	+6	+8	+22	+44	+55	+63	+82	+95	+136	+168	+162

* Some of the figures are provisional
Source: Calculated from *IMF Yearbook*

Italy and Spain are the two countries in which tourism contributes the largest surplus on the travel account. In the early 1960s Italy had by far the largest travel surplus in Western Europe; but since 1964 Spain has become much more popular and its surplus in some years has been marginally above that of Italy, and the difference was quite substantial in 1970. Apart from the more important position of Spain in international tourism, several other salient features emerge from the table. For example, Yugoslavia, Greece, and Portugal have shown a rapid rate of growth in their surplus on the travel account. On the other hand, in Switzerland and to a lesser extent in Austria, the rate of increase in the travel surplus has been less conspicuous though in absolute terms it has been substantial. Since 1962 Austria's surplus on the travel account has exceeded that of Switzerland and it received a special boost in 1970. The position of France has fluctuated from a surplus up to the end of 1964, to a small deficit in occasional years in the late 1960s, but by 1970 it was back in surplus again.

Those countries which had a deficit on the travel account at the beginning of the last decade, such as Germany and Sweden, tended to have an even larger deficit by the late 1960s; for example, revaluation of the Deutsche Mark in October 1969 contributed to a considerable increase in Germany's deficit on the travel account in 1970. An important exception to this generalization was the UK whose position will be examined in more detail in a later section.

Table 4.2 shows the influence of tourism on the current account of the balance of payments.

In 1968 and 1969 international receipts reduced the deficit on the goods and services account of eight countries; for example, it covered 55·5 per cent of the deficit in Spain, 54·0 per cent in Yugoslavia, and 112·0 per cent in Austria in 1969. Tourism reduced the surplus on the goods and services account of seven countries in 1968 and of five countries in 1969; for example, in Germany by 20·7 per cent and in the Netherlands by 75·8 per cent in 1969. In the case of two countries in 1968, and four countries in 1969, tourism added to the existing surplus on the current account of the balance of payments; these countries were Italy and Switzerland, plus the United Kingdom and Finland. However, in only one case did tourism provide a real disequilibriating force. That was reflected in the position of Iceland in 1968 and Sweden in 1969.

These findings must be qualified by the fact that they only refer to the balance of payments on current account, and travel has been deducted from the current account total. In addition, the short-run position has been shown only for two years 1968 and 1969, and countries can switch positions between the four categories which have been outlined. However, an examination undertaken of earlier years to 1960 suggests that relatively few countries have moved their positions. In only one other country, Finland, did tourism appear to be exercising a significant disequilibriating force for much of the 1960s, but by the end of the decade it had succeeded in obtaining a surplus on its travel account.

In those countries which tended to have a travel account deficit, tourist expenditure as a percentage of their expenditure for goods and services from abroad was generally quite low; for example, in 1969 it was 6·0 per cent in

Table 4.2

Tourism and the Equilibrium of the Balance of Payments in 1968 and 1969 ($m.)

Countries	Balance on goods and services excluding travel		Balance on Travel account		Effect of Tourism (travel account balance as a % of the balance on goods and services) The 4 group categories are shown in brackets*	
	1968	1969	1968	1969	1968	1969
Austria	−567	−437	+430	+489	75·8 (1)	112·0 (1)
Belg-Lux	+208	+338	−124	−138	59·6 (2)	40·8 (2)
Denmark	−259	−392	+3	+12	1·2 (1)	3·1 (1)
Finland	+67	+2	−2	+1	3·0 (2)	50·0 (3)
France	+56	−774	−133	+33	237·5 (2)	4·3 (1)
W. Germany	+5,308	+4,753	−674	−985	12·7 (2)	20·7 (2)
Greece	−554	−731	+78	+102	14·1 (1)	14·0 (1)
Iceland	−44	+5·4	−3	−1	6·8 (4)	18·5 (2)
Ireland	−248	−377	+95	+97	38·3 (1)	25·7 (1)
Italy	+1,224	+903	+1,112	+1,139	90·8 (3)	126·1 (3)
Netherlands	+250	+140	−116	−106	46·4 (2)	75·8 (2)
Norway	+161	+145	−1	−2	0·62 (2)	1·4 (2)
Portugal	−364	−435	+144	+93	39·5 (1)	21·4 (1)
Spain	−1,819	−2,155	+1,110	+1,195	61·0 (1)	55·5 (1)
Sweden	+52	−161	−199	−238	382·7 (2)	147·8 (4)
Switzerland	+399	+462	+404	+368	101·3 (3)	79·7 (3)
UK	−49	+1,519	+27	+84	55·2 (1)	5·5 (3)
Yugoslavia	−311	−311	+136	+168	43·7 (1)	54·0 (1)

Source: Calculated from *IMF Yearbook*
*(1) Tourism reduced the deficit on goods and services;
(2) Tourism reduced the surplus on goods and services;
(3) Tourism added to the surplus on goods and services;
(4) Tourism increased the deficit on goods and services.

Germany, 5·1 per cent in Sweden, and 4·4 per cent in the Netherlands. This is shown in Table 4.3.

In those countries heavily dependent on tourist earnings, receipts from this source were a significant proportion of their receipts for goods and services. This was most evident in Spain where tourist receipts were over one-third of its total receipts from goods and services, and in Austria where they were over one-fifth. In Ireland, Portugal, Greece, Italy, and Yugoslavia tourist receipts tended to provide one-tenth or more of total receipts from goods and services.[12]

Table 4.3

International Tourist Expenditure and Receipts Related to
Total Expenditure and Receipts for Goods and Services

	Tourist expenditure as a % of expenditure for goods and services		Tourist receipts as a % of receipts from goods and services	
	1968	*1969*	*1968*	*1969*
Austria	8·3	8·5	23·2	22·2
Belg-Lux	4·6	4·4	3·2	3·0
Denmark	6·1	5·7	6·5	6·5
Finland	3·6	3·6	3·4	3·7
France	7·0	5·2	6·2	6·0
W. Germany	6·1	6·0	2·6	2·6
Greece	2·9	2·9	12·3	14·3
Iceland	3·2	2·5	2·0	2·0
Ireland	6·1	5·5	14·2	13·5
Italy	3·0	3·3	10·1	9·6
Netherlands	4·4	4·4	3·2	2·7
Norway	2·8	3·1	2·8	3·0
Portugal	4·3	4·4	15·3	12·6
Spain	2·5	2·4	36·1	33·6
Sweden	5·1	5·1	1·8	1·8
Switzerland	6·0	5·8	11·8	11·3
UK	2·8	3·1	2·9	3·3
Yugoslavia	2·5	3·0	9·8	10·3

Source: Calculated from *IMF Yearbook*

Tourism has undoubtedly been an important factor in improving the balance of payments position of several less-developed countries in southern Europe. It has also contributed to the rapid average growth rates achieved per annum. Between 1960 and 1968 these were 7·7 per cent in Spain, 6·7 per cent in Yugoslavia, and 7·3 per cent in Greece;[13] in the latter, the tourist multiplier,[14] which will be discussed later, has been estimated at 1·2 to 1·4. Tourist receipts should

[12] For earlier figures see IUOTO, *Economic Review* (1970), *op. cit.*, pp. 33, 34.

[13] A. Maddison, *Economic Progress and Policy in Developing Countries* (1970), p. 29.

[14] The tourist multiplier, or more accurately here, the tourism income multiplier, is a factor by which the direct expenditure by tourists increases as a result of subsequent diffusion through the economy. *Eds.*

also in future years maintain these trends and also enable some other countries to improve on their growth rates; for example, Turkey's growth rate was 5·2 per cent a year on average during this period,[15] but in 1970 its tourist receipts recorded one of the most rapid rates of growth among the OECD countries and rose by 39 per cent over the 1960 figure.[16]

Tourism in the Developing Countries

The receipts from international tourism can provide a valuable source of foreign exchange for many developing countries helping to mitigate the pessimistic 'Prebisch thesis'. Although tourism is sensitive to the level of economic activity in the tourist generating countries, it provides more stable earnings than primary products. Although tourism was not a spectacular net earner of foreign exchange for developing countries as a whole in the '60s, it has tended to increase at a higher rate than merchandise exports in a number of countries; it has also been important for those countries near the main tourist generating areas; for example, Mexico's tourist receipts as a percentage of its merchandise export receipts rose from 67 per cent to 94 per cent between 1960 and 1968 as indicated in Table 4.4.

Table 4.4

Tourist Receipts for Selected Developing Countries as a Percentage of their Merchandise Export Receipts

	1960	*1968*	*1969*	*1970*
Mexico	67	94	89	103
Morocco	7	19	25	27
Israel	13	15	12	13
Jamaica	24	40	36	34
Kenya	10 ('63)	20	19	19

Source: Calculated from *IMF Yearbook.*

Expenditure on international tourism by the USA in the 1960s meant that it had a larger deficit on its travel account than all the West European countries added together. In 1967 the USA travel deficit was $1,549 million; in 1968 it was $1,247 million and in 1969 $1,332 million. Apart from Mexico, other countries in close proximity which benefited included the West Indies, Bermuda, and the Bahamas; for example, in Jamaica tourist receipts as a percentage of its merchandise export receipts rose from 24 to 40 per cent between 1960 and 1968.

Tourist receipts also contributed to the impressive annual average growth rates achieved by countries like Mexico and Israel – 6·4 per cent and 8·3 per cent

[15] *Ibid.*
[16] See 'International Tourism in OECD Member Countries', *OECD Observer*, No. 54, October 1971, pp. 14–17.

respectively between 1960 and 1968.[17] However, it is in the African continent, and areas like Morocco and Kenya that tourism has begun to expand with tourist receipts as a percentage of merchandise export receipts rising from 7 to 27 per cent and from 10 to 19 per cent respectively as indicated in Table 4.4.

North Africa is the main beneficiary of this comparatively recent trend.[18] Morocco is followed in order of tourist receipt importance by the UAR, Tunisia, and Algeria. East Africa is also growing rapidly as a tourist attraction and although it accounted for fewer tourist arrivals than Southern Africa, it was responsible for marginally higher tourist receipts.[19] The development of tourism in countries such as Kenya was originally fairly sluggish. Overseas visitors merely tended to replace former European colonial visitors resident in Africa, and it was not until 1965–6 that accommodation shortages became acute. Meanwhile the former colonial regimes had left behind little expertise in tourism, and this in addition to capital and skilled labour shortages tended to constrain development.[20] However, it is now recognized that tourism can provide valuable development assistance not only via the balance of payments, but more directly via production (the capital/output ratio) and via employment (the capital/employment ratio). The incremental capital output ratio of tourism in Kenya has been estimated at 2·5 to 3·0 compared with 4·4 for manufacturing activities.[21] The employment-creating effects of tourist expenditure in Kenya are manifested by the fact that every $2,400 of tourist expenditure has apparently created an additional job.[22] Tourist multiplier effects have been calculated for a number of countries, though the estimates vary over a wide range.[23] For example, the indirect or induced effect of tourist investment via the multiplier has been calculated at 0·9 to 1·3 for the island of Hawaii, where one would expect considerable leakages. This is a good study,[24] but multipliers generally may be higher than this since Hawaii is part of a customs union with a federal tax system. For Pakistan the multiplier has been estimated at 3·3[25] and for the East Caribbean re-calculated multipliers have been put at 1·0 compared with earlier estimates of 2·3.[26]

Given the induced effects of tourism on other activities such as building, agriculture, and infrastructure, some employment can be provided outside the main

[17] Maddison, *op. cit.*

[18] As defined in IUOTO, *Pilot Study of Africa's Tourism Prospects* (1966), Appendix 10.

[19] *Ibid.*, Appendices 10 and 13.

[20] *See* F. Mitchell, *The Costs and Benefits of Tourism in Kenya*, Institute of Development Studies (Nairobi, 1968).

[21] *See* F. Mitchell, 'The Value of Tourism in East Africa', *Eastern Africa Economic Review*, Vol. 2, No. 1, June 1970, p. 9.

[22] *Ibid.*

[23] M. Peters, *International Tourism* (1969), pp. 238–40.

[24] Note that mistakes have been made in calculating some tourist multipliers: for example, *see* H. G. Clements, *The Future of Tourism in the Pacific and Far East* (Washington DC, US Dept of Commerce, 1961); also H. Zinder and associates, *Essential Elements of a Tourist Development Programme – A Critical Commentary* (Washington, October 1968).

[25] IUOTO, *Economic Review* (1968), *op. cit.*, pp. 38, 39.

[26] K. Levitt and I. Gulati, 'Income Effect of Tourist Spending: Mystification Multiplied. A Critical Comment on the Zinder Report', *Social and Economic Studies*, Vol. 19, No. 3, September 1970.

tourist season. With its further tendency to be labour-intensive it is surprising that many countries have not spent more on investments in the tourist sector of their economies. Labour-intensity measured by the ratio of man-years of labour to units of $10,000 of capital for travel services in the USA resulted in a ratio of 1·43 compared with an average for all activities of 1·034.[27] The travel ratio was compiled on the basis of three categories: eating and drinking places, hotels, and other personal services with respective contributions of 25 per cent, 30 per cent, and 45 per cent. This labour intensiveness of travel activities is likely to apply also in less-developed countries, though the provision of some minimum capital requirements may have tended to restrict the development of tourism in the past.

The benefits from tourism, however, should be kept in perspective, if only to avoid unrealistic developments. For some countries where tourist earnings have risen only slowly, the temptation sometimes arises to over-accelerate projected developments. In the case of Ceylon, earnings from tourism have been relatively low and as much as 70 per cent to 80 per cent of the foreign exchange earned has leaked into the black market and out of the banking system.[28] Furthermore Ceylon's recent ten-year plan proposing to increase the number of visitors from 24,000 in 1967 to 307,000 in 1976, seems over-optimistic.[29]

Developing countries should recognize that in a partial equilibrium framework, the possibility of the simultaneous creation of significant competitive capacity by other developing countries has been ignored. This can result in over-investment and excess capacity in the industry. Those countries whose main tourist asset is climatic may find that considerable price flexibility may not overcome seasonal problems. Also, such countries cannot expect to achieve such a rapid growth of tourist potential until the greater part of the non-reproducible resources, e.g. beaches, ancient ruins, situated between them and the tourist-generating centres have been developed and are being utilized at a satisfactory rate. Though a reduction of transport costs will facilitate the development of more remote areas, existing tourist areas will also benefit from cheaper transport. However, those tourists constituting the 'fashionable' element of demand will probably be induced to travel farther. The places of those displaced in the nearer and more established tourist areas will then tend to be filled by new 'band-wagon' tourists. But it is apparent that international tourism, in the short run at least, is unlikely to transform the economies of less-developed countries distant from the main tourist-generating countries; but it will be of growing importance in the long run.

Economic considerations are of paramount importance to maximize returns from tourism. International trade theory has been constructed on the virtual inability of factors of production to move across international boundaries; yet international tourism involves the movement of labour, albeit as a factor of consumption, instead of a factor of production.[30] International tourist flows and

[27] H. P. Gray, *International Travel-International Trade* (1970), pp. 21, 22.
[28] *See* D. P. Guneratne, *An Analysis of Tourist Arrivals in 1965 and Foreign Exchange Earnings from Tourism* (Ceylon Dept of Census and Statistics, No. 14: 1967).
[29] Gray, *op. cit.*, pp. 133, 134.
[30] Gray, *op. cit.*, p. 3.

patterns can be explained by relative costs based on the factor input mix, in which demand-adjusted factor supply differences determine tourism similar to the way in which they determine trade.[31] In addition, economic techniques provide the means of assessing the viability of tourist developments and of ensuring their most effective contribution to the economy.

It is necessary initially to identify the main tourist attractions which a country possesses, to consider the opportunity costs of tourism, and to conduct a cost benefit analysis of the returns. If the prospects seem promising, then it is likely that the government will have a major role to play in providing the pre-conditions for tourist development, particularly the infrastructure. Afterwards it can be left more to the private entrepreneur both from home and abroad to develop the potential. The latter are more likely to provide realistic assessment, know-how, and knowledge of the requirements of tourists; they may also help to ensure that over-expansion does not ensue as a result of too many countries over-investing for the limited volume of tourist demands.

Further government intervention will be necessary to ensure that the widespread provision of new jobs is not accompanied automatically by excessive local price increases. There is considerable scope for government fiscal policy to readjust prices;[32] to reduce the pressure of local demand; and to redistribute income elsewhere in the economy consolidating the 'spread' effects of the tourist complex. Governments must be in a position to collect any rise in income through taxation, according to the formula, $T = E_f K_t p$ where $T = $ tax revenue, E_f is expenditure by international tourists, and K_t is the tourist multiplier (after allowing for the import content of tourists' expenditure); $p = $ the proportion of national income accruing to the government through taxation.[33] Government taxation of profits also appears superior to a policy of price controls by hotels since the latter might deter investment by creating uncertainty about future rates of return. This does not mean, however, that hotels should not be encouraged to publish their prices since that can be very beneficial.[34]

Co-operative promotion campaigns between tourist countries to provide a comprehensive tour of regional attractions might be more useful than competition.[35] Yet in East Africa, for example, Uganda actually withdrew from the East African Tourist Travel Association in 1963, partly because of the difficulty in ensuring an optimal division of the gains between the various countries.[36]

Superior marketing might help to extend the tourist season and thereby the duration of hotel occupancy. To show a reasonable profit new hotels require a minimum occupancy of 100 per cent for eighty days.[37] However, although tables

[31] *Ibid.*

[32] *See* P. Diamond, 'On The Economics of Tourism', *Eastern Africa Economic Review*, Vol. I, No. 2, December 1969.

[33] Peters, *op. cit.*

[34] *See* H. D. Davis, 'Investing in Tourism', *Finance and Development*, March 1967.

[35] IUOTO, *Pilot Study, op. cit.*, p. 61.

[36] Mitchell, *Eastern Africa Economic Review, loc. cit.*, p. 14.

[37] IUOTO, *Economic Review of World Tourism* (1970), pp. 24, 25.

exist of international hotel occupancy, meaningful comparisons cannot be undertaken since high occupancy rates may be merely a result of scarce accommodation.[38] To achieve maximum returns from tourist investment it is necessary to concentrate it in priority areas where consumer preferences may have already been shown or are likely to be expressed, and in which scale economies can be reaped. The creation of micro-urbanization developments[39] would provide the linking of industrial and agricultural activities to tourism. Within such a spatial settlement a mixed composition containing not only hotels[40] but also real estate for quick sale would result in the most rapid amortization of capital. The development of such a residence, or enclave industry, would make better use of infrastructure and be contra-seasonal. However, such developments seem more appropriate for countries near the main tourist generating areas; for example, in Spain on the coasts of the Alicante and Malaga provinces, and in areas in close proximity to the United States. Such non-hotel accommodation might go as high as 90 per cent of total development of 10,000 beds. It would provide full employment for approximately 2,400 people, and enable aircraft to be used at an efficient level. It might also form the basis for further peripheral zone development to create a tourist complex of 30,000–40,000 beds.[41]

Finally, developing countries might consider the potential value of a national flag airline and though it involves the costly import of aircraft, it can confer several benefits. It provides publicity and marketing image, and such companies would generally survive with IATA rates.

The United Kingdom's Position and Performance in International Tourism

The United Kingdom has traditionally tended to have a deficit on the travel account of the balance of payments. Such a position could be expected, given that the United Kingdom has a relatively high income per head and lacks the climatic attractions which are possessed by more southerly countries. During the early 1960s the travel account deficit continued to widen, and the government decided that some restriction in expenditure abroad was required by the introduction of a travel allowance. Despite the substantial increase in travel debits, however, the widening of the travel deficit can be attributed more to the slow growth of travel credits, up to 1967. This is indicated by the statistics in Table 4.5.

International comparisons also suggest that the percentage increase in tourist expenditure abroad by British citizens between 1958 and 1967 was less than in any other major tourist-generating country except Canada.[42] Meanwhile, though total British expenditure and spending per tourist was quite high by international standards in the middle of the last decade, per capita spending of

[38] *Ibid.*

[39] I. E. Galeotti, 'Industrialization of Tourism in the Developing Areas', *Supplement to IUOTO Travel Research Journal.*

[40] *Ibid.*

[41] Note that with package holidays medium-priced rather than luxury hotels will be needed.

[42] OECD, *Tourism in OECD Member Countries* (1968), p. 24.

Table 4.5

The UK Balance of Payments on the Travel Account (£m.)

	Credits	Debits	Net
1960	169	186	−17
1961	176	200	−24
1962	183	210	−27
1963	188	241	−53
1964	190	261	−71
1965	193	290	−97
1966	219	297	−78
1967	236	275	−39
1968	282	271	+11
1969	359	324	+35
1970	433	388	+45

Source: Economic Trends (1961–1971)

the population was relatively low. Furthermore by 1967 spending both per tourist and per capita of the population had been reduced to such an extent that the United Kingdom had fallen to eleventh position in the table of twelve major tourist-generating countries.[43]

Table 4.6

Total and Per Capita Expenditure on Foreign Tourism
by the Main Tourist Generators
Expressed in US $ (Excluding International Fare Payments)

Countries	Total expenditure (m.)		Spending per tourist		Per capita population spending	
	1965	1967	1965	1967	1965	1967
USA	2,438	3,195	112·4	115·9	12·5	16·2
UK	812	763	107·8	66·8	14·9	13·9
France	939	1,097	93·9	82·1	19·2	22·2
W. Germany	1,370	1,532	63·3	65·9	24·1	25·7
Canada	677	654	101·5	74·7	45·3	32·6
Belg/Lux	282	370	74·4	95·5	28·8	37·5
Netherlands	309	380	75·8	86·3	25·1	30·4
Italy	227	298	72·3	72·5	4·4	5·7
Switzerland	209	235	95·2	83·4	35·2	39·1
Denmark	165	225	120·7	235·8	34·7	46·9
Austria	141	219	67·8	90·3	19·4	30·0
Sweden	207	287	144·7	295·3	26·8	36·8

In 1967 the United Kingdom still had a travel account deficit in spite of the fact that the travel debit was reduced in absolute terms for the first time in many years. The continuing deficit can be mainly attributed to the relative failure of

[43] IUOTO, *Economic Review* (1970), *op. cit.*, p. 32.

the United Kingdom to increase substantially its share of tourist receipts. Despite the absolute growth of tourist receipts between 1958 and 1967 the percentage increase for the United Kingdom was less than in practically any other major country, with the exception of Belgium.[44] Tourist receipts as a percentage of British GNP remained constant over this period at 0·6 per cent whereas in most other countries they increased.

Thus the resort to travel restrictions to secure a quasi-adjustment in the balance of payments represented an unfair discrimination against British tourists. Their expenditure had not grown excessively and policy should have been more concerned to accelerate the growth of tourist receipts in this country. However, the considerable antagonism against travel restrictions ensured that it would only be a temporary measure and removed relatively quickly.

The travel allowance itself was certainly effective, more so than was expected or so generally believed,[45] though it was accompanied by deflation which added to its effectiveness. However, deflation alone would probably have been insufficient since overseas tourists may be retired people, or have run down their savings, or are less likely to be made unemployed. The year 1967 probably provides the best year in which to assess the effects of the travel allowance since devaluation did not occur until November 1967 and seems unlikely to have significantly affected expenditure abroad in that year. Although the number of visits abroad rose from 6·5 million in 1966 to 7·2 million in 1967, travel debits were reduced by £22 million over 1966. This may be partly explained by the publicity for and greater availability of holidays abroad for under £50, despite the incentive to visit the Sterling Area. The removal of travel restrictions in 1970 resulted in a rapid and substantial increase in travel debits of £64 million compared with the previous year, and more expenditure outside the Sterling Area.

Some indication of the effects of policy measures on British tourist expenditure abroad is given by measuring this as a percentage of the total value of imports. This rose from 4·9 per cent in 1960 to 6·0 per cent in 1965, but in 1968 it was reduced to as low as 4·1 per cent.

Table 4.7

British Tourist Expenditure as a Percentage
of the Total Value of Imports

1960	4·9	1965	6·0
1961	5·5	1966	5·9
1962	6·6	1967	5·1
1963	6·0	1968	4·1
1964	5·5	1969	4·7

Source: Calculated from the *Monthly Digests of Statistics.*

[44] OECD, *Tourism in OECD Member Countries* (1969), p. 24.
[45] *See* F. R. Oliver, 'The Effectiveness of the UK Travel Allowance', *Applied Economics*, Vol. 3, No. 3, September 1971.

Over the five-year period from 1965 to 1969 inclusive, the number of visits abroad by residents in the United Kingdom increased each year, but relatively slowly in 1967 and 1968. Furthermore, an index of travel expenditure, taking 1965 as 100, was reduced to 94 in 1967 mainly as a result of travel restrictions; it fell to 93 in 1968 with the additional impact of devaluation. This is indicated in Tables 4.8 and 4.9.

Table 4.8

Distribution of Visits Abroad by UK Residents 1965 to 1969 (per cent)

	1965	*1966*	*1967*	*1968*	*1969*
N. America	2·3	2·4	2·9	2·9	2·9
W. Europe	66·1	67·6	65·8	64·2	66·1
Other non-sterling area	2·2	2·4	2·3	2·7	2·6
Overseas sterling area	27·8	26·0	27·0	28·4	26·6
Total as a per cent of 1965 value	100	107	111	112	125

Source: Percentages calculated from absolute figures on 'Foreign Travel and Tourism', in the *Board of Trade Journal*, 27 August 1969, pp. 1–8, and 23 September 1970, pp. 656–63.

Note that the percentages in some of these Tables do not add up to 100 per cent because of UK residents holidaying on cruise ships, not assigned to particular areas.

Table 4.9

Distribution of Expenditure Abroad by UK Residents 1965–1969 (per cent)

	1965	*1966*	*1967*	*1968*	*1969*
N. America	4·8	5·3	6·2	5·6	5·3
W. Europe	65·0	64·6	59·5	58·5	60·4
Other non-sterling area	4·5	4·7	4·7	4·5	5·0
Overseas sterling area	25·7	25·4	29·6	31·4	29·3
Total as a per cent of 1965 value	100	102	94	93	112

There was some reorientation of visits, and particularly of expenditure, towards the Overseas Sterling Area which was most marked in 1968. The percentage of visits to Western Europe tended to stagnate between 1965 and 1969, and in 1967 and 1968 the percentage declined; this was most evident in the reduction in the percentage of UK expenditure in Western Europe which fell from 65·0 in 1965 to 58·5 in 1968 and rose to 60·4 in 1969. Over the five years Italy and Switzerland actually recorded an absolute reduction in the total number of visits from the United Kingdom and in addition to those two countries, France, Belgium, Luxembourg, the Netherlands, and Austria also registered absolute reductions in the total amount of British expenditure there. One of the reasons why Western Europe's share of United Kingdom visits and expenditure did not fall even further was because of the growth in popularity of Spain after devaluation. In 1966 Spain accounted for 13·9 per cent of total United Kingdom visits abroad and 14·5 per cent of their expenditure, and by 1969 this had increased to 18·6 per cent and 19·1 per cent respectively.

The effects of sterling devaluation, however, apart from its 'income' effects on expenditure, are more apparent as an independent factor on the United Kingdom's receipts from international tourism. The extent of the increase in the percentages of visits and expenditure from abroad is illustrated in Tables 4.10 and 4.11.

Table 4.10

Overseas Visitors to the UK 1965 to 1969 (per cent)

	1965	1966	1967	1968	1969
N. America	24·9	26·4	25·8	25·7	28·4
W. Europe	40·9	41·4	42·4	44·0	44·0
Other non-sterling area	5·0	5·4	5·7	5·8	6·2
Overseas sterling area	29·2	26·8	26·1	24·5	21·4
Total as a per cent of 1965 value	100	110	119	134	162

Table 4.11

Expenditure by Overseas Visitors to the UK (per cent)

	1965	1966	1967	1968	1969
N. America	31·9	32·4	33·5	32·8	35·2
W. Europe	28·3	29·0	29·6	31·1	31·1
Other non-sterling area	7·2	9·0	8·3	9·5	9·2
Overseas sterling area	32·6	29·6	28·6	26·6	24·5
Total as a per cent of 1965 value	100	114	122	147	187

The percentage increase in expenditure by overseas visitors has grown even more rapidly than the percentage increase in the number of visits. Before devaluation British tourist receipts had been growing relatively slowly, and less than those of OECD countries as a whole. However, after devaluation the United Kingdom's tourist receipts tended to rise faster than those of other countries, like the OECD members; this was despite the lower rate of economic activity which tended to slow down the aggregate growth of world tourism in 1967 and 1968.

International tourism appears to be highly sensitive to exchange rate changes.[46] Devaluation achieves its results in a variety of ways. It has made the United Kingdom a cheaper country to visit relative to staying at home or visiting other countries. It has also encouraged visitors to spend more money, since they can

[46] *See* A. S. Gerakis, 'Economic Man: The Tourist', *Finance and Development*, March 1966; also Gerakis, 'Effects of Exchange – Rate Devaluations and Revaluations on Receipts from Tourism', *IMF Staff Papers*, XII (November 1965). J. R. Artus, 'The Effect of Re-valuation on the Foreign Travel Balance of Germany', *IMF Staff Papers*, XVIII (November 1970).

buy cheaper goods than at home, and this has been shown in the previous tables. In addition, the statistics usually under-record tourist expenditure here since shopping expenditure is only included if the articles are transported in passenger's baggage, and the bigger items exported separately are not recorded in the tourist trade returns. Yet tourists attracted by tax advantages probably buy at least 20,000 motor cars each year in the United Kingdom, but these are included in the records of physical exports and not in tourist receipts.[47] There is also evidence that visitors have been encouraged to make more short shopping trips to purchase goods in the United Kingdom since devaluation. Such visits tend to provide a demonstration effect to other prospective tourists. Some tourists visiting two or more countries have also tended to switch more of their expenditure to the cheaper one.

As a result of the above factors, the United Kingdom, after a relatively poor performance in the early 1960s, has started to develop fully its tourist potential since devaluation. It has achieved a surplus on its travel account probably for the first time in its history.[48] Over the three years 1968–1970, the surplus was £91 million, and the increase in credits from tourism in the latter year alone exceeded those from 1960 to 1967, inclusive. The United Kingdom's remarkable performance makes it, in terms of credits, a bigger tourist country than Spain, and its growth rate is roughly double the global average.[49] By the end of the last decade travel credits (excluding fare payments) accounted for 9·5 per cent of total invisible receipts compared with 7·7 per cent in 1960 and only 6·8 per cent in 1965. Thus the United Kingdom has added another invisible item to the surplus which it derives from invisible trade.[50]

Conclusion

International tourism has generally provided a useful equilibrating mechanism in the international economy. This has manifested itself between Western European countries and particularly for developing countries. There is now almost an automatic channel of financial flows from richer countries to poorer ones, raising the latter's export earnings and rate of economic growth. These returns from tourism can be maximized more effectively, particularly by factors such as active government intervention, co-operative promotion campaigns, and a mixed composition of tourist facilities.

The United Kingdom position in international tourism is now rather anomalous. This can be mainly attributed to the belated devaluation of sterling and greater government appreciation of the macro-economic benefits from tourism. It has provided a real British 'success story' and although travel restrictions and deflation made an effective contribution to this, one would like to see the current

[47] Unpublished Draft Statistical Book on Tourism by L. J. Lickorish given at SSRC Seminar.
[48] M. Panić, 'Britain's Invisible Balance', *Lloyds Bank Review*, July 1968, p. 17.
[49] *Financial Times*, 11 May 1971.
[50] E. Merigo and S. Potter, 'Invisibles in the 1960s', in OECD *Economic Outlook, Occasional Studies*, July 1970.

trends maintained in the future by positive rather than negative policy measures. Furthermore, it does seem that if the United Kingdom's rate of growth continues to grow more slowly than the growth rate abroad,[51] then the current surplus on the travel account can probably be maintained. If so, the government should concern itself more with policies to deal with the micro-problems of the spatial distribution of tourists between holiday centres in the United Kingdom.

Provided these problems are tackled, international tourism should be fostered for its benefits which have been outlined in this article. One aspect which has not been mentioned is the undesirable externalities which have been stressed by some writers.[52] It is suggested that the pricing of travel has been well below the social costs incurred and that the cost to the marginal tourist does not consider the additional congestion costs and the destruction of natural assets. But any proposal for a ban against all air travel[53] on this basis alone seems ludicrous. It is just a particular value judgement; it seems to forget the benefits derived by millions of tourists; also it does not mean that the growth achieved already exceeds the ideal level or that welfare must decline.[54] Indeed in some countries, by bidding resources away from other uses, tourism is helping to preserve the ecological heritage.[55] In addition, there are sociological and political gains to be reaped from tourism, but a discussion of these is beyond the scope of this article.

[51] *See* the table in W. Beckerman, 'Why We Need Economic Growth', *Lloyds Bank Review*, October 1971.
[52] E. J. Mishan, *The Costs of Economic Growth* (1967), pp. 103–6.
[53] *Ibid.*
[54] Beckerman, *loc. cit.*
[55] Mitchell, *Eastern Africa Economic Review, loc. cit.*, p. 3.

Part III
Dimensions of Tourism

Introduction

Our two contributions in this Part of the book have a common ground in making cross-country comparisons drawing on available statistical surveys. However, their intrinsic concern is different.

Schmidhauser points out the need to recognize the growing incidence of more than one annual holiday away from home in developed countries in drawing conclusions from national travel surveys about holiday propensities of resident populations. He distinguishes between the net and the gross travel propensities and the travel frequency. The travel frequency is often described in the English language as travel intensity, but as intensity is used in German to describe propensity, this translation of Schmidhauser's material avoids the use of the word intensity. After examining these indices of participation in tourism for a number of countries, he confirms usefully a number of economic and social determinants in tourism.

The report by the Research Department of the British Tourist Authority brings together what is known about the incidence of self-catering holidays in a number of countries in Western Europe and about self-catering holidays of overseas visitors in Britain. The report is concerned only with the demand for self-catering holidays, but it indicates sources of information about the supply of facilities, and represents a valuable survey of this important market.

The growth of holiday propensities has led to an increase in the volume of tourism, the growth of self-catering holidays to its greater diversity. Both have contributed significantly to the impact of tourism on generating and on the receiving areas and on the areas through which tourists travel.

Although this is not their concern, the two contributions read together do raise interesting speculation about the relationship between the growth in holiday propensities and frequency and the growth of self-catering holidays. The price of holidays is recognized as a major determinant in tourism and the lower price of self-catering accommodation has undoubtedly contributed to the popularity of this type of holiday.

5 Travel Propensity and Travel Frequency

BY H. SCHMIDHAUSER
(Translated from German text by Professor S. Medlik)

From Festschrift zur Vollendung des 65. Lebensjahres von O. Prof. Dkfm.
Dr Paul Bernecker, Institut fuer Fremdenverkehrsforschung, Hochschule fuer
Welthandel in Vienna, 1973

Introduction and Definitions

In household inquiries about holiday and travel behaviour of residents, which
are carried out in most European countries, travel propensity is one of the most
important indices. In this it is necessary to distinguish between net travel
propensity, gross travel propensity, and travel frequency.

This distinction has come into use only in the last few years and has not by any
means been generally accepted. However, as it is likely to gain ground rapidly in
the future, it is desirable to clarify briefly the concepts and interdependence
between both travel propensities as well as travel frequency.

By net travel propensity (*taux net de départ, Nettoreiseintensitaet*) we mean the
proportion of the total population or of a particular group in the population
who have made at least one trip away from home in the period under investigation (normally twelve months), i.e. one or more trips as defined for the purposes
of the inquiry. Over the years the working definitions of a trip have been considerably adapted and today require in almost all countries that the trip (including the stay) should last at least 4×24 hours and that it should not be undertaken for business or vocational reasons.[1]

Net travel propensity can be represented by a formula as follows:

$$\text{Net travel propensity (as a percentage)} = \frac{p}{P} \times 100$$

where

p = the number of persons in a country or in a particular population group
who have made at least one trip away from home in the period under investigation, as defined for the purposes of the inquiry, and

P = total population of the country or of the particular group.

On the other hand we mean by gross travel propensity (*taux brut de départ,
Bruttoreiseintensitaet*) the total number of trips in relation to total population,
which were undertaken by those participating in tourism in the period under
investigation, according to the formula:

---

[1] Whether the deliberate exclusion of trips of less than four nights (or five days) is meaningful and whether it should be adhered to in the future, is outside the scope of this discussion.

$$\text{Gross travel propensity (as a percentage)} = \frac{Tp}{P} \times 100$$

where
Tp = the number of trips, as defined for the purposes of the inquiry, which were undertaken by those persons of a country or of a particular population group participating in tourism in the period under investigation, and
P = total population of the country or of the particular group.

If we divide the gross travel propensity by the net travel propensity (or the number of trips by the number of those participating in tourism), the outcome is the travel frequency, i.e. the average number of trips undertaken by a person participating in tourism in the period under investigation:

$$\text{Travel frequency} = \frac{Tp}{p} = \frac{\text{gross travel propensity}}{\text{net travel propensity}}$$

where Tp and p have the same meaning as above.

The concept of travel frequency has been used in a different sense, for example, by the Federal Statistical Office in Wiesbaden. This office understands by it 'the proportion among all travellers who make two or more trips'.[2] This would seem a better description.

Sauer[3] also defines travel frequency as we do, as 'trips per traveller'. He draws attention to the fact that the usage of the Statistical Office of the Federal Republic of Germany merely shows how many tourists made more than one trip; the same travel propensity, as defined by the Statistical Office, can represent different numbers of trips according to the distribution of travellers who made two, three, four or more trips.

The postulated relationships can be clarified in a simple example: Let us assume the population of a country is 10 million. Of these 2·5 million make one trip (of at least four nights away from home), 1 million two trips, 500,000 three trips, and 100,000 people four trips in a year:

2,500,000 people × 1	trip	= 2,500,000 trips
1,000,000 people × 2	trips	= 2,000,000 trips
500,000 people × 3	trips	= 1,500,000 trips
100,000 people × 4	trips	= 400,000 trips
4,100,000 people × 1·56 trips		= 6,400,000 trips

This means that
p = 4,100,000 travellers (participants in tourism)
Tp = 6,400,000 trips
P = 10,000,000 population

[2] Statistisches Bundesamt, Wiesbaden: Urlaubs- und Erholungsreisen 1972, Sonderbeitrag zur *Fachserie F, Reihe 8: Fremdenverkehr*, Stuttgart und Mainz 1972.
[3] Sauer, W., *Prognosen über die Entwicklung des Tourismus*, Sonderdruck eines Vortrages, gehalten am 3.3.1972 im Rahmen des Kongresses der 6. Internat. Tourismus-Börse ITB in Berlin, herausgegeben vom Studienkreis für Tourismus, Starnberg, und der Deutschen Airbus GmbH, Munich.

$$\text{Net travel propensity} \quad = \frac{4,100,000}{10,000,000} \times 100 = 41\%$$

$$\text{Gross travel propensity} = \frac{6,400,000}{10,000,000} \times 100 = 64\%$$

$$\text{Travel frequency} \quad = \frac{6,400,000}{4,100,000} \times \frac{64}{41} = 1{\cdot}56\%$$

The net travel propensity is, therefore, of interest, because it tells us what proportion of the population of a country or of a particular market segment participates at all in travel (as defined for the purposes of the inquiry). The index provides a first rough assessment of potential demand. That is how, for example, Koch[4] estimated the tourist demand of the European population in 1969 on the basis of available data of net travel propensity (which he described simply as travel propensity). On the other hand, gross travel propensity, which gains increasingly in significance with the growth of second and third trips, tells us how many separate trips – i.e. purchases – we can assume per 100 population. With this approach it is not evident whether, for example, 60 people make one trip or 30 people make two trips each; in both cases there is a demand of 60 trips.

The travel frequency, the connecting element between the two travel propensities, is a suitable measure for the frequency of the travel consumption within the period of inquiry.

Growing Significance of Gross Travel Propensity

The net travel propensity will never reach 100 per cent, because there will always be people who will not or cannot for various reasons travel away from home (accident, illness, old age, lack of money, lack of time, etc.). It is estimated by experts that the attainable optimum may, according to country, lie between 70 and 80 per cent and that this level can only exceptionally be exceeded.

However, this does not mean that there are narrow limits to the future development of tourism and that it is necessary to expect stagnation.

The gross travel propensity can in some countries within a few years reach values between 100 and 200 per cent; it presupposes that participants in tourism travel away from home not only once a year, but twice or more often; and the trend is clearly in this direction (longer holidays, more free time, more freely disposable purchasing power). For example, in Switzerland already in 1970 a participant in tourism made 1·5 trips and in 1972 1·6 trips away from home.

The statements by Koch[4]

that it can be generally postulated 'that only a relatively small proportion of holidaymakers make more than one holiday trip';
that the number of holiday trips is about 10 to 15 per cent higher than the number of holidaymakers;

[4] Koch, A., Die touristische Nachfrage der europäischen Bevölkerung, in: *Jahrbuch für Fremdenverkehr*, 17. Jahrgang, (Munich 1969), S.3ff.

that it can be further postulated 'that in case of two or more holiday trips only one will be made abroad';

might have been quite true for 1966/67, but must be regarded as out of date, at least in the case of the Swiss.

The latest inquiry into travel behaviour of the Swiss resident population in 1972[5] disclosed that

no less than 39 per cent of those who travelled away from home made two or more trips of 4×24 hours' duration;
the total number of trips (inland and abroad) is 62 per cent higher than the number of travellers;

the number of trips abroad (gross travel propensity abroad) alone exceeds the number of travellers abroad (net travel propensity abroad) by 27 per cent.

Structural analyses of travel propensities disclose the following relationships between socio-demographic characteristics and the disposition to go away from home, which have been established also in other countries.

The highest travel propensity (both net and gross) is shown by
recipients of high incomes;
the professions, entrepreneurs, directors, and senior employees;
residents of large urban areas;
age groups between 20 and 45 years;
members of small households (gross) as well as families who have only children of school age (net).

The lowest travel propensity is recorded by
recipients of low incomes;
farmers, labourers, retired retailers, artisans;
small children and persons over 75;
residents of villages with less than 2,000 inhabitants;
members of large households (with more than 5 persons).

For example, members of households with a monthly income of more than 5,000 Swiss Francs achieve a net travel propensity of 84 per cent and a gross travel propensity of 189 per cent, with an average of 2·26 trips per traveller (travel frequency).

By contrast those engaged in agriculture have a net travel propensity of only 24 per cent and a gross travel propensity of only 30 per cent, with an average of 1·29 trips per traveller.

It must be added that the disposition to travel among the Swiss (including foreigners living in Switzerland) appears well above average in comparison with the rest of the world and must be regarded even in Europe as atypical at present. However, there is no reason why the other Western industrialized nations should not sooner or later reach similarly high indices. The growing difference between

[5] Schmidhauser, H., *Reisemarkt Schweiz 1972*, Institut fur Fremdenverkehr und Verkehrswirtschaft an der Hochschule St. Gallen, Mai 1973.

the net and gross travel propensities is, therefore, not only a Swiss, but a generally valid phenomenon.

Correlation between Net and Gross Travel Propensity

In other words: the growth of tourist demand is based not only on the recruitment of new strata of population who have so far not gone away from home, but equally on the enhanced travel activity of the already experienced participants in tourism.

The appropriate values for net and gross travel propensities of the various population groups can be recorded in a scatter diagram. Although for individual countries they will slope differently, the diagram will show regression lines, which represent pure linear functions. The scatter delimited by the extreme values of the investigated countries gives the width of the band, within which the individual values are distributed.

It is interesting to note that the scatter diagrams for France[6] and Switzerland[5] move approximately along or just underneath the middle line of this band, whilst the values for Germany[4], Belgium[7] and the Netherlands[8] are rather concentrated in the lower half of the scatter.

This may be connected to a certain extent with the varying popularity of winter sports holidays in the individual countries, with the varying density of second homes and, in the case of Holland, with the fact that in contrast to the other four countries, visits to relatives and friends are not included in the inquiry.

The extreme values at the upper end of the scatter emanating from the Swiss inquiry are accounted for by the retired or persons over 65 and at the other end by professional people or their dependants from the highest income group (with a monthly income over 5,000 Swiss Francs):

Table 5.1

Population Group (Switzerland 1972)	% Travel Propensity Net	Gross	Travel Frequency
Retired or persons over 65 years old	53–55	94–96	1·73–1·78
Professional people and their dependants	77	177	2·29
Persons from households with a monthly income over 5,000 SF	84	189	2·26
For comparison: Total population	66	107	1·62

[6] Pierre le Roux: *Les vacances des Français en 1969*, No. 32 des collections de l'INSEE, série M, No. 6, Nov. 1970.

[7] N. Vanhove: *Structure des vacances et dépenses touristiques de la population belge*, Westvlaams Ekonomisch Studiebureau (WES, Brugge, 1969).

[8] Centraal bureau voor de statistiek: *Onderzoek naar vakanties en uitgaan 1970*, 's-Gravenhage 1972.

Obviously these groups represent the most mobile part of the population, stimulated on the one hand by the availability of time or flexibility in the use of time, and on the other hand by the financial means at their disposal.

In the over 65 group one is not so surprised by the absolute travel frequency (1·73–1·78), as by its relative level in comparison with the below average travel propensity (net and gross).

We may presume that three categories have to be distinguished in this group of people, namely

(a) people over 65 who can afford to travel because of time, financial and health reasons, and do so very actively;

(b) people over 65 who could well afford to travel on time and financial grounds, but do not do so for health reasons;

(c) people over 65 who largely for financial reasons do not travel.

In spite of the above average travel frequency of group (a), the substantial weight of group (b) depresses the net as well as the gross travel propensity of the retired under the general average for the total population.

This statement holds good not only for Switzerland, but also for the Federal Republic of Germany, Belgium, and the Netherlands:

Table 5.2

	% Net Travel Propensity	% Gross Travel Propensity	Travel Frequency
FR Germany 1971			
(a) Total population	42·2	51·1	1·21
(b) People over 65	31·8	41·5	1·31
Netherlands 1970			
(a) Total population	45·9	56·9	1·24
(b) Retired	25·8	32·5	1·26
Belgium 1967			
(a) Total population	34·3	42·1	1·23
(b) People over 70	14·5	18·2	1·26

In all three countries the values of travel frequency for the retired are above, but the values for the travel propensies below the general average.

Conclusions

It is possible to generalize from scatter diagrams that the first decisive change occurs with a net travel propensity of about 55–60 per cent and a second one probably when the net travel propensity reaches about 75–80 per cent.

When these turning points are reached, empirically a tendency appears for the travel frequency to increase. This is clear from the study of the five countries (Belgium, France, Germany, Holland, and Switzerland).

Whilst there is little or no correlation between net travel propensity and travel frequency below a net travel propensity of about 55–60 per cent, the picture

Table 5.3

Relationships between the Growth of Net and Gross Travel Propensities

	Probable range of		Changes in travel propensity				Elasticity of growth of gross propensity against net propensity	
	Gross Travel propensity	Travel frequency	net		gross			
Assumed average net travel propensity of a country			absolute	%	absolute	%	absolute (6) ÷ (4)	% (7) ÷ (5)
(1)	(2)	(3)	(4)	(5)	(6)	(7)	(8)	(9)
40%	45–53%	1·125–1·325						
50%	60– 70%	1·2 –1·4	10%	25%	15–17%	33%	1·5–1·7	1·32
60%	78– 93%	1·3 –1·55	10%	20%	18–23%	30–33%	1·8–2·3	1·5–1·65
70%	98–116%	1·4 –1·65	10%	16·67%	20–23%	25%	2·0–2·3	1·50

changes when this level is exceeded. On the basis of the Swiss example it may be supposed that a further change may be expected with a net travel propensity of about 75–80 per cent.

It will be possible to test this hypothesis more accurately only when net travel propensities of substantial population groups also reach this magnitude in other countries.

Should the relationships postulated here be confirmed in the future, it would be possible to deduce from them the information in Table 5.3, which shows the elasticity of growth of the gross travel propensity against the growth of net travel propensity. For example, if the net travel propensity of a country rises from 50 to 60 per cent, 100 new travellers – irrespective of population growth – bring about between 180 and 230 additional trips. In percentage terms a 20 per cent increase in the number of travellers can be compared with a 30–33 per cent increase in the number of trips.

These conclusions make it clear that it will not be sufficient in the future to regard net travel propensity as the focus of market or forecasting studies; to an increasing extent it will be necessary to differentiate between net travel propensity, gross travel propensity, and travel frequency.

6 Self-catering Holidays

BY RESEARCH DEPARTMENT, BRITISH TOURIST AUTHORITY

From *British Tourist Authority Research Newsletter* No. 11 Winter 1973–4

Introduction

The general rise in levels of holidaytaking in recent years has been in many cases more than matched by the increasing popularity and demand for self-catering accommodation.

The aim of this report is to collate available data on self-catering holidays in Europe and to examine the part they play in overseas tourism to Great Britain. Some of the surveys have been carried out by the BTA itself, others have been carried out by official organizations or by commercial companies in the countries concerned. Further research work is planned.

Definition

The term 'self-catering' is by no means self-explanatory since it can cover a wide variety of both accommodation and facilities. In a standard and simple form self-catering accommodation can be defined as any accommodation where a meal service is not provided as an integral part of the service. Cooking facilities sometimes will be provided but these may not be extensive. In some cases restaurant facilities may also be available at or near the place of accommodation but these facilities are not, however, included in the accommodation offered.

There are also overlap areas within some categories of accommodation, e.g. a number of hotels and motels in North America provide cooking facilities in guests bedrooms giving them the option of serviced or self-service catering arrangements. Similarly some holiday camps in Britain and elsewhere offer serviced or self-serviced catering. For the purpose of this article the following categories of accommodation have been considered 'self-catering':

1. second or holiday homes;
2. rented chalet, house, flat or bungalow;
3. camping and caravanning.

In order to give a general picture of self-catering holidays both at home and abroad information is shown on all major European nationals. Where possible the pattern of behaviour of the same people on holiday in Britain is discussed.

This article concentrates solely on the demand aspects of the self-catering market. An examination of the supply of self-catering accommodation in this country is outside the scope of the current study. Investigations are being carried out by the Tourist Boards within their own areas. The reports that have been published are listed below:

Self-catering Accommodation in the North East Scotland by Scottish Tourist Board

Static Holiday Caravans and Chalets by the English Tourist Board

Caravan Pitches in Wales by the Wales Tourist Board

Tourist Accommodation in the West Midlands by the West Midlands Tourist Board.

The use of self-catering accommodation among holidaytakers from most West European countries is relatively high although the specific type preferred varies between countries according to local custom.

Table 6.1 shows the level of self-catering holidaytaking by West Europeans and Table 6.2 refers to the type of self-catering accommodation most widely used. The data for most countries derives from national surveys carried out either by official organizations or by commercial companies. Information on Denmark, Italy, and Spain derives from BTA surveys which in the case of the two Mediterranean countries sampled only the top 30 per cent of the population in socio-economic terms – the more affluent people.

In France,[1] holidaytaking is characterized by two main features, the large proportion of the population (55 per cent in 1969) which traditionally does not take a holiday thus inhibiting the overall growth of the market and the relatively high degree of usage of a second or holiday home, usually in France.

Between 1964 and 1969 the proportion of self-catering holidays within France increased slightly from 32 per cent of all domestic holidays to 37 per cent. Although use of the second home showed some increase the most marked trend was the rise in popularity of rented accommodation abroad from 6 per cent to 11 per cent. It may be that the custom of owning a second home has established a preference for similar catering arrangements when abroad by way of rented accommodation.

The level of self-catering holidaymaking is lower in Germany than in most of the other European countries and does not appear to be increasing.[2] In 1970 self-catering accommodation accounted for 16 per cent of the accommodation used at any time during a holiday in either Germany or abroad. In 1972 15 per cent of the main types of accommodation used on holiday were self-catering of which 8 per cent were caravanning or camping facilities and 6 per cent rented houses or flats.

The Dutch are probably the most widespread users of self-catering accommodation in Europe.[3] The tradition for domestic holidays of this type is a well-established part of Dutch life which is also strongly carried over into the abroad holiday sector.

Camping and caravanning features strongly in holidays taken both at home (25 per cent) and abroad (31 per cent). It seems that the Dutch family that moves

---

[1] INSEE Survey of French Holidaytakers 1964/69.

[2] Reiseanalyse 1970/1972

[3] Survey of Dutch Holidaytaking 1971 – Nederlandse Stichting voor Statistiek.

Table 6.1

The Level of Self-catering Holidaytaking by West Europeans

Country	Survey date	Self-catering			Not Self-catering		
		All Holidays %	Domestic %	Abroad %	All Holidays %	Domestic %	Abroad %
Norway	1970	52	54	34	48	46	66
Netherlands	1971	51	na	47	49	na	54
Belgium	1971	45	na	na	75	na	na
Switzerland	1972	39	50	22	70	51	94
Sweden	1970/71	na	na	38	na	na	96
France	1969	35	37	25	65	63	76
Italy [a]	1968	na	37	10	na	62	70
Italy (top 30%)	1972	na	33	na	na	70	na
Spain (top 30%)	1972	28	28	28	73	71	75
Denmark [b]	1971/72	na	21	16	na	82	86
Germany	1972	15	na	na	85	na	na
Britain	1971	na	37	13	na	76	99

a The figures for Italy (1968 survey) refer to days spent in self-catering accommodation. Other figures refer to holidays taken.
b The figures for Denmark may underestimate the proportion of self-catering holidays since the category 'Second or holiday home' was not used in the survey.

Table 6.2

Type of Self-catering Accommodation Most Widely Used

Country	Second Home			Rented Accommodation			Camping/Caravanning			Total Self-catering All Holidays
	All Holidays	Domestic	Abroad	All Holidays	Domestic	Abroad	All Holidays	Domestic	Abroad	
	%	%	%	%	%	%	%	%	%	%
Norway	18	20	2	14	16	4	20	18	28	52
Netherlands [a]	10	na	3	10	na	12	28	na	31	51
Belgium	4	na	na	26	na	na	15	na	na	45
Switzerland	9	12	4	23	33	9	7	5	9	39
Sweden [b]	na	23	8	na	16	7	na	20	17	na
France	na	11	2	na	12	11	na	14	12	35
Italy [c]	na	13	2	na	22	3	na	2	9	na
Italy (top 30%)	11	na	na	15	15	na	7	na	na	33
Spain (top 30%)	9	9	10	14	15	13	5	4	5	28
Denmark [d]	na	na	na	na	8	4	na	13	12	na
Germany	1	na	na	6	na	na	8	na	na	15
Britain	na	na	1	na	10	4	na	27	8	na

a The boat was considered as a separate self-catering category for the Netherlands and is included in the 'total' figures.
b The figures refer to 'stationary' holidays only i.e. more than four consecutive nights in one place.
c These figures refer to days spent in self-catering accommodation other than holidays taken.
d The Danish survey excluded a category for second or holiday home.

under canvas during the summer months in Holland is equally well disposed to live in similar fashion when holidaying abroad.

Although few Belgians appear to actually own and thus use a second home for holiday purposes, the level of use of self-catering accommodation is still fairly high through use of rented accommodation.[4] In 1971 26 per cent of accommodation used at any time on all holidays was in rented property, 15 per cent in camping or caravanning and 4 per cent in second homes. Since a similar survey carried out in 1968 showed virtually the same overall pattern, there does not appear to be any growth in general or towards one particular form of self-catering accommodation.

Swiss holidaytaking in 1972 showed a relatively high level of self-catering accommodation used on all holidays (39 per cent) but considerably less for holidays taken abroad (22 per cent).[5] This is due to widespread use of the family (12 per cent) or rented (33 per cent) holiday home within Switzerland. Camping and caravanning are less widely used and are more popular on holidays taken abroad (9 per cent) than they are on those taken in Switzerland (5 per cent).

There is no data on any of the Mediterranean countries from national surveys except for a limited amount on Italy.[6] A survey of Italian holidays in 1968 showed that 37 per cent of days spent in the accommodation used most frequently on holiday in Italy could be described as self-catering. Within this overall category 22 per cent of days were spent in rented accommodation and 2 per cent in camping or caravanning. The remaining 13 per cent of days were spent in a house owned by a member of the immediate family which would thus include a number of people who stayed with close relatives and who are therefore not technically self-catering holidaytakers. As a result the actual level of self-catering holidaytaking may be somewhat lower than the figures suggest. The level of self-catering holidaytaking by Italians outside their own country is considerably lower accounting for only 10 per cent of days spent in the main type of accommodation of which 5 per cent were in camping and caravanning.

In 1973 BTA commissioned attitude surveys into holidaytaking among affluent Italian and Spanish nationals,[7] i.e. the top 30 per cent of the market. The data derived from these surveys was thus unrepresentative of the total population but reasonably representative of the holidaytaking market in these countries.

Among affluent holidaytakers in Italy 33 per cent used a form of self-catering accommodation at some time during their holiday. A second home was used for 11 per cent of holidays, rented accommodation 15 per cent, and camping or caravanning a further 7 per cent.

In Great Britain in 1971 37 per cent of accommodation used at any time on holidays within the country was self-catering. Of the holidays 8 per cent were in camping, 19 per cent caravanning, and 10 per cent in rented accommodation.

The British on holiday abroad in 1971 by comparison used self-catering to a

[4] Aspemar Holiday Survey 1968/1971.
[5] Reisemarkt Schweiz 1972.
[6] Survey of Italian Holidays 1968 – Istituto Centrale di Statistica.
[7] BTA Surveys of Italian/Spanish attitudes to travel.

lesser degree (13 per cent), of which 8 per cent were in camping and caravanning, 4 per cent in rented accommodation, and 1 per cent made use of a holiday home.

Among affluent Spaniards a second home represented 9 per cent, rented homes 14 per cent, and caravanning or camping 5 per cent of accommodation used on all holidays. The same proportions apply for both home and abroad holidays.

Swedish holidaytakers appear to use self-catering accommodation to a fairly high degree, particularly within their own country.[8] On 'stationary' holidays within Sweden, i.e. four consecutive nights in the same place, 23 per cent used a second home, 16 per cent rented accommodation, and 20 per cent camping or caravanning. When holidaying abroad camping remains relatively popular, accounting for 17 per cent of 'stationary' holidays and 35 per cent of touring holidays.

In Norway, similarly, use of a personal (20 per cent) or a rented holiday cabin (16 per cent) is widespread among domestic holidaytakers.[9] When abroad, however, camping and caravanning (28 per cent) tends to be preferred. It should be remembered, however, that relatively few Norwegians take holidays abroad (probably less than 300,000 per year).

It would appear that the level of self-catering among Danish holidaytakers (21 per cent in Denmark, 16 per cent abroad) is lower than the average both for Scandinavia and the rest of Europe.[10] The data, however, derives from a survey which does not include a category for the second home. This undoubtedly could have deflated the level of self-catering holidaytaking since the unspecific 'other' category accounts for 18 per cent of home and 9 per cent of abroad holidays.

Self-catering Visitors to Great Britain from Western Europe

In general terms self-caterers tend to be found among those visitors who spend a reasonable length of time on holidays in Britain, probably touring around, in some cases quite extensively.

If it is assumed that the proportions of self-catering European visitors are relatively constant, it is possible to obtain some indication of the numbers involved in a particular year. If for example those proportions are applied to the relevant holiday tourist arrival figures for 1971, the estimated number of European holidaytakers mainly using self-catering facilities in Britain at that time would be in the region of 135,000 to 140,000. It seems likely that with the extra numbers of people who use such facilities in addition to their main choice of accommodation, together with the steady increase in tourist traffic, these figures would currently represent a minimum number of self-caterers per year.

BTA Surveys carried out among the main European nationalities between 1968 and 1972 indicate a relatively low level of use of self-catering facilities within Britain particularly in rented accommodation. Table 6.3 shows that the

[8] Ake Sundelin – Survey of Swedish Holidaytaking 1971/77.
[9] Survey of Holidaytaking 1970, Central Bureau of Statistics.
[10] BTA Danish Travel Survey 1971/72.

Table 6.3

Use of Self-catering Accommodation by European Visitors to Great Britain

Country	Year of Survey	Used Mainly			Used at any time		
		Total %	Rented Accommodation %	Camping/ Caravanning %	Total %	Rented Accommodation %	Camping/ Caravanning %
Netherlands	1969	12	2	10	15	2	13
France	1969	8	1	7	13	2	11
Sweden	1970	6	2	4	9	2	7
Germany	1968	6	2	4	9	2	7
Norway	1970	7	2	5	9	3	6
Belgium	1969	4	1	3	5	1	4
Denmark	1972	4	1	3	4	*	4
Switzerland	1969	3	2	1	6	4	2

* Less than 0·5%

rented sector accounted for only 1 per cent to 2 per cent of the main types of accommodation used on holiday whereas camping and caravanning appear to be somewhat more popular particularly among the Dutch (10 per cent) and the French (7 per cent).

Self-catering Holidaytaking in North America[11] [12]

Although use of self-catering accommodation has not developed to the same extent in North America as it has in Western Europe it is nevertheless fairly popular particularly in Canada where facilities are being introduced into the national parks. In 1970 32 per cent of Canadian domestic holidaytakers used self-catering at some time on their vacation trips.

In the United States, staying in hotels or with friends and relatives remains the most usual type of holiday. However in 1970 research showed that 16 per cent of all holidays used mainly self-catering accommodation evenly divided between camping and rented or owned cottages.

Self-catering Visitors to Great Britain from North America

From the BTA survey of summer visitors to Britain in 1971 it appears that only a small percentage of all Americans and Canadian visitors use self-catering accommodation facilities while on holiday in Britain. Among these summer visitors 2 per cent of Americans and 4 per cent of Canadians camped at some time during their stay (no other type of self-catering accommodation was covered). If it is assumed that over the year as a whole these proportions would be nearer 1 per cent and 2 per cent respectively, this would give a minimum number of around 20,000 campers alone from North America (i.e. using mainly camping facilities during their holiday).

[11] Newsweek Travel and Vacation Study 1970.
[12] Canadian Tourism Facts Book 1972, BTA Nationality Surveys 1968–72, British National Travel Survey 1971.

Part IV
Passenger Transportation

Introduction

Transport is a necessary condition of tourism. For the greater part of contemporary tourism, transport means the airlines and the private car.

There is abundant literature on transport, particularly on the economic and operating characteristics of the various modes of transport. However, there is much less available on the role of transport in tourism, and recognition by airline managements that they are 90 per cent of the time in tourism has been slow in coming.

Wheatcroft's paper which forms Chapter 7 is an early and a noteworthy discussion of the mutual dependence of transport and tourism on each other. He clearly sees transport as a component in a total travel package. He relates demand for travel and tourism to the level of personal incomes and stresses the price-elasticity of demand for tourism. The lessons he teaches have perhaps not been entirely learnt yet, but the great increase in the inclusive tour (package holiday) traffic since Wheatcroft's paper was delivered has been due to the tour operators' recognition of the truth of his arguments. It is of interest to note that his observation that 40 per cent of holiday prices is attributable to the transport element is as valid for inclusive tours (where the tourist himself does not realize it) as for other forms of holiday, and his plea to deal with seasonality by offering low prices in the off-season has been answered by the introduction of very cheap winter air inclusive tours.

In Chapter 8 Dr Abrams analyses the effects of car ownership on leisure trends in the UK generally. Car ownership in the developed countries has increased rapidly, and for countries with land frontiers (e.g. Canada/USA or Western Germany/France) the car is the principal mode of transport for holiday tourism. This is, of course, an effect of the economic growth of the last twenty-five years.

Dr Abrams points out that within the overall increase in prosperity there are other factors at work, for example, the intensity of car ownership varies with socio-economic class, occupation, and so on. A most illuminating analysis is his discussion of the effect of life cycle stage on car ownership and use. He also discusses briefly the effect of car ownership on the demand for recreational and leisure facilities in the future.

The growth in mobility and developments in transport have been some of the main preoccupations of planners in recent years. They are also some of the most significant factors in the changing patterns of tourism and in the management of tourist flows.

7 Transport and Tourism

BY S. F. WHEATCROFT

From a paper presented to a Study Course on the Tourist Industry organized by the British Travel Association at the BEA Training Centre Southall on 25–27 September and 30 October–1 November 1964.

Analysis of Holiday Expenditure

I propose to examine, first of all, the place of transport costs (i.e. fares) in the general pattern of tourist expenditure. As a broad generalization one can say that holidaymakers travelling abroad spend rather less than half their total holiday money on transport and travel, and rather over half on accommodation and other activities. To be more precise, travel costs are typically about 40 per cent of total holiday expenditure.

In the case of inclusive tours it is, of course, difficult to separate the travel element of tourist expenditure. But, in the case of independent travellers, the fare element on average is about 43 per cent of total expenditure on the holiday. An interesting point about this is that the detailed figures published by BTA show that the travel proportion of total expenditure did not vary much from 40 per cent irrespective of the form of transport which the travellers used, whether travel was by sea, by air, or by coach, or by private car. There is, moreover, a general similarity in the pattern of North Atlantic tourist expenditure. Figures published by the US Department of Commerce show that US travellers to Europe spend about 40 per cent of their total holiday money on the fare. As a matter of fact, these US figures show that the fare proportion of total expenditure has tended to increase over the past ten years. But the basic fact remains that fares are less than half of total tourist expenditure.

This raises an interesting philosophical question. Why should it be that, on average, holidaymakers tend not to spend more than half of their total holiday money on transport? One of the basic explanations for this is, I think, purely psychological: most of us have an underlying preconception of what is a worthwhile outlay on fares. Most of us would agree that to spend (say) £50 on a fare for a weekend trip would be an unreasonable relationship of travel cost to the total cost of the excursion. If we are going to spend that amount of money on the fare then we want to have a longer time available to make the fare seem worthwhile.

I do not want to suggest that there is any hard and fast rule about this. But I do think that there is a general attitude of mind about the relationship of travel expenditure to the total cost of the holiday. If this is true, it has some important implications in the pattern of tourist expenditure and development. One implication is that, as the level of fares comes down, there is a tendency for shorter visits to become more worthwhile even on longer routes. There is clear evidence that this has happened. On the North Atlantic route, for example, the figures for the past thirteen years – from 1950 to 1963 – show that there is a marked correlation between the reduction in fare level and the reduction in holiday trip time. The average level of air and sea fares has been reduced by about 25 per cent over these thirteen years. (This is the reduction in real terms, that is to say taking into account the falling value of money.) Over the same period the average length of stay of US visitors to Europe has also been reduced by about a quarter. I do not attach any significance to the coincidence of the two figures, but the important fact is that, as the average fare level has come down, it has become worthwhile for people to take shorter trips. The importance of this tendency for the future development of the tourist industry is obvious.

The North Atlantic development which I have just described was influenced, to some extent, by the fact that over this period of time the proportion of people travelling by air grew very substantially. This change in the mix of travel has had an influence on the average length of stay because air travellers on this route have always tended to make shorter visits to Europe than sea travellers. I think that this can be explained by another psychological factor: the unwillingness of the average person to devote too large a proportion of his holiday to the travel portion.

Cruises or coach tours, on which people spend virtually all their time travelling, are an obvious exception to this. But in general, there appears to be a psychological tendency to regard travel time (as well as travel costs) as a sort of overhead of the trip, and this overhead has to be spread over a reasonable length of visit to make it seem worthwhile. Speed of travel, as well as the cost of travel, therefore influences the pattern of tourist expenditure.

Let me illustrate this point by reference to a personal experience last year when I went out to Singapore for a one-day visit. It took about twenty-four hours to get there and twenty-four hours to come back – just for a one-day visit. All my instincts rebelled against this, and, although the trip was worthwhile, it was difficult to escape the feeling that it was silly to spend so much time on travel for such a short visit. If the journey had only taken, say, six hours each way, I do not think that I should have had the same feeling. This attitude of mind is one of the explanations of the fact that, as fares come down, and consequently more people are able to afford to go further afield for their holidays, the time element becomes increasingly important in travel. Since there are relatively few people who have more than about three weeks available for their holiday, it is obvious why air travel has become such an important means of tourist travel on long distance routes.

Travel and Income

Another aspect of the general relationship between travel and tourism is the way in which travel grows in relation to national income. I have not got time to offer more than pontification on this subject, but I will make one or two comments later.

As a broad generalization, one can say that expenditure on holiday travel is functionally related to income level: as personal income increases so does the amount of travel expenditure. But travel expenditure increases at a substantially faster rate than the increase in total income. This means that expenditure on travel is very much the reverse of what economists sometimes call 'Giffen goods' (after Sir Robert Giffen, a nineteenth-century economist who drew attention to the fact that the proportion of income spent on basic necessities, like bread, tends to fall as income rises). What we need here is a new term to express the reverse of this – the 'anti-Giffen-goods', if you like – the goods on which we spend more of our income as we get richer. The available evidence leaves no room for doubt that recreational travel is one of the things that people want more of as incomes rise.

The proportion of income which people spend on different things is a fascinating subject. A recent study made by the Stanford Research Institute of California analyses the proportion of income spent on a whole range of items – food, furniture, clothing, transport and communications, motor cars, radio and television, etc. – in many different countries. What they have done is to compare the amount spent on these items in about twenty-five different countries and relate these expenditures to the level of income in those countries. This gives a 'cross-country' relationship from which an income elasticity coefficient can be derived. An analysis of the same kind for recreational travel suggests that the income elasticity coefficient for this type of expenditure is about 2·0: that is to say that expenditure on travel increases at about twice the rate of increase in income.

A point which follows from this relationship is that as national income increases there is likely to be a steady development, at the top end of the market, of the number of people who want to go further afield. To assess the extent of this market we must examine the pattern of income distribution and the distribution of holiday expenditure. Some extremely interesting data on this subject is given in the BTA holiday survey for 1963, to which I referred earlier. The survey shows how much various sections of the public spend on their overseas holidays. From this data it is possible to construct a distribution curve showing the amounts spent by different numbers of people.

It can be seen that the average amount spent in 1963 was about £60. The numbers of people spending larger amounts naturally tend to fall and there are relatively few spending as much as £200. But as the general level of incomes increases there is a tendency for this curve to shift to the right, though its shape will remain broadly the same. As the curve shifts to the right, the tail end of the curve, which represents small numbers of people spending large amounts of money, will inevitably show a much greater proportionate increase than the average increase in holiday expenditure.

This is an extremely important factor in explaining why we have seen, in 1964, such a large increase in expenditure in long-haul travel from this country: the increase in travel to North America being a very substantial part of this. An implication of this aspect of the developing pattern of tourist expenditure is that, as people are willing and able to spend more money on their holidays, and if they are limited in the time available for those holidays, there is bound to be an increasing use of air transport for longer-distance holidays.

Elasticity of Demand

I should now like to say something about price elasticity of demand for travel. I do not want to leave the impression that there will be a large and automatic increase in holiday travel solely because of increases in national income. I must say something about the influence of price on the growth of the travel market.

Expenditure on travel is competitive with all other consumer needs and this is particularly true, I think, of the competition between expenditure on travel and on consumer durables. It has been argued that the very large increase in expenditure on some forms of consumer durables in 1964 was a major reason why some sectors of the holiday market developed less rapidly than might reasonably have been expected.

There is little doubt that a change in price of the total holiday has a significant influence on the growth of the travel market. And changes in relative prices can have an even more direct influence on the share of the holiday market going to particular regions, to particular types of accommodation, and travelling by different forms of transport. I am referring here to the total price of the holiday, which means the fare plus the cost of accommodation and all other facilities on which holidaymakers spend their money. Fares, as I mentioned earlier, are only about 40 per cent of total holiday expenses and it is a mistake to think about the influence of prices in the holiday market exclusively in terms of fares: accommodation costs are at least as important. There is support for this statement in the way in which the European travel market has developed in the post-war years. Areas with low accommodation costs have developed much more rapidly than high costs areas, even though fares to the former may have been higher than to the latter. The growth of travel to Spain and the relative decline of travel to France illustrates this point very clearly.

The relationship between price level and the volume of demand is referred to by economists as the 'elasticity of demand'. This expresses numerically the relationship between a change in price and the volume of goods sold, whatever they may be.

If price is reduced by 10 per cent, and sales increase by 20 per cent demand is said to be 'elastic'. If price is reduced by 10 per cent and sales increase by less than 10 per cent demand is said to be 'inelastic'. In the elastic case total revenue has been increased by the price reduction: in the inelastic case total revenue has been reduced.

The evidence suggests that the demand for travel is fairly sensitive to the price level; in other words we are dealing, in the travel industry, with an elastic demand. I have spent some time during the past year studying the elasticity of travel on the North Atlantic route. My investigations leave me with no doubt that this has been a market in which the level of fares has had a substantial influence on the volume of traffic carried each year; this has been a fairly elastic market over the last fifteen years. This probably sounds like a revelation of the blindingly obvious. But if this conclusion applies, as I think it does, to the whole travel market, its truth has not been universally accepted in practice. It has, for example, taken the French tourist industry a long time to recognize this simple truth; that the price level has a considerable effect on the number of customers who buy the product.

One must, of course, add that quality is also an important factor to be taken into account: the influence of price level on the volume of demand must be related to the quality of service provided. One must not oversimplify the picture of the holiday market. The travel industry does not sell an homogeneous product: in fact it sells about as varied a product as any other industry in the country. Individual preferences concerning the quality of the holiday product are very varied and obviously play a considerable part in determining the shape and direction of the development of the industry. Price is not, therefore, the only factor. But there is ample evidence that when the relative price levels for different types of services get out of line with consumers' evaluation of what those different qualities are worth, there is a rapid change in the sales of the different types of service. A good illustration of this point has been the change in demand for first class travel on the North Atlantic route. The difference in the fare for first class travel compared with economy class travel became substantially greater than the evaluation which previous first class travellers thought worth-while. A marked decline in the numbers of people buying first class tickets indicated that the fare differential was out of line with the quality differential and, as a matter of interest, the airlines have taken effective steps to correct this imbalance.

Factors Influencing Transport Costs

I now want to say something about cost factors in the transport business. I have argued that holiday travel is sensitive to price and, since transport is a substantial element of total holiday cost, I now want to examine the factors which cause the costs of transport to be high or low. I want also to consider the ways that the level of fares might be reduced by the creation of conditions conducive to low operating costs. There are five factors which, in all forms of transport, are fundamentally important in influencing the level of operating costs. They are:

1. vehicle size;
2. utilization of vehicles and operating crews;
3. load factor;
4. utilization of terminal facilities;
5. route traffic density.

There are, of course, substantial technical differences between each form of transport but these technical differences are, I think, less important than the basic economic similarities summarized under these five headings. Let me say just a few words about each.

First of all, vehicle size. In all forms of transport there are economies arising from the use of larger transport units: larger trains, larger buses, larger ships, larger aeroplanes, all have lower costs per available seat mile than smaller vehicles of the same kind. The economies of using a large vehicle derive partly from economies in capital costs: a larger ship costs less per ton of payload than a smaller one. Then, secondly, there are weight economies in a larger vehicle which usually produce a better relationship between payload and gross weight. Thirdly, there are power economies because larger engines are almost invariably more efficient in terms of horse-power produced per pound of fuel consumed than smaller power units. Finally there are economies in the crew of a larger vehicle; crew weights and crew costs do not rise proportionately with increase in size of vehicle. I am not saying that it will always be cheaper to use a larger vehicle than a smaller one – this will depend upon the availability of traffic – but cost per available unit of capacity will almost invariably be lower for a larger vehicle than a smaller one.

Utilization of vehicles and crews is the second factor determining operating costs. The economic advantage of larger vehicles will depend on whether there is enough traffic, all the year round, to enable them to be utilized at a high rate. The capital costs of the vehicle – depreciation, insurance, and interest on the money invested in the equipment, which are substantial costs in all forms of transport – these costs are spread over a large number of revenue-earning hours as the utilization of the equipment is increased. Hence the greater the number of revenue-earning hours operated by each vehicle each year the lower are costs arising from ownership when these are expressed as costs per unit of capacity produced.

The same is true of the costs of operating crews: an increase in the utilization of crews – whether they be pilots, ship's officers, train crews or bus drivers – produces a lower cost per revenue-earning hour.

Load factor is the third cost consideration listed. Its importance is obvious. If a 30-seater coach can be operated on a certain route for £15, the operator can charge a fare of 10s. [50p] if all the seats are filled, but must charge £1 if only half the seats are filled. This simple example shows the immediate relationship between the unit cost level and the load factor at which the vehicle is operated.

The fourth factor listed above is the utilization of terminal facilities. In general terms (although this is subject to several important qualifications), terminal facilities become cheaper per unit of traffic as throughput is increased. Here again this generalization is valid for all forms of transport. Moreover, another aspect of terminal costs which holds good for all forms of transport is that, as the length of haul increases, these costs are spread over a larger number of revenue-earning miles; thus a longer haul journey has a lower terminal cost per mile than does a shorter journey.

Fifthly, there is the factor of route traffic density. Track costs – the costs of permanent way, the costs of signalling, and so on – these all tend to fall per unit of traffic carried as the traffic density over the route increases. Again there are qualifications to this generalization, but it represents a broad truth about the operating economics of most forms of transport.

Let me now review, very briefly, some of the operating conditions and circumstances in which transport costs are likely to be high or low. A primary condition conducive to low costs is a high volume of traffic, because this makes possible the use of large vehicles. A regular flow of traffic is conducive to a high utilization of vehicles and crews. And thirdly, balanced flows of traffic – an equal flow of traffic in each direction of the route – is an important factor because this is essential to enable the operator to achieve a high load factor.

On the other side of the penny, the circumstances in which operating costs will be high can best be illustrated by two examples. First of all, suburban services operated by bus or rail. Demand conditions for such services produce a one-direction peak of traffic in the morning and again in the evening. As a result, the operator gets low utilization of vehicles, low utilization of crews, and low average load factor on this type of service.

Another example, and one of great importance, is the provision of highly seasonal holiday services. These give rise to high operating costs, first of all, because extra vehicles and crews are required only for the peak time, and hence low average utilization of vehicles and crews is inescapable. Secondly, because there is a tendency for traffic to be one-directional at the beginning and end of the season, and this gives rise to low average load factor at those times. Thirdly, because terminal facilities have to be adequate to meet the peak demand, and therefore are more than are needed at other times of the year and under-utilized on a year-round basis.

The Beeching Report gave some startling data of the way in which seasonal traffic peaks cause high costs in railway operations. The utilization of British Railways rolling stock in 1959 was astonishingly low. In that year British Railways had about 18,500 coaches allocated to fast and semi-fast trains. Of these coaches only 5,500 were required for year-round services and 8,900 (about half of the total) were required only for peak summer services. There were over 2,000 coaches which were only used on ten occasions during the course of the year. It would be difficult to find more dramatic figures illustrating the way in which seasonal peaks give rise to low vehicle utilization.

Co-operation for Lower Holiday Costs

To conclude I should like to say a few words about the ways in which the different sections of the tourist industry could co-operate to produce conditions in which transport costs might be reduced to the lowest possible level. It is painfully clear that the circumstances in which transport costs tend to be high are the natural conditions of the holiday travel market, particularly conditions of high peak demand. This problem can be offset to some extent by achieving very high load factors at peak times. Charter operations and other forms of group travel are means by which high load factors can be achieved in peak holiday travel. But co-operation between the providers of hotel and other accommodation and the transport operators could also assist in achieving conditions in which transport costs are kept to the lowest possible level. It is obviously desirable for all sections of the tourist industry to try to spread the holiday season. People in the industry have talked about this for years but very little has yet been achieved.

There seems to be a general feeling that not much can be done. I think that is a great pity and I think that we should take encouragement from the evident success in 1964 of an attempt by airlines to change the pattern of North Atlantic travel. Lower fares have been successful in stimulating additional traffic during the so-called 'shoulder months' of the year. Traffic increased by 44 per cent in May, 38 per cent in June, 23 per cent in July, 34 per cent in August, and 41 per cent in September. These figures show that the increases in travel, compared with the same month in 1963, were much greater at the beginning and end of the summer season; which is exactly what the excursion fare inducements set out to achieve.

There is, I think, a strong case for very much greater co-operation between travel agents, transport companies, and hoteliers to offer price inducements which will encourage new traffic at the beginning and end of the existing season. But this policy could be extended even further by a big increase in the effort devoted to winter holiday promotion. I am well aware that the 'conventional wisdom' holds that the winter holiday market is insensitive to price reductions. But I am rather sceptical about this, particularly after making my study of elasticity of demand on the North Atlantic route. It appears to me that winter non-business travel across the North Atlantic has been just as responsive to fare reductions as summer traffic. I would suggest that the travel industry should direct more of its marketing activity towards the encouragement of winter travel and that, in doing this, it should aim its message at wives.

I think that the people who sell central heating could give us a lesson here. They have directed a large part of their advertising on the female head of the family, and with considerable success. The travel industry should do the same thing because there is, I believe, a strong desire amongst middle-class housewives to get away from the chores of the home and kitchen for a short break in middle of the winter. They do not necessarily want to go to some exotic spot to lie in the sunshine; they just want to be looked after in a comfortable hotel for a few days.

In most of these matters the interests of the transporters and the hoteliers are identical. There is, however, one problem which is not shared by the hotelier. This is the question of spreading the load throughout the week. The peaks which occur at weekends are a major problem for the transport companies and they must spread loads more evenly throughout the week if they are to reduce costs. This problem does not arise in the same way in the hotel business, because a hotel can run quite efficiently by having the total occupancy changed each Saturday. What is needed here is a much greater sympathy in the hotel business with the need of the transporter to spread the load throughout the week.

Although this does not appear as an immediate problem for the hotelier, it is, in the long run, a problem for the whole industry because it influences the total cost of the holiday package and hence the aggregate level of demand. It is essential that all sections of the industry should consider not just their own immediate problems, but co-operate in achieving a pattern of development which will be of long-term benefit to the growth of holiday travel.

8 Trends in Car Ownership and Leisure

BY DR M. ABRAMS

From a paper presented to a Conference on Roads and Leisure organized by the British Road Federation and the British Tourist Authority in association with the Ministries of Transport and of Housing and Local Government at the University of Keele on 14 July 1970.

Currently well over half of all persons in Great Britain aged 16 or more are members of households that own at least one car; their proportion has more than doubled over the past decade and is still increasing steadily.

Table 8.1

Percentage of persons 16 and over in Car-owning Households

	%
1958	26
1963	40
1968	54
1973 (est.)	63[1]

Source: National Readership Surveys; 1973 author's estimate.

Car Ownership by Class

Over the decade the rate of growth in ownership has been high in all socio-economic grades, but naturally it has been lowest in the middle classes (since they started with a high level of ownership), and highest in the working classes. The *National Readership Surveys* divide the population into four main socio-economic grades along the following lines:

Designation	Class	% of all adults
AB	Middle and upper	12·5
C1	Lower middle	23·5
C2	Skilled manual	30·0
DE	Unskilled, pensioners	34·0
		100·0

[1] The 1973 actual percentage of persons aged 16 and over in car-owning households was 61 per cent instead of the estimate of 63 per cent. The main reason for this shortfall was the fact that in the *AB* grade there was practically no increase between 1968 and 1973 in the proportion owning at least one car. *Eds.*

The proportions over the past decade of car owners in each of these grades are shown in Table 8.2. It will be seen that in 1968 almost three-quarters of all those

Table 8.2

Car Ownership by Socio-economic Grade

	1958 %	1963 %	1968 %	1973 (est.) %
AB	66	79	84	90
C1	31	51	68	75
C2	20	40	60	70
DE	10	17	30	39
Total	26	40	54	63

in the middle classes (i.e. *AB* plus *C1*) were in car-owning families (73 per cent), and even among skilled working class adults three out of every five were car owners. The rough estimates made for 1973 suggest that by then the proportion of car households will have reached saturation levels in the *AB* grade, and that in the two middle bands of the population (*C1* and *C2*) approximately three out of every four will have access to a family car.

Car Ownership by Life-cycle Stages

Past and present differences in rates of car ownership between the socio-economic grades are not surprising since these grades are initially defined by occupation and hence indirectly by income. There are, however, other variables related to differences in rates of car ownership, and perhaps the most important of these are connected with age and domestic circumstances.

In these terms we have divided the 16 and over population of Great Britain into six groups:

(*a*) Unmarried, aged 16–24. Currently this group comprises 12 per cent of the total population aged 16 and over; for the most part they are junior members of families where irrespective of occupation the parents have reached, or almost reached, their maximum earnings; there are few or no dependent children in the family, and those aged 16 to 24 not only have independent earnings of their own, but are also highly likely to spend a large part of their leisure time outside the home in gregarious activities.

(*b*) Unmarried (including widows, divorced, etc.) aged 25–64; these constitute 10 per cent of the adult population; they are mainly women and middle-aged and on both counts are less likely than other people to be car owners.

(*c*) Married, aged 16–34. They form 18 per cent of the adult population; almost all of them are parents of young children; for the whole family to move around both as a group and comparatively cheaply, both at week-ends and for holidays, the ownership of a car has considerable attractions. Moreover, in the interests of their young children an unduly high proportion live in the suburbs, the New Towns, and the smaller towns where not only is a garden available, but also car parking is cheap and there is easy access to the country for family excursions. On all these counts we can expect car ownership to be high in this group in spite of the fact that in their budgets the ratio of income and assets to liabilities and outgoings is likely to be well below average.

(*d*) Married, aged 35–44. These form 16 per cent of the adult population. Most of them are young enough to have been teenagers in the post-war world and therefore to take car driving and car ownership as part of the everyday world. For most of them their children have either left home or else are at work; they are not house-bound and, with few dependants, income per head is likely to be high. In short, they are more likely than most people to be car owners.

(*e*) Married, aged 45–64. These constitute 28 per cent of the adult population. Although they grew up at a time when car ownership was an expensive novelty limited to a small minority they find that at this stage in their lives they are almost entirely without any dependent children and with earnings and assets at their peak. These advantages are sufficient to overcome the handicap of age and we can expect them to show a car ownership level well above the average.

(*f*) All 65 and over. These form 16 per cent of the adult population. Because of their age, their relative poverty, and the fact that nearly two-thirds of them are women, the rate of car ownership among them will certainly be well below average.

In order to hold constant the variable of socio-economic grade, Tables 8.3*a* and 8.3*b* show separately trends of ownership rates for grade *AB* and grade *C2* by life cycle stages.

Table 8.3a

Grade *AB* Car Ownership by Life Cycle Stages

		1958 %	1963 %	1968 %	1973 (est.) %
Unmarried	16–24	75	83	90	95
,,	25–64	50	64	76	85
Married	16–34	64	78	87	92
,,	35–44	76	89	92	95
,,	45–64	73	86	90	92
All 65 and over		44	56	58	63
All *AB*		66	79	84	90

In 1968 of the six life cycle groups, car ownership was above the average in four of them – the young unmarried and the three married groups of 16 to 64. In the other two – the middle-aged single and the very elderly – the proportions were well below average, and in the second of these expansion is almost at a standstill.

Table 8.3b

Grade *C2* Car Ownership by Life Cycle

		1958 %	1963 %	1968 %	1973 % (est.)
Unmarried	16–24	25	48	63	75
„	25–64	23	37	44	50
Married	16–34	22	41	65	70
„	34–44	26	43	63	75
„	45–64	24	41	62	75
All 65 and over		20	25	35	40
All *C2*		20	40	60	70

Among adults in the skilled working class the pattern of differences is the same; among the young unmarried and among married adults below the age of 65 ownership rates in 1968 were above average and over a ten-year period has risen rapidly from ratios in the middle twenties to ratios in the middle and lower sixties. Among unmarried adults aged 25 to 64 and among all those aged 65 and over the proportion of car owners was, in 1968, well below average and showed least expansion over the decade.

If, bearing in mind this general pattern of car owning by age and domestic circumstance, we look forward to the year 1981, it seems that the potential for growth in total car ownership is comparatively slight. According to the Registrar-General's latest estimates (*Monthly Digest of Statistics, 1970*) between now and mid-1981 the United Kingdom total population will show an increase of approximately 3 million people (or just over 5 per cent) – from 55·9 million to 58·9 million. However, over this period, on present marrying trends, the number of married people under 65 years of age (i.e. the bulk of those with above average car ownership ratios) will remain practically stationary. At least two-thirds of the total increase in population, it is estimated, will take place among those under school-leaving age and those who have reached and passed retirement age.

In short, as far as demographic factors are concerned much of the potential for growth in car ownership has already reached its peak; in future, growth will depend almost entirely on any rise that takes place in the real net personal income of the average married couple. The experience of the past twenty years suggests that this is very unlikely to exceed a modest $2\frac{1}{2}$ per cent per annum. But even on this basis it is probable that by 1981 roughly 75 per cent of all adults will be in car-owning families; and if those over pensionable age are excluded, then the ratio of car owners among the rest of the adult population may well be as high as 80 per cent.

In terms of cars on the road, this probably means that, after allowing for the two-car family, the number in Great Britain will be of the order of 17 million as compared with today's $11\frac{1}{2}$ million – or an increase of almost 50 per cent.

Leisure

For most people the experience of the past ten to fifteen years has been that real income in goods and services has increased faster than income in the form of leisure, and that this trend in the ratio of income to leisure looks like continuing. The average weekly hours worked by adult male manual workers in 1961 were 47·4; by October 1969 this weekly average had declined by 50 minutes to 46·5 hours. A much more important source of leisure has been generated by the changing occupational structure of British industry. Over the past decade the total work force has remained almost stationary; but at the same time the number of salaried employees in industry and of white-collar workers outside industry has expanded by 25 per cent – and practically all these are on a 40–hour week; most of them have the weekend clear from work and usually their paid annual holidays are appreciably longer than those of manual workers.

Leisure and Cars

In the white-collared middle classes (*AB* plus *CI*) not only is there more than the average amount of leisure, but, as we have seen, more than three-quarters of them today have a car. The relationship, therefore, between car owning on the one hand and, on the other, the amount and pattern of leisure is a very close one.

Some of the details of this relationship were made clear in the report *Planning for Leisure* based on the research in 1965–66 of the Government's Social Survey. Some of the findings of this study can be summarized as follows:

1. Car owners in general were found to spend four times as many leisure periods on excursions to the country or to the seaside than did the rest of the population.
2. Within each socio-economic class people with cars were much more likely to be members of clubs. This contrast between car owners and non-car owners was greatest for young married people with children and for the elderly.
3. Car owners were much more prone than others to go further afield in their excursions and also to visit a wider variety of these places.
4. Participation in and expenditure on sports and games were much higher among car owners; these held true within each age group and each social class.

All the preceding finds strongly suggest that with future increases in car ownership we will see an appreciable rise in outings, in club membership, and in participation in sports and games. If side by side with the higher rates of car ownership there are significant increases in the real standard of living of the average family then the expansion in outings, sports, and games will be particularly rapid in those where the monetary costs are relatively high – far-ranging trips involving overnight accommodation, golf, sailing, etc.

5. When people take part in physical recreation they almost invariably go by private transport if they are able to do so, *regardless of the distance they have to travel*. This indicates the growing importance of providing adequate car parks adjacent to all sports and games facilities.

6. Among the most popular activities, the greatest distances were travelled by those taking part in water sports (i.e. rowing, canoeing, boating, sailing, and pleasure cruising). Car owners who participate in water sports go much further afield to enjoy these activities than do non-car owners pursuing the same activities.

7. The rate of participation in all forms of physical and outdoor recreation is highest among those under 22 years of age – irrespective of whether they have a car or not; but from that age on car ownership becomes very important; the decline among car owners is comparatively slight; among non-owners it is sharp and falls away rapidly.

8. In considering attitudes to participation in sports and games men's interest in the social/competitive aspects of these activities declined rapidly with age, and instead much greater stress was given to the opportunities these provided for getting out into the open air either alone or with one or two friends, or else with members of their own family.

Summary

1. Over the past ten years the proportion of adults living in car-owning families has doubled, and by the end of this year may well be as high as 60 per cent.

2. In the middle classes (*AB* and *C1*) the ratio today at 4 out of 5 is rapidly approaching saturation point; and among skilled workers and their families the figure already exceeds 3 out of 5.

3. In all social classes the highest rates of car ownership are found among married people under 65 years of age. Their total numbers ten years hence are likely to be much the same as they are today and therefore any increase in the number of cars on the roads will be largely determined by growth in the number of two-car families and by increases in the average real incomes of working class households.

4. In the past much of the increase in the total amount of leisure time has come not from any all-round reduction in working time (including travel to work) but from changes in the structural composition of the occupied population. These changes are still taking place and may well accelerate.

5. In all social classes and at all stages in the life cycle the ownership of a car substantially affects leisure behaviour. With a car people cease being predominantly house-bound and sedentary in their leisure time; less of it is spent on watching television and reading; much more is on excursions and physical recreation; they range further afield, they visit more places, and they are more prone to pursue the minority, informal, non-competitive activities. A motor-owning population is one that spreads its leisure over the whole country in the pursuit of variety, autonomy – and parking facilities.

Part V
Accommodation and Catering

Introduction

In this Part we have included one contribution on catering and one on accommodation with a common focus on marketing. As elements in the tourist product, catering and accommodation raise particular problems of availability, capacity, and standards, the need for harmony with other elements of the tourist product, and, therefore, the need for co-operation between their providers.

In spite of increasing activity in tourist research, as far as we know no study has been made of the needs of tourists when eating away from home. Longden's contribution represents the only attempt known to us to examine the catering element in the tourist product. It postulates what the tourist's needs are in an eating-out situation and how they differ from those we have when we are not on holiday. It pays particular attention to the special needs of tourists and how they may be met effectively. Although this paper relates primarily to Britain, the issues raised are relevant to any country which genuinely seeks to meet the requirements of its tourist traffic.

Pickering's contribution recognizes that small firms face particular problems and that some of them may be overcome by co-operation between them. He distinguishes between area marketing, group marketing, and other co-operative activities of value to hotels and restaurants, and examines the characteristics of three hotel group marketing schemes in Britain, their benefits, and the problems they encountered. Co-operatives of small businesses have been common in several fields, including retailing, and have not been confined to Britain. But this article based on a close investigation of existing co-operative action of hotels represents a significant contribution to our understanding of this field, and we are grateful to the Controller of Her Majesty's Stationery Office for permission to reproduce it here.

9 Catering for the Tourist

BY J. P. LONGDEN

From a paper presented to a Short Course 'Tourism in Britain' organized by the University of Surrey at Richmond, England, on 2–6 January 1967.

Introduction

Under all that mohair, behind that Leica, somewhere, deep down, there's a person. Not so deep down, in fact. The tourist disguise is less than skin deep. The person, the essential humanity, very quickly emerges. And, in reality, when you come to consider it, the barrier to identification lies not so much in their now familiar appearance as in our unchanging attitudes, our determination never to lose the caricaturist's image of the typical tourist. And we so easily forget that for a few weeks in the year we ourselves, or at least most of us, are tourists. This alone should convince us that tourists are people.

In any industry involving large numbers of human beings, the entrepreneur is faced with the task of producing customer satisfaction not only on a large scale but also, and, perhaps especially, in individual cases. The efficiency of catering for a group of a hundred might easily be judged by the manner in which its one vegetarian member received his requirements – precisely, without fuss or delay – rather than by the fortunes or misfortunes of the other ninety-nine. Minorities tend to be vocal; minorities of one, stridently so.

The caterer is familiar with this problem; to reach markets of substantial size he must deal with the general; to maintain the highest standards he must be obsessed fastidiously with the particular. In this sense, the best caterers are those who survey their markets bi-focally, who discern both the woods and the trees, the groups and the persons, the types and the individuals. The secret of success is simple: mass production of the personal touch. Primarily, the tourist, like any other catering consumer, is an individual person.

The first question to be asked about catering to the tourist market is: What do we know about the tourist market, and to what use do we put that knowledge?

In many respects, our knowledge is more precise about tourist markets than it is about home markets. We have accurate assessments of numbers, countries of origin, average duration of stay. Empirically, over a period of years a pattern (albeit a changing pattern) has emerged of localities favoured, seasonal peaks and troughs, even national peculiarities and preferences. Socio-economic levels are easily discernible from the methods of travel and types of accommodation chosen. In fact, for large parts of his stay, the tourist is captive or semi-captive, to his catering requirements, to his travel and accommodation arrangements.

Moreover, tourists tend to behave in groups and families rather than as single persons. Spending power is normally self-evident, sometimes pre-stated. Research surveys have been made not only of the foreign tourist, but also the domestic tourist, and these yield quite a useful amount of information. Taken together, these migratory data form a sufficient body of knowledge to make the tourist a fairly predictable phenomenon, in many ways much more predictable than our own domestic consumer.

Classification of Tourist Needs

But these are all predominantly external aspects of the tourist. It is internally – to the inner man – the inner man in the truest and fullest senses – that the caterer should address himself. Internally, the tourist consists of a complex of needs which the caterer should strive to satisfy efficiently and profitably. The catering needs of a tourist fall into three somewhat elastic categories:

1. Needs which the tourist has in common with all catering consumers: for instance, to eat, drink, rest, be served, be sheltered, get good value. The identification of tourist needs with common-consumer needs is, of course, almost complete when the tourist is, in fact, touring in his own country – and this accounts for a very significant part of the tourist market.
2. Consumer needs which take on an added emphasis and importance in the tourist situation: e.g. to be entertained, interested, distracted, involved in novel eating experiences.
3. Needs which are the particular prerogative of tourists: e.g. to understand menus and be relieved of currency conversion problems.

A priori, one would expect that the third category, the special needs of the tourist, would be the most difficult to satisfy and therefore the one in which some degree of failure would be understandable, if not forgivable. However, the critics of British catering – and particularly British catering to tourists – might easily claim that our failures embrace all three categories; that our particular failure to satisfy tourist needs is only part of a more general insensitivity to consumer needs as a whole. Taking a less cynical view, I would say that the catering operations which seem to satisfy tourist clientele most, are also those which satisfy domestic clientele most, and I do not know of any restaurant which is conspicuously good at catering to tourists and conspicuously bad at catering to its home clientele – or, even the reverse.

It may well be that the primary breakdown of catering markets should not be by nationality or even 'tourist and non-tourist', but rather by socio-economic levels of international validity. In this way, there would be not only an international élite, but also an international middle class, an international working class, and international versions of all those gradations of class which we have in our so-called classless society.

The caterer's business consists of satisfying the catering needs – precisely and appropriately – of each class. And it would seem that these 'class needs' are of even greater importance than the characteristic national needs.

The caterer, then, should regard the tourist firstly as a person, secondly as a consumer with common-consumer needs, thirdly as a representative of a certain sector of society with special needs, and fourthly as a person in transit at home or abroad.

Addictive and Experimental Needs

We saw that the caterers' 'identikit' of a tourist should consist of three strata of needs. Let us look at his need to eat and drink – the basic requirements of the eating-out situation. The controversy which normally arises here is as to whether the tourist should be given as near as possible what he has at home, or whether he should be given characteristic samples of the national fare of the country he is visiting. We often get the wrong answers to this question. Largely because it is the wrong question.

The right questions to ask are:

1. At what level in a tourist's personality do his addictive needs give way to his experimental needs?
2. Do we fully realize that every tourist has both kinds of needs – in varying proportions?
3. And do we apply ourselves adequately to both?

By 'addictive', I mean those needs or taste preferences which are sufficiently insistent to make one search for normal fulfilment even in a foreign country; most tourists are addicted, for instance, to the newspapers and cigarettes of their countries of origin.

In the field of consumables, the first striking observation is that tourists are more likely to be addictive in their drinking habits, alcoholic and otherwise, than in their eating. Methods of preparation of coffee and tea, the availability of iced water, the importance of cocktails in relation to beverage wines, the correct temperature at which all drinks are served: these are subjects of comparatively strong national conservatism. Since, apart from our beers and whisky, we, in Great Britain, have little in this field to offer as a bait towards experimentation, this tendency is perhaps not surprising.

In matters of food as opposed to drink, it is the tourist's willingness to experiment which predominates; and this desire is frequently under-rated by restaurateurs who insist on offering indifferent sauerkraut to German visitors, tinned spaghetti to Italians, and seven-year-old bogus Beaujolais to Frenchmen.

Addictive taste preferences are likely to assert themselves in what might be described as 'faddy' eating – concepts of nutrition based on considerations of health and medicine. In this way, tourists may easily request special modes of food preparation such as grilling or poaching, salt-free cooking, processed breads, processed coffees, sugar-free sweeteners, and so on.

Coincidentally, the easy availability of 'fad-foods' and such things as a wide variety of international sauces and side-dishes seems to help in making basically English food acceptable to a wide variety of foreign palates. Unrelated but parallel is the tourist's, especially American, requirement of the availability of Kosher food for orthodox Jews. This, and other sectarian regimes, must be regarded, of course, as outright addictions.

On the whole British caterers should beware especially of the dangers of under-rating the foreigner's desire to experiment. The British tourist going abroad has in the past acquired the reputation of being more addictive than experimental. We are all familiar with the picture of the English dowager-duchess transporting her own very personal – and very English – mattress from hotel to hotel, washing her teeth in mineral water and supervising the preparation of her morning por-ridge (lest garlic should be added!). It is perhaps true that we are less adventurous as tourists than most nationalities. What is certain is that it is a mistake to attribute this same conservatism to our foreign visitors. The mistake is in fact twofold – that of confusing Anglo-Saxon attitudes with foreign attitudes, and that of confusing consumer attitudes with supplier attitudes.

More numerous and important than the outright addictions of tourists are the semi-addictions – the food and drink preferences which somewhat reluctantly they are prepared to sacrifice during a visit to Britain, but which form a none the less significant substratum of unsatisfied needs. Americans, for instance, after some weeks in Europe, will confess that what they yearn for most is a real American hamburger and a chocolate malt; Italians after a while pine for a truly *al dente* pasta, and so on.

The ratio of addictive needs to experimental needs is largely influenced by the socio-economic status of the consumer; by and large, it seems that the higher income groups tend to be more experimental – always excepting the international 'beatnik' who has devised his own brand not only of extreme poverty, but also of extreme experiment. Further complicating factors which influence this ratio of experiment to addiction are, of course, the tourist's purposes. It is usual to divide these purposes into 'business' or 'pleasure', with 'visiting friends or relatives' as a kind of non-committal compromise. In analysing consumer needs, these rough categories are, of course, inadequate. What of the Jekyll and Hyde tourist who normally comes on business and sometimes comes on pleasure? What of the visitor who combines both or even all three activities in the same trip?

The refinement of study which might be devoted to this pattern of motives, circumstances, and resulting needs is almost infinite. And it will only be when such a study has been made scientifically and its results made generally available that the British catering industry will be able to address itself precisely to the task of catering for the tourist. In the meantime, it is, perhaps, permissible to make one or two commonsense observations.

Meeting the Tourist Needs

Firstly – what should the British caterer do about addictions and semi-addictions? Several things –

    1. Where possible and financially feasible, produce the genuine article.

2. Where this is not possible, produce alternative British foods and drinks of sufficient interest and sufficiently well prepared to compensate the tourist's loss of addictive pleasure by supplying him with an experimental pleasure. These native alternatives must be excellent of their kind. The aim should obviously be to offer the best standards of British cuisine, incorporating, as this does, international elements, and taking advantage of our immensely rich natural resources of fish, meat, vegetables and fruits.

What he should not do is to produce either:

(*a*) poor imitations of the foreign foods; or
(*b*) less than excellent versions of our national dishes.

I shrewdly suspect that what the tourist objects to primarily is bad food; the fact that it is also strange is merely a secondary affront. Even the maligned British coffee, instant or cona, can be acceptable to foreign palates if it is well made by our own standards (and there are virtually absolute standards of taste: it should, obviously, be hot, nutritious, flavourful).

It is perhaps relevant to note at this point that the traditional gulfs separating the national palates of the world seem, to some extent, to be diminishing. The increasing availability and use of processed foods throughout the world is bringing about a levelling out of palates, and forms, in a way, a kind of gastronomic esperanto of universal validity. The touring American is thus comforted to find that the controversy is no longer whether he should be given *Crème Portugaise* or *Crème Andalouse*, but rather whether Campbell's Tomato Soup is better than Heinz.

To some extent, the higher income groups of foreign tourists are protected by their own affluence from indulging in the degree of experimentation which they would like to enjoy. Generally speaking, they are more sophisticated, more articulate and discriminating with greater appetites for novelty than their poorer compatriots. Yet, because they stay in expensive hotels (sometimes owned by companies of their own nationality, e.g. Americans staying at the Hilton) they can afford and are offered either:

(*a*) food similar to that of their country of origin; or
(*b*) food drawn from the international repertoire of the so-called classical cuisine.

Ironically, because of their wealth and spending power, this class of tourist has difficulty in breaking through these protective barriers to the experimental pleasures of the authentic foods of the land he is visiting. Rich tourists, in my experience, yearn to share in the domestic eating experience of the country they are visiting, to sit down with a family at home and taste an ordinary meal. And it is only very rarely that they witness authentic forms of domestic eating, or even substitute domestic eating.

Ironically, these pleasures tend to be reserved for those least able to survive them. The lower income groups, coming on the cheapest of inclusive tours, having lower levels of sophistication and discrimination, less appetite for novelty, are very often plunged brutally into British domestic food because they cannot afford anything else.

It would be naïve and inappropriate to consider catering merely as the provision of food and drink; we all know – and in recent years, at least, have shown our knowledge – that it also means the provision of service and atmosphere. Fifteen years ago, the expression 'restaurant atmosphere' would have brought to most British minds a vivid recollection of the odour of stale cooked cabbage. Today, it means something entirely different.

The success stories in British catering in the past decade have been the stories of those organizations who have marketed service and atmosphere sensitively, who have taken the trouble to find out how people liked to be served and in what settings, and have provided the consumer with what he wants. This process is by no means complete and has only been applied occasionally to our tourist catering. American visitors are, it seems, immensely sensitive to restaurant atmosphere and have great appetites for the enjoyment of settings, décor, gimmicks, theming and so on for their own sake. Continental visitors are perhaps less initially susceptible to this form of catering by suggestion but, equally, tend to succumb to it in the end. It should be remembered that, to many tourists, a holiday is a series of meal experiences made more or less memorable by aspects not only of food and drink, but also service and atmosphere. This need to be entertained, intrigued, surprised, and even instructed is one of the characteristic catering consumer needs which gains especial importance in the tourist situation.

The consideration of atmosphere leads naturally to a consideration of our attitude to brochures, menu cards, and other souvenirs – formerly guarded zealously, now in enlightened quarters freely given to restaurant customers as a most potent source of sales persuasion.

As everyone knows, there are varying degrees of Britishness. There is the normal, even sub-normal level of Britishness which embraces a whole gamut of eating experiences including, shamefully, egg and chips, toad in the hole, beans on toast, reheated, cold-sliced, roast beef, the infinite metamorphosis of bread and potatoes, the bottomless cup of tea. And then there is the more-British-than-British style – the Hollywood view of British catering, in which, endlessly, we toss the gnawed remains of haunches of venison over our shoulders, dab trickles of claret away from our chins and cause havoc amongst the serving wenches.

Are either of these extremes acceptable to the tourist? Not, I would say, to any very marketable extent. The 'beans on toast' style has normally the bad characteristics of poor service and atmosphere value, even when the food value is good. The 'haunch of venison' style, rich in atmosphere, howsoever spurious, is often poor value in food content.

The tragedy is that there is, between these two extremes, a whole range of genuinely British foods which are capable of being cooked, served, and presented in ways which combine both intrinsic value and extrinsic interest. In the past ten years there have been signs in some of our restaurants, like the Hunting Lodge, of an understanding of this need, and of a will to supply it. I think we have only begun to exploit its possibilities.

At a certain level of sophistication the customer has an even greater need to experiment in the eating situation. There is ample evidence to suggest that as a result of his desire for novelty and change, he tends to under-utilize the restaurant facilities of the hotel where he is staying. Subtly and perhaps subconsciously, the restaurant of his own hotel is down-graded to the level of a substitute domestic facility. In these circumstances he tends to take only the cheapest of meals 'in'; if he feels like spending a little extra he automatically assumes that he gets better value by going outside. The grass is greener. This is a characteristic of all kinds of hotel guests which gains added emphasis in the tourist situation where the variety of experiences obtained is one of the first criteria by which a tour is judged.

I might cite as an example of this the London Airport Excelsior Hotel – where the luxury restaurant, the Draytone Room, is full – not necessarily of residents of the Excelsior Hotel – but also of residents of other hotels and local business-men. The old-fashioned policy of hoteliers and restaurateurs used to be to attempt to make the tourist as 'captive' as possible. Nowadays more enlightened caterers only 'capture' by adding attractions and facilities to their hotels, and not by aiming at restrictive pension or demi-pension terms. Thus they are able to profit from the migratory instincts of tourists by erecting more hotels and restaurants (up to a certain point) in the vicinity of existing ones. In other words, they establish 'tourist eating localities'. Thus, by relaxing traditional jealousies, and accepting as a fact of tourist life the interchange of consumers, restaurateurs can, in fact, increase their own turnover, and, collectively, give better value to the tourist.

Special Needs of Tourists

What of the special needs of a tourist – the need to identify, to understand, be understood, communicate generally, the need to evaluate accurately and without embarrassment, the need to pay?

The need to identify is certainly very strong in the tourist situation; strangers in a foreign land would gladly grasp at identifiable persons and reputable names in whom they could trust. Yet our style of restaurant management, ownership and administration is reticent, self-effacing almost to the point of anonymity. With a few very notable exceptions, we tend rather to manage from behind the scenes, hoping to achieve miracles of remote control and throwing the onus of customer contact on to the lower echelons of staff; i.e. precisely that sector of our labour force which might be ill-equipped, by nature and by training, to accept this responsibility. We tend, in other words, to let the tourist fight his own battles. It is to be hoped that the discreet, non-committal, even obscurantist style of restaurant operation will continue to give way to a more open and in-formative style in which the identity, facilities, and prices of restaurants will be clearly and accurately proclaimed by public advertising, and modern methods of merchandising.

It should not be necessary for a tourist (or indeed any customer) to spend two hours and several pounds to find out what a restaurant is like. It should be made obvious to him before the moment of decision. This form of experiment – especially when unsuccessful – is particularly productive of tourist displeasure.

And what of communication? The English people in recent centuries has neglected its vocabulary of food, drink, and taste to such an extent that there remains only a pale shrunken nucleus of 'native' words to describe the eating experience. To supply this deficiency, we now borrow foreign and predominantly French expressions; which does not help our transatlantic visitors, and makes us mildly ridiculous in the eyes of the continentals whose vocabularies we somewhat inexpertly plunder.

We really need to make up our minds about this. In the majority of cases, menus should be expressed in English, anglicizing by usage only those foreign words which are untranslatable, and reviving many of our own forgotten foodwords. Then, foreign languages should be used only for foreign menus. As a parallel movement, we should, of course, intensify our efforts to encourage in management and staff the study of foreign languages as a means of general communication.

A far greater degree of helpfulness could also be achieved in the question of evaluation. The process of converting mentally every dish on an *à la carte* menu from one currency into another is sufficiently laborious to discourage some of our visitors from eating at all. And I am sure that this is the explanation behind the figure of the much-maligned tourist who sits down in a British restaurant and defiantly orders an omelette with nothing else. It is not that he is not hungry or even, possibly, that he cannot afford more. He is just not prepared to commit himself to the labyrinthine puzzle of vegetable charges, cover charges, and so on. A bit like the Englishman in a French hairdressers. The remedy is simple – more table d'hôte menus, more fixed and inclusive charges, more composite dishes with an overall charge including vegetables.

We seem now to be out of the naïve frame of mind in which the credit card bearer is automatically a second-class citizen or, more to the point, a second-class customer. Credit is a commodity and a sales promotion facility which, like any other commodity or facility, must be paid for, presumably by the caterer, possibly, in the long run, by the customer. The cost of credit facilities may diminish the caterer's percentage of profit, but if, at the same time, it produces sufficiently larger volume of business, it may well be that the amount of his profit, in actual money, rather than as a percentage, is greater. It is for the caterer to assess this feasibility and act according to his findings.

By and large, this lesson has probably been absorbed by catering management, but there lingers in the attitudes of catering staff a certain amount of distrust, even disbelief, in the little plastic name cards which are now produced by tourists almost as commonly as traveller's cheques. Presumably this is a question of time and attrition which could be expedited by the precept and example of management.

It is not, I think, possible to over-state the tourist's preoccupation with cost; the extent to which costs are planned and comparisons made not only during their visit but also, and perhaps especially, during the planning and preparation which precedes it. How often are their theoretical expectations of cost precisely realized by their actual experiences? Very rarely, it seems. And, we do not appear to go out of our way to help them in the difficult process of evaluation. For instance, in selling an inclusive tour, how careful are tour operators to specify the things which are not included in an inclusive tour? What provision do they make for instance to cover room service for meals in hotels?

Whilst discussing money matters, it is permissible to ask another rhetorical question. What have we done in Great Britain to make our system of tipping rational, uniform, and trustworthy? Do we encourage the tourist to feel that he has 'done the right thing' (remembering the tourist's phobia of appearing ridiculous) and do we inspire confidence in the fact that gratuities levied inclusively are in fact distributed wholly to the staff?

Conclusions

I return to what is really the fundamental burden of this thesis. That, predominantly, what tourists need is what all consumers need – good value, both real and apparent – only more so. And that by making our catering more consumer-orientated, we will, automatically, make it more tourist-orientated.

It should be noted in this connection that, to the commercial caterer, tourism is only one sector of the market – albeit a very important one and one with enormous potentialities. Especially in our present economic climate, it is natural that caterers, before committing themselves to the heavy capital investment necessary to create facilities specifically for tourists, should ask themselves whether the money would be better spent if applied to a more numerous, less seasonal market. At present, this agony of choice does not present itself on an important scale, merely because, in principle, it seems that a good British restaurant is automatically a good tourist restaurant.

In 1959 a BTHA (as it was then) survey of Belgian, Dutch, and German visitors to Britain contained the following findings:

'Food, drink, or accommodation were favourably mentioned by 11 per cent of Belgians, 13 per cent of Dutch, and 10 per cent of Germans.

'The general opinion of British food was favourable. Over half of those interviewed remembered meals they had particularly enjoyed – mostly in restaurants and hotels – and the majority liked the English breakfast.

The meals particularly enjoyed were usually described as "traditionally English".'

This is not a very inspiring testimonial. Some progress – and, in fact, a lot of progress – has been made since 1959. The sincerest compliment we pay to the tourist restaurants of other countries is to create imitations of them in our own land. Here, we relive the pleasures of eating experiences abroad, and refresh our optimism in life by rehearsing for the next visit to the country of our choice. If we cannot afford this, we smoke Gauloises, or drink Campari, or watch Antonio's Flamenco dances. But, by and large, the most complete form of 'static tourism' is the meal in a foreign-style restaurant.

When there are, in Paris and Rome, as many English restaurants as there are now French and Italian restaurants in London, then I think we will have tangible evidence, by inference, that we have, in reality and on a significant scale, been catering for tourists.

10   *Co-operation and the Small Business*

BY DR J. F. PICKERING

From *The Small Firm in the Hotel and Catering Industry* by J. F. Pickering, J. A. Greenwood, and Diana Hunt, published as *Research Report No. 14* for the Committee of Inquiry on Small Firms (Her Majesty's Stationery Office, London, 1971).

Much interest has been shown in the possible scope for the development of co-operative activities in the hotel and catering industry. This emphasis seems to be particularly justifiable where there are large numbers of small firms unable individually to obtain full economies of scale and placed in unfavourable bargaining positions with powerful buyers and sellers in the market place. Through co-operation some of the inherent disadvantages can be overcome and greater benefits obtained from smaller individual marketing and other outlays. Whereas the growth of large organizations is often said to be a means of 'internalizing externalities', it is perhaps not incorrect to suggest that the co-operative movement is 'externalizing internalities' and so offering to individual firms benefits that their own size alone would not allow them to achieve.

Similar developments appear to be taking place in other countries, for example, a trade mark for independent German hotels is currently suggested and co-operation in the exchange of information, advertising, selling, marketing, accounting, and purchasing is being advocated. We believe that the co-operative movement in one form or another has considerable importance for the small firm. It does, however, seem appropriate to indicate certain caveats throughout this section as we discuss particular forms of co-operation.

It is important that co-operative schemes should be based upon discovered facts about the nature and economics of the operation and a clear identification of those areas where co-operation may be expected to prove beneficial. In Torquay, for example, it was the collection of information as a result of inter-firm comparisons that revealed the common problem of low off-peak occupancy and led to joint promotional activities by the hoteliers and in conjunction with British Rail. It is also necessary that co-operation should be based upon clearly identified objectives. In most cases the primary objectives will be to improve profitability through the attraction of additional trade, especially at times when demand is slack. Other objectives may be the achievement of lower operating costs and the establishment of a corporate image.

Area Marketing

Marketing effort concentrated on a particular town or group of towns in an area can be beneficial especially where the objective is not merely to sell room space but where attention is also paid to the infrastructure of amenities and entertainments in the area. Co-operative marketing on a wide scale then becomes possible to secure maximum impact and the manning of a central reservations system offers benefits.

Although in principle this sounds attractive, there may be difficulties since co-operation means promoting one's competitors as well as oneself: '. . . each productive unit has a considerable interest in publicizing its own product but a much smaller interest in promoting the area in which it operates since there exist in that area other units which are either actual or potential competitors'.[1] But this attitude is, to say the least, remarkably shortsighted and the IUOTO seems rather to rule out the possibility of co-operative promotion by area other than by public authorities for this reason. While some operators no doubt do take this view, particularly where local hotel associations are weak or focusing on the wrong objectives with little orientation towards the market, we do not think it is a true assessment of the situation. Indeed if the small hotel is to survive in some areas at all, and with it much of the local economy, it cannot afford to allow this to be the case.

Some local groups are active in marketing their services. For example, in Brighton the local restaurateurs publish a guide to eating places for delegates attending conferences in the town and various promotions are organized from time to time. Groupings of hoteliers in the New Forest and in the Thames Valley are marketing their area to foreign visitors. The New Forest scheme is particularly aimed at off season trade from France and from reports in the trade press has been well planned. In Torquay a small group marketing scheme called Torquay Leisure Hotels has been developed arising out of the inter-hotel comparison activities in Torquay. A sense of mutual confidence has been established and the scheme has been extended to collective buying which also yields significant benefit. Because the BTA did not favour the inclusion of individual hotels in its workshops a consortium of Sussex hotels called The Sussex Resorts and Hotels Association was formed in order to obtain representation at these workshops.

Local authorities have a substantial economic interest in the benefits of tourism to their areas and many are actively involved in promotional activities through publicity, central reservation, and information bureaux and general provision of entertainment facilities. Some local authorities are very well orientated to this work, others appear to be far less interested. The EDC study *More Hotels?* contained the following comments on the Nottingham Publicity and Information Department: 'The department sees its role as a means of pro-

[1] IUOTO, Technical Commission on Research, *IUOTO Economic Review of World Tourism* (Geneva, 1969), p. 31.

viding information on Nottingham's activities and advice on problems affecting the citizens and visitors rather than an agency for the promotion of the city as far as visitors are concerned'. The department does apparently produce lists and information leaflets that are relevant but these do not represent 'a serious attempt to positively attract leisure visitors to the City . . . The Corporation's present view is that it would not be viable to adopt a more positive approach towards the attraction of tourists to the city, at least within the foreseeable future.'[2]

Malvern on the other hand is reported to have conducted a cheap but effective campaign to sell capacity in the town in June. This sort of limited promotion may be particularly attractive and effective where it is used to top-up business at a time when capacity utilization is normally below the desired level.

Regional marketing is considered to be particularly important for the future because of the benefits offered by additional scale. Area marketing appears to be extensively organized in France and much interest is being shown in this sort of activity in the Lake District where the Lakes Travel Association is engaged in giving promotional and publicity assistance to hotels in the area.

Group Marketing

The term group marketing is used here to indicate the grouping of non-competing units into a common marketing scheme. In this way a group marketing scheme may have members scattered all over the country and is to be contrasted with area marketing schemes where the participants are all in the one geographical area and may be considered to be more directly competitive with each other. The concluding pages of this chapter contain notes on three group marketing schemes in the hotel industry, Prestige Hotels, Interchange Hotels, and Inter Hotels. There appear to be others which so far are less highly developed, such as the Historic Hotels of Britain consortium. In addition, the British Motel Federation seems to be operating as a co-operative group operating package tours and a central reservation office.

Franchising of restaurants and hotels also offers many of the benefits of group marketing such as the establishment of a corporate image, controls over standards, benefits of countervailing buying power, and a centralized referral system.

Many people seem to view the co-operative group movement as the key to the future of the independent in the same way that it has been with the symbol groups in the grocery trade. This does not however seem to be a valid analogy. First, it is probably true to say that the grocery voluntary groups are primarily concerned with countervailing buying power for goods sold and only secondly with marketing their members' products. The emphasis in hotel co-operatives is reversed. Secondly, it should be noted that the most successful form of voluntary group in the grocery trade is wholesaler sponsored whereas the hotel co-operative movement is more akin to the less effective retailer sponsored groups. Thirdly, there is a greater need to maintain comparable standards in the hotel

[2] Hotel and Catering EDC, *More Hotels?* NEDO (HMSO), p. 50.

co-operatives because of the importance of the package tour and referral opportunities. The co-operative movement in the hotel and catering industry must therefore be based upon the particular features of that industry.

If this is achieved, substantial opportunities clearly present themselves. The basis of the schemes so far developed is that non-competing hotels[3] of similar standards and attractiveness join together in a common promotional activity, aimed particularly at overseas travel agents and tour operators. The ability to offer suggested package tours around the various hotels in the group in different parts of the country is an important selling point. Central reservation systems are employed and standards of participating hotels closely controlled. The negotiation of favourable buying terms is a secondary, though often important, activity.

So far those schemes that exist in this country have had a relatively short life. It takes many months to bring a group together and it will take several years before the real payoff in terms of travel agent acceptance occurs. Those that do exist account for a very small proportion of the total hotels in the country and there does not at the moment appear to be any rush to emulate them. Inevitably the hotels that do join the co-operatives will be the higher quality, better-managed ones most of whom have an AA listing or some mark of approval.

We can perhaps, however, begin to identify some features that will have a bearing on the overall success of the scheme.

1. To be successful, the co-operative must be strong. It cannot afford to be simply a loose confederation of members. It must be able to ensure the participation of all its members in promotional activities. As the groups get larger so personal contact will need to be replaced by tighter central control and supervision of standards. All this implies that participants in co-operatives will have to be prepared to concede some independence.[4]

2. The need to offer a large number of bedrooms in London as a necessary condition for the interest of overseas travel agents has important implications for the basis of the scheme on the independent hotel. Some sort of link between London hotel companies and independent hoteliers in other parts of the country may become increasingly important.

3. The *raison d'être* of the co-operatives so far is seen primarily in terms of the attraction of foreign tourists. It is probably equally important at least in any other groups that may be formed to pay attention to the British user of hotels for business or holiday purposes.

4. The future vitality of the groups may well depend on the extent to which they do in fact co-operate in other areas such as the provision of operational data to each other, the use of advisory services, etc.

5. The negotiation of terms with both bulk purchasers of hotel services and with suppliers of hotel equipment is an important activity for co-operatives.

[3] Though this is changing, *see* description of three hotel groups on pages 105–7.
[4] 'If the idea of co-operatives for independent hoteliers is to really produce substantially higher profits, then hoteliers must be prepared to accept a slight loss in independence.' R. Cornwall and M. Greene, *Improving Hotel Profitability* (Northwood, 1968), p. 70.

There appear to be limits to the extent to which it will be possible to require members to use standardized equipment and furnishings in order to obtain even better terms.

6. The essence of the schemes will remain the marketing of hotel services. The building of a group identity preferably with a common tariff must remain a central feature. It cannot, however, be relied upon to do more than provide the marginal boost to occupancy rates that makes the difference between breaking even and achieving satisfactory profits.

So far the co-operatives that do exist appear to have made good progress but it is far too early to comment on the potential for a much wider development. If an assessment had to be made it would be that for a small minority of good quality independent hotels they offer substantial advantages. The vast majority of independent hotels should however look to area rather than group marketing as a means of improving their capacity utilization. For this to be successful will require a greater sense of interdependence between local hoteliers, a reorientation of the thinking of many local hotel associations and in some cases greater involvement by local authorities.

Co-operative marketing of restaurants in the same way is less probable. Area marketing is more likely on condition that restaurateurs will work together. Restaurants are heavily dependent upon good publicity in the press and guides such as the *Good Food Guide, Inns of Britain* and the *Egon Ronay Guide*. It does not look as though significant large scale changes here are likely in the near future though it may be that groups of restaurants of a similar standard could operate some common promotion with a form of package built in. We certainly found some interest in such a possibility. We also heard of a group of restaurants that is endeavouring to establish a package scheme and agent's manual whereby a customer would obtain vouchers allowing a choice between the various restaurants in the group. It should be noted that in the catering trades franchising offers an independent franchised operator many of the benefits that co-operative marketing and buying schemes seek to confer.

Other Co-operative Activities

One recent suggestion in which much interest has been shown is for the development of centralized kitchens for the preparation of foods which would then be frozen and delivered in bulk to individual restaurants. The justification for this suggestion is that the skills required are in the preparation of food and that skilled chefs could be used more economically in this way. It is argued that these skills are needed many hours before the finished product is required and that the finishing of food is not something that requires considerable skills. While this appears initially to be an attractive proposal, it has not received much support in the industry. The objections are that the additional costs of transport, etc. outweigh the cost savings offered by the scheme and that it would unduly restrict the range of choice which individual menus could offer.

Various co-operative buying schemes are organized in the industry. These seem to be successful and offer worthwhile savings. The British Hotels and Restaurants Association and the Caterers Association also run a members' buying scheme but only on a small scale and it is understood that the savings are small. They do not handle any goods themselves and the level of costs that would be involved rather preclude consideration of developments in this respect.

Whereas the multiple hotel and catering groups are able to place large scale orders for standardized linen, crockery, etc., this is not a possibility with independent units that wish to preserve their individuality. The future for co-operative buying by independents therefore looks as though it will be more concerned with the negotiation of favourable discounts than with the actual placing of large scale orders and so the economic benefits will inevitably be fewer.

There does not appear to be much scope for co-operation in the buying of foodstuffs. Most caterers have their own agents in the wholesale markets and integration is unlikely. Cash and carry warehouses are increasingly opening specialist catering sections. According to the Crosse and Blackwell national cash and carry survey, 238 outlets now have a separate catering section out of a national total of 610 cash and carry grocery outlets.[5] Whether this will ever be a major source of supplies for hotels and restaurants remains uncertain. We found the potential users tended only to use them in an emergency on the grounds that visits to the cash and carry outlet were time consuming and the prices of goods bought there were not particularly favourable.

We also feel that there may be some merit in a suggestion put to us by a consultant that in order to help meet the financing problem, a group financing scheme might be established whereby a group of independents would all take a stake in each other. This would inevitably necessitate some loss of independence but would improve the group's access to funds and the terms on which these were made available.

There does therefore appear to be a substantial scope for the development of co-operative activities in the industry for the benefit of the owner-managed organization. In most cases it seems to us that the co-operation must be on a local basis although the group marketing schemes offer important benefits for a small number of good class independent hotels. If it is agreed that greater co-operation is an important key to the small firm's prospects (though by no means the only one – managerial attitudes and skills must surely have the first priority) we have to ask where the innovative activity is to come from that will encourage the spread of co-operation. From some individual hoteliers? The local hoteliers' associations? The national trade associations? The EDC, the industry training board, the hotel schools? It is far less likely to be imposed on the industry from outside in the way that the airlines and travel agents are influencing the activities of the larger hotel groups. Ideally all the sources mentioned should show some initiatives in the matter. If the small unit is to survive as an economic unit in the industry action needs to be taken. There is no room

[5] Reported in *Caterer and Hotelkeeper*, 24 May 1970.

for any group simply to pass the buck in the hope that somebody else is doing something about it! If anything, there may well be a danger at the present time of a proliferation of organizations involved in this field without the necessary co-ordination to ensure that resources in advice, research, and training are optimally utilized. The establishment of a clearing house to assist in the co-ordination of such work may well be desirable at this stage.

Some Notes on Three Hotel Group Marketing Schemes

Within the last five years three major hotel group marketing schemes, Prestige Hotels, Interchange Hotels, and Inter Hotels, have been formed in this country[6], primarily to help the owner-managed independent hotel to obtain the advantages of large-scale marketing, referral business, etc. that is naturally available to the larger multiple-hotel groups. This section provides information on each of the groups and offers comments on some of the benefits and problems that appear to exist in them. It is, therefore, relevant to the discussion of the general case for group marketing schemes contained above. It should be emphasized that the interpretation of the benefits and difficulties is that of the writer of this report, not the group members.

FOUNDING AND SIZE

Prestige was the first group, founded in 1966, followed by Interchange in 1968, and Inter in October 1969. They all had between ten and twelve members initially but whereas Prestige has doubled its size to twenty-four, Interchange now has fifty-one and Inter eighty-three members. The rate of growth of Interchange and particularly Inter has been very rapid and indicates a rather different outlook on ultimate size from that held by Prestige. Interchange certainly appears to be looking for more new members and Inter plans to expand to at least one hundred. So far there have been few resignations from any of the groups; mergers and declining standards are the main causes of those withdrawals that have occurred.

REASONS FOR FOUNDATION

Two main reasons appear to be fairly common to all three groups. Firstly, there was a response to the economic pressure associated with a general weakening of the home market. This was perhaps less important to Prestige than to the other two groups. Secondly, there was a clear awareness of the positive advantages to be gained from collective marketing, especially overseas. The ability to offer a group of hotels with some guarantee of standards, with package tours around the country and ease of booking were held to be important selling points with overseas travel agents. In addition, it was recognized that a group of hotels could spread basic marketing costs over the whole membership and could therefore offer an important saving in overseas marketing.

[6] There is also an historic hotels consortium which does not as yet appear to be as extensively organized as the three under discussion here.

BASIS OF MEMBERSHIP

The basic principle was that the membership of each group would be restricted to independent hotels (defined as those which were not part of a large hotel group) with some degree of geographical protection to avoid having member hotels too close to each other. This policy does, however, appear to be undergoing some modification at the present time.

Prestige aims to have up to about thirty hotels of roughly 4-star standard, giving a national coverage. They do not operate a formal franchise arrangement but try not to have too many hotels too close together. Amongst their members is the Carlton Tower Hotel in London which is part of an American hotel group. It has been included because of the need to have a hotel in London within the group.

Interchange was initially aimed at 2- and 3-star hotels but has now broadened its base to include any hotels that are 'good within the style they set out to be in'. They are emphasizing the need for good quality, energetic management, and a rigid inspection system is adopted. The group members are primarily privately owned hotels but the need to have access to rooms in London in order to attract travel agents has led to the acceptance of some small multiple hotel groups. The Associated Hotels chain is also linked with Interchange for the same reason.

Two recent developments in the Interchange operation are potentially of considerable significance for the future basis of similar group marketing schemes. Although it had originally sought to avoid having closely competing hotels within the group, in one town it does now have two hotel members. This seems to be working well and is leading to a change in the climate of opinion regarding 'close' competitiveness amongst group members. The second development has been concerned with the establishment of three strong regional areas: the South-West; Cotswolds and Shakespeare country; the North-West. Each area is autonomous and responsible for developing its own promotional material. The success of this move may well have contributed to the changed climate of opinion regarding close competitiveness among group members and is a pointer to future developments in the organizational structure of co-operative groups.

Inter has grown fastest of all. All its members are privately owned, of 2- or 3-star standard, and are vetted and subject to continuous checks. They also aim to have only one hotel in an area but will accept 'affiliated' additional members in an area. Their policy is being reconsidered because of the need for access to beds in London.

PRICES

None of the groups operates a standard tariff throughout its membership though both Interchange and Inter have a standard touring tariff of £3 for bed and breakfast.

COSTS OF MEMBERSHIP

All the groups have a joining fee and an annual subscription. Inter charges £25 membership and £100 annual subscription. Interchange has a £110 initial charge and £250 a year, and Prestige has a £50 joining fee and an annual subscription based on the number of bedrooms and on location. For most members the annual subscription to Prestige would probably be a little in excess of £300.

SERVICES OFFERED

The range of services offered at present tends to vary from group to group and seems to be very much a function of the perceived needs and opportunities for each group. On paper, Prestige appears to operate less extensively as a group but this is probably explicable in terms of the size of the group and the absence of a full-time secretariat. Overseas marketing is very much the key to all three groups though the domestic business conference and travel market is now being developed. There appears to be considerable scope for the negotiation of favourable discount terms with suppliers of equipment, without the necessity for the groups to engage in any physical handling of the goods purchased.

Prestige members do not feel that a central secretariat is required at the present time and group interests are cared for by about four group members who represent the group at overseas workshops, etc. In so doing they are saving several thousand pounds a year in the short run but are losing the possible benefit of having a staff wholly devoted to the interests of the group as a whole. The whole subscription income is devoted to various forms of promotional activity. A central booking office in London and New York handles Prestige bookings and is considered to be very important. In an effort to achieve off-peak sales the business houses market is being developed, as are specialist weekends at individual Prestige hotels, so far with encouraging results.

Interchange, by virtue of a full time marketing director, is able to offer a more extensive research and consultancy service to members. Marketing the packages of tours to major travel agents and tour operators either through BTA workshops (where these are considered to be worthwhile) or individually is considered to be a most important element in the total activity. The group also runs its own workshops. A central reservations system is run from the London office. While hotels within the group are naturally given the first opportunity of these bookings the office tries never to refuse a booking even if it means placing it with a non-Interchange member in order to encourage the agent to use Interchange for subsequent bookings.

Inter has two full-time staff. Although it had only been in existence for less than a year at the time of this research it seems clear that a similar range of activities will be developed through a standard brochure, attendance at workshops, and the arrangement of discounts with suppliers.

LINKS WITH OTHER ORGANIZATIONS

Links with major tour operators, car hire firms, and airlines are important aids to the marketing of the groups' package tours. In addition, Inter has developed links with similar hotel groups in other countries – Bonne Chaine, Tulip Inns, Inter hotels France, and Friendship Inns – in an effort to obtain the benefits of international referrals and recommendations.

Benefits of Group Marketing Schemes

It is really rather too early to begin to comment on the exact extent of the benefits achieved. Such schemes have to be seen as long-term investments and the real pay-off will come when a group's identity and reliability of standards have been permanently established in the eyes of tour operators and travel agents. The short-term gains are already becoming clear – increased numbers of foreign tourists, falling costs per reservation secured, significant benefits from the exercise of countervailing buying power, the development of a corporate identity which makes publicity and marketing much easier. It is generally agreed that the regular meetings of members are also particularly valuable in allowing the opportunity for an exchange of views and ideas. It appears that even if only the direct benefits of improved discounts and other cost savings from consultancy assistance offered by some of the groups are taken into account the annual subscription is a very small cost and can quickly be recouped.

Problems Arising from Group Marketing Schemes

The basic problem with any such scheme is the individualism of its members. This makes it more difficult to obtain agreement on basic issues of policy such as standard tariff rates, whether to accept credit cards, etc. It is clear that mutual responsibility and interdependence is a crucial element in such a scheme and without this recognition on the part of its members the effectiveness of the group will be much reduced. Control of standards also remains a problem and as groups get larger so the contact between members and the central secretariat will become less and less. Whether a central secretariat itself is desirable would appear to be open to different views. On the one hand it means that overhead costs have to be borne which could otherwise be used for direct promotion. On the other hand it means there is less problem of the time of individual hoteliers being taken up with group administration. It is also probably easier for a central secretary to undertake the general organization and harrying that such a group requires, though if members are not willing to co-operate this can be a thankless task. The need for adequate access to beds in London in order to have a strong selling point with travel agents appears to be crucial. The absence of independent hotels in London that meet the requirements of the groups has already led to some modification of the basic essence of the scheme and is clearly something that is likely to become increasingly important and would pose even more serious problems for later groups operating on the same sort of basis.

Part VI
Tour Operation

Introduction

Some kind of regulation for economic reasons has been a constant feature of transport and hence of tourism. The regulation of air services is of paramount interest to the practitioner and to the student of tourism. The United Kingdom shares with the United States the distinction of making economic regulation a matter for quasi-judicial tribunals (Civil Aviation Authority in the UK, Civil Aeronautics Board in the USA). The major development in European tourism in the years immediately before and after 1970 was the air inclusive tour. The Civil Aviation Act 1971, which created the Civil Aviation Authority, brought tour operators within the Authority's jurisdiction, thus recognizing that external factors, in this case the charters of aircraft, can exercise a profound influence on air transport.

In Chapter 11 Boyd-Carpenter, the first Chairman of the Civil Aviation Authority, surveys the general position of civil aviation in the economy. In particular, he examines how fares are compiled by the airlines and professes himself readier to regulate capacity than fares. The current regulation of air fares has become nearly unenforceable and the distinction between scheduled and non-scheduled services has become blurred. The introduction of new kinds of service and of new kinds of fares is examined, and it is concluded that so far as possible the licensing procedure should leave the airlines free to follow their own commercial judgement.

The principal factor in the growth of holidays taken abroad by the British tourist is identified by Burkart in Chapter 12 as the air inclusive tour. The low prices made possible by charter operation are at the heart of this development. The tourist generating power of the large tour operator leads naturally to a new role for national tourist offices in the generating countries. This new role will be to facilitate the operations of the reliable tour operator, rather than to appeal directly to the public. Moreover, the tour operator alone produces a complete tourist product, and the tour operator is basically a marketing man. The national tourist offices should ponder carefully how tour operations have transformed tourism in the generating countries of north-western Europe.

11   The Contribution of Civil Aviation to the Economic Strength and Well-being of the UK

BY LORD BOYD-CARPENTER

From the 29th British Commonwealth Lecture given at the Royal Aeronautical Society on 11 October 1973 and published in *The Aeronautical Journal*, Vol. 78, No. 761, May 1974.

If one studies the economics of contemporary Britain one is forced more and more to the conclusion that her future lies less and less with heavy manufacturing industry and more and more with the so-called service industries. There are, of course, significant exceptions to this. There are certain manufacturing industries in which we still do very well. There would indeed be more of these if some of them were not so startlingly susceptible to industrial disputes. But the broad trend is there. In manufacturing industry, as compared with our rivals, we increasingly lack the competitive advantages to be obtained on the one hand from a massive capacity to invest and at the other extreme from competitively low wage levels. We still have in certain trades the inherited and acquired asset of skilled craftsmen. But these skills are, in manufacturing industry, increasingly relevant only to the higher grade and expensive product and are less and less significant in the great areas of mass production. This general tendency is reinforced by our lack of indigenous natural resources with the exception of our old friend coal and our exciting new friend North Sea oil. On the other side of the picture, the service industries offer a much more cheering picture. In general they demand not mass production, but skill; they need to draw upon an educated and sophisticated population. They are an area in which an acquired reputation and tradition of service are becoming more rather than less important. Increasingly Government statistics underline the increasing dependence of our balance of payments on the so-called invisible exports. Banking and insurance, brokerage and commercial services loom larger and larger. The other great field for services is the transport industries. British shipping is still a major factor in our economy, although menaced by flags of convenience. (There is a warning to civil aviation here for those who have ears to hear.) Civil aviation and its associated tourist industry is already a major factor in the British economy. Tourism to this country is already the fifth largest earner of foreign exchange for Britain. In this day and age, with the exception of a limited amount of very short-hauls from north-west Europe, tourism means carriage by air. The British civil aviation industry itself earned net in 1972 £320 million. But this is only one element in its contribution. If it did not exist, the traffic would either come by foreign airlines with the loss to our balance of payments equivalent to British civil aviation's overseas earnings, or a greater loss would be suffered by reduction in our tourist trade. Probably the truth would be a combination of the two. But it doesn't stop there. The manufacturers of British aircraft were earning last year at a rate of some £500 million a year in exports. It is difficult, and could be contentious, to estimate how much of that massive contribution is shared by the British civil aviation operators. But it must be true that were there no British customers for our manufacturers, and no shop window created by their use of British aircraft, the position of the manufacturers would be very different indeed.

Another interesting point is the increasing part in our economic effort played by air cargo. In terms of value, which is what really matters, Heathrow became last year Britain's second cargo port. Only the Port of London handled more cargo last year, and in the course of last year Heathrow pushed the great port of Liverpool into third place.

So we have here, in British civil aviation, an indispensable part of our nation's economic effort. It is fortunately an activity in which we are well fitted to participate. Except for fuel, it is not an economic activity dependent on the import of foreign raw materials. It is an activity involving professional skills and high technological achievement. Though it may be unfashionable to be so immodest, it is a thing we are rather good at. Our flight deck crews know their business. The sight of a British captain up front is a very reassuring thing to many people of many nationalities, particularly when the weather is bad and conditions difficult. And our cabin crews have a way with them, perhaps inherited from the great passenger liners of the past, which is unique in the world and which I know appeals especially to discriminating American travellers. Miles Thomas once told me of a flight he made with a certain foreign airline, when the Chief Steward greeted the passengers on the public address system with 'Howdy folks, I'm Bob, this is Rosie – if you want anything just buzz' and then disappeared into the galley for the rest of the trip. Service in the cabins of British airlines, be they publicly or privately owned, is the very antithesis of this and an immensely strong selling point.

The diagnosis is therefore clear. Civil aviation is what the authors of *1066 and All That* called 'a good thing'. It is good for Britain's struggling economy and every effort should be made to expand it and develop it profitably. But diagnosis is one thing; devising the proper treatment quite another. I always like the story of the old doctor seeking to reassure a nervous woman patient who had said to him 'Doctor, I have heard that doctors sometimes treat a patient for pneumonia and the patient dies of typhoid', to which, in his best bedside manner, the doctor replied, 'Dear lady, don't worry, if I treat a patient for pneumonia, he dies of pneumonia'.

What then is the right treatment to induce profitable growth in British civil aviation? I stress the profitable – expansion at a loss is a quick-growing plant that quickly withers. It was said by cynics of the late David Lloyd-George's farm at Churt that he was determined that it should pay regardless of cost! That is an awful warning.

Profitable growth is then the objective. It is achievable only as a result of the combined efforts of Government, regulatory bodies, airline managements, air crews and ground crews, and the public at large. The last named, of course, is the ultimate master of all the others. Public opinion in a democracy can be thwarted and defied for quite a time, but if it persists it always wins in the long run. One of its manifestations at present is very relevant to my theme. That is what I may call environmental extremism. Some years ago the public mood went perhaps too far in pursuit of economic efficiency and damn the environment. Excess in one direction inescapably creates an excess in the other and to some extent aviation is at risk from this excess. There are a number of people, mostly comfortably circumstanced, who feel that we should all live in peaceful old world villages, in cottages adorned with thatched roofs, climbing roses and bearded oldest inhabitants. While that is absolutely splendid, and a very agreeable way of life, it is only possible if we are prepared to pay for it. That price is enormous. It implies the emigration of some three-quarters of our present population and acceptance by the remainder of greatly reduced standards of life. It is, in fact, wholly unacceptable. If our large population is to remain and grow and continue to improve its standards of life, economic efficiency has got to receive very high priority. The results of this are often disagreeable, particularly in a small and crowded country. But it is really no use our kidding ourselves that we can enjoy the amenities of modern industrial civilization – the individual motor transport, the labour-saving devices, the television sets, and the holidays on the Costa del Sol, unless we are prepared to accept and work the economic and productive activities as a result of which these boons can be purchased. Coming down to brass tacks, there are powerful lobbies in this country which seek to restrict aviation activities in the name of environmental considerations. They want those horrid noisy aeroplanes taken away – except of course when they want one to take them on holiday. There are real dangers of excessive pressures on Government to restrict airport development in convenient places; to force greatly increased costs of operation on airlines; and to seize any opportunity to ban aircraft movements at night. Of course we all accept that there must be a balance between amenity and efficiency and that aviation has no divine right to do as it pleases and let everybody else be damned. But it has the right to point out that, for example, reducing the utilization of expensive aircraft during the periods of peak demand during the summer can very quickly undermine the opportunities for profitable use of these aircraft. Profitable airline operation depends very much on maximum utilization of immensely expensive equipment at the times of year when public demand is at a peak. Preventing the use of this equipment for considerable periods over the twenty-four hours can have quite an adverse effect. Even worse would be the effect if British restrictions were to stimulate the owners of foreign airports served by British aircraft to bestow upon us the flattery of imitation. Particularly with very fast aircraft like Concorde, bans on night operation at major airports in several countries can severely restrict utilization. For it is not only a case of preventing take-off during night hours. It is also that a ban is effectively imposed on take-off during daylight hours in the country in which the journey starts if arrival at the destination, allowing for time differences, would then be at night. Above all, in the case of British civil aviation the great majority of whose operations go overseas, the greatest caution is needed lest well-meaning attempts marginally to improve amenities in certain localities set off a world wide repercussive effect. I am sure that those with responsibility in these matters will have these considerations very much in mind and act with prudent caution in respect of any restrictions which they are under pressure to impose.

I am not for one moment underrating the social and personal effects of aircraft noise. I live myself under one of the approach tracks to Heathrow when the wind is westerly. But there are more ways than one of securing improvement. There is the carrot of unlimited freedom of operation for really quiet aircraft as well as the indiscriminating stick of general bans. It is also fair to comment on the apparent discrimination against aviation as a noise producer as compared with the treatment of other creators of noise nuisances. Monstrous lorries can roar and vibrate down village streets or through centres of great cities at any hour of the day or night without any restriction whatsoever. No one stops railways operating or shunting at night or interferes with young gentlemen showing off the noise-producing capacity of their car or motor-bike to those who are trying to sleep in residential areas. Or prevents public utilities making the day hideous and work impossible with pneumatic drills. Personally I hate all noise but one has to accept that a certain amount of it is inevitable in big cities. But if restriction is to be applied, as in many cases it should be, there should be no discrimination against aviation. I would indeed be delighted to join any society dedicated to the prohibition of the pneumatic drill or the night operation, or any operation in big cities, of monster lorries.

Profitable operation involves careful consideration of the way in which fares are determined and capacity decided upon. I believe that capacity is here the key. It is excessive capacity, either on a particular route or through misjudgement in the ordering of aircraft, which causes fares to be cut to levels which cannot produce a profit even with a full aircraft. The deceptive doctrine of marginal costs in such a situation produces decisions to offer fares for which there is no economic justification even in lasting promotional advantages. But if capacity is right, no one has any motive to take fares lower than a sensible judgement of the market would dictate. I must confess to a preference for leaving airlines as responsible businesses to determine both the capacity they offer and the price they charge for it. But if extraneous circumstances, circumstances such as either misjudgements in aircraft purchases or national pride insisting on uneconomic operations, make some interference by regulatory authorities inevitable, I find control on capacity much more attractive than attempted control of fares. For one thing it is possible to regulate capacity as we do in this country both in respect of ABC Charters [Advance Booking Charters] and on certain scheduled services. But fares if they are fixed higher than economic forces would determine are susceptible to innumerable variants of cheating. If an airline wants to sell a fare lower than has been fixed, and there are willing buyers, no regulatory system in the world can really prevent it from doing so. As far as scheduled services are concerned this is IATA's great problem. If airlines, for one reason or another, seek to peg air fares above what is really the market rate and everybody knows that, neither IATA nor anybody else can effectively enforce this. I wish IATA would look afresh at its role. I think it could learn a good deal from the techniques used in the heyday of North Atlantic passenger travel by sea. Then the North Atlantic Conference to which all the major shipping lines belonged fixed fares. But they fixed them with a good deal of sophistication. A first class fare on a very luxurious and fast ship like the *Queen Mary* was fixed a good deal higher than the top class fare on say the *Laconia* or the *Sylvania*. And the North Atlantic Conference having fixed a fare, did not attempt to interfere with the amenities which for competitive reasons the shipping lines offered to their passengers. Fares were fixed on a realistic basis; and amenities and entertainment competition flourished. There were no such nonsenses as compelling airlines to charge for films (logically perhaps there should be a charge on those of us who wish to avoid seeing a film!) and I understand that at one time IATA seriously concerned itself with the precise dimensions of the morsel of smoked salmon which airlines offered with their pre-dinner canapés. In any event, the advent of Concorde will offer IATA the opportunity to look again at the idea that fares should be graded in accordance with the type of aircraft offered. I hope they may take the opportunity to look again at their whole system and to consider whether, as I have suggested, they cannot learn something from the former practice of the shipping lines.

In any event the arrival on some of the main traffic routes of Concorde will have a considerable impact on the structure of the industry. As I see it, on a number of main traffic routes there will be a 'top persons' service operated by Concorde. This will attract a substantial proportion of the traffic at present travelling first class and on certain routes, notably the North Atlantic, will undoubtedly generate new traffic. An example of the latter is the top executive, Minister or civil servant who will find it worthwhile to go to a meeting in New York if he can sleep in his own bed in London both before and after the meeting, but who feels he cannot spare the two or three days, plus adaptation to time zone changes, required at present. I have no doubt at all that there will be an adequate supply of top industrial and commercial brass, Ministers, civil servants, and 'Show Biz' to fill Concorde on the main routes. I am only surprised at the modesty of the suggested 10 per cent premium on ordinary first class fares. The point of flying for passengers of this sort is speed. Very few of them pay their fares out of their own pockets and those they work for plainly indicate by the salaries that they pay them that they think their time is immensely valuable. I hope that Concorde operators will not be too modest in their calculations of capacity and willingness to pay in respect of this special kind of traffic.

The main bulk of the traffic will travel in wide-bodied subsonic aircraft. I hope I am not treading on anybody's toes in pointing out that aviation as it becomes middle-aged is tending to indulge in what the doctors call middle-aged spread. But the economic attraction of the increasingly large aircraft is very strong and I think if one is in pursuit of profitable operation one should regard it as the main instrument for the maintenance of services, both scheduled and charter, on the more popular routes. The narrow-bodied aircraft, even if given the so-called wide-bodied look, should increasingly revert to the lower density routes and of course to the opening up and development of new ones.

As I see it these wide-bodied aircraft would, on the main routes, still carry a certain amount of first class traffic, at a fare below the supersonic rate and catering for those people who prefer a good deal of space, separate lounges, and so on, to speed. There may well be a particular appeal for this sort of service on such routes as eastbound at night over the North Atlantic. But the great numbers will be in other classes and if the scheduled services are really to prosper in the wide-bodied age they will have to carry large numbers of passengers at rates which are competitive with those which can be offered by their charter competitors. For the purpose of my argument it does not matter whether these cheaper fares come within such categories as APEX or IT or indeed part-charter. They can be somewhat higher than the majority of charter rates since people are prepared to pay something for the greater regularity of a scheduled service aircraft operated by a major operator. But they must bear a sensible relationship to charter rates.

Both scheduled and charter operators (and as I see it, the distinction between them is blurring every day) if they want to stay in profitable business have got to face the fact that the growth end of the market is the bottom end. It is all very well for state-owned, state-supported airlines to seek in IATA to maintain a high fare regime and support themselves on their own, for practical purposes, conscripted passengers. But airlines that are going out for major international traffic cannot do this and they cannot afford to allow the unanimity rule in IATA to thwart them in serving the great new and growing mass market. The growth already of the air holiday movement has been one of the phenomena of the age. Young people whose parents felt that it was quite a travel adventure to take their annual holiday in Cornwall or the Lake District, now regard an annual visit to the Mediterranean or the Alps almost as a matter of right. Large numbers go to the Caribbean, East Africa and now, with its fine new airport, to the Seychelles. The world is now being opened up to the ordinary man, and still more perhaps to the ordinary girl, in a way undreamt of even ten years ago. The appetite, as the poet puts it, grows by that it feeds on. The travel industry, which whatever else it lacks does not lack initiative and salesmanship, is stimulating that appetite. The arrival of the large aircraft which can be operated economically if it is very full provides an instrument for the economical gratification of that appetite. It would be a great mistake if we allowed our judgement of this development and its potentialities to be obscured by certain recent difficulties and in particular by the excessive rate-cutting of airlines which, through their own misjudgement, had acquired excessive capacity. Cheap fares of course do not mean operating at a loss, except perhaps in an early promotional phase. But they do mean taking advantage of the low seat mile costs of the big new aeroplanes to fill them with the big new public that, at the sort of rates which are now profitably possible, wishes to see the world.

If one steps back for a moment from this concentration on the economics of the industry, one can surely feel a moment of pleasure at the immensely valuable social consequences of this opening of new horizons for the great mass of our people and of the peoples of the advanced nations. It is the kind of thing that the social reformers of a century ago would have frankly regarded to have been much too incredibly good to ever be possible at all.

Progress in exploiting this opportunity is very much tied up with getting the fare situation right. There are still strange and awkward anomalies. For example, in Europe the general level of fares on a seat mile basis is high. This is only partly explained and justified by the admittedly higher cost per seat mile on short haul operations. This level of fares in Europe has produced the curious situation that it is in many cases cheaper to take an inclusive tour ticket covering both air transport and hotel accommodation than just to take a ticket entitling one to air travel. In other words, no doubt in breach of the regulations, a traveller can save money by booking on an inclusive tour and then throwing away the hotel part of what he is entitled to under his ticket. This is, as Euclid put it, absurd, and it is a standing temptation to people both in the trade and among the public to break the rules. It is very foolish for any authority to set up and try to operate regulations which seek to thwart economic forces and the perfectly reasonable wishes of individuals. It would be much better to organize a system of cheaper travel-only fares in Europe subject to reasonable conditions as to advance booking and length of stay than to continue a situation in which the good name of the inclusive tour business is damaged, individuals encouraged to cheat, and the law made to look silly. At the same time we want to see genuine inclusive tour arrangements develop, undertaken by reputable organizers – and it is the duty of the CAA under the air travel organizers' licensing system to secure that only reputable organizers organize. It could do an enormous amount to facilitate holiday travel particularly for that large section of travellers who require an economical holiday or who are unfamiliar with the technique of making arrangements for themselves in foreign countries. IT must certainly expand but it is legitimate IT that we want to see develop. It is in line with the philosophy of seeking to avoid unenforceable regulations, for which the ordinary public has nothing but contempt, that we have taken steps to replace affinity group charters by advance booking charters. The affinity group was a nonsense from the beginning. Why on earth should a citizen who has the good fortune to belong, and to have belonged for six months, to his local caged birds society be able to travel cheaper than the equally worthy citizen who has not that distinction. Besides that the system is wide open to every form of cheating. Its good point is of course that cheap fares rest on the sound economics of a full aeroplane. But that same aim can be achieved in many other ways. By insisting on advance booking – which itself can be enforced by the simple expedient of requiring the submission of a passenger list in advance – it is perfectly possible for organizers to be able to plan the filling up of aeroplanes, while not diverting into those aeroplanes business traffic the bookings for which have to be made at short notice. That is why the CAA took the lead in developing ABCs. We are very gratified by their success on the Canadian run. We are not at all surprised that the American TGC, which has a number of unfortunate features, has proved something of a flop. We very much hope that the CAB will feel that there are practical lessons to be learnt from our joint experience and will find ways of avoiding the stumbling block of pro-rating. For our part we want to see ABCs perhaps modified in certain ways, applied on further routes. I believe that there is a real opening for them on the route to Australia. East Africa too has its possibilities and although Europe is very much the preserve of inclusive tours, I know of no reason why before too long the alternative of the ABC might not appear in Europe.

The essence of what I have been trying to say about fares, and its relevance to my main theme, is that if any business is to be profitable it must study and cater for the interests and wishes of the customer. But part of the trouble with aviation in the past is that it has tended to regard the operation of services, particularly scheduled services, as an end in itself. I would like to see it become much more customer-orientated and more effort given to market research and to efforts to find out what the customer really wants. It was because we believed that Mr Laker had done just this in his Skytrain proposals that caused us to grant him a licence to operate this new kind of service aimed at a new type of customer who wishes to travel between this country and the USA. The least happy aspect of our relations with that great country is that which relates to the way in which their authorities have treated the Department of Trade and Industry's designation of Laker to operate that service under our Air Services Agreement with the United States. Four American companies operate scheduled services to this country under permits issued speedily and helpfully by the Department of Trade and Industry to them when they were designated by the American authorities under our Air Services Agreement. But Laker's Skytrain, which will be only the third British scheduled operator on the route, though designated under the agreement in February of this year, is now facing only the beginning of prolonged proceedings before organs of the CAB. If British airlines, duly designated by the national authorities and whose affairs have been scrupulously examined by those authorities, are to be subjected to prolonged and detailed inquisitions not only into every detail of their own affairs but as in this case also into the policies of their government, it may be difficult to satisfy British airlines, and indeed British public opinion, that it is fair that American airlines seeking to operate here should be allowed to continue to receive their permits so quickly and with so little fuss as they have in the past.

The right policy must then be customer/consumer orientated, alert to new opportunities and moderate in its fare demands. The CAA in this country will operate the licensing system so as to help airlines that seek to operate in this way and our system is flexible enough to enable us to do this effectively.

There is one other necessary condition for success. Airlines must in general be free to purchase the equipment which in their judgement is what they need to operate their particular routes. They ought not to be inhibited in the choice of their equipment by questions of the interest of national aircraft manufacturers. I say this despite the fact that I was a member of the Cabinet which overruled the then board of BOAC's decision to cancel their VC10s and go all Boeing. This was a bold decision, but of all the decisions with which I have been associated in my public life it is the one about which I have the least doubt. The Cabinet appreciated, as BOAC's board did not, the great passenger appeal of the VC10, and we did BOAC an immensely good turn by overruling its considered judgement.

But exceptions to a general rule prove nothing. In general governments should accept the judgement of airlines as to what they need to do a job. If a state airline is involved and the government has no confidence in the decision of that board it has the power to get a new board. If a private airline is involved it should remember that it is the shareholders' money which is being risked. In present circumstances it is essential to the prosperity of British civil aviation that British airlines should be free to buy the aircraft they want on their technical merits. If a man is denied the tools he needs he has the best possible excuse for falling down on the job.

It has been the theme of this lecture that British civil aviation must not be allowed to fall down on the job. Granted the conditions I have set out, I believe it has a very great future and that in the latter years of this century it will be seen to be playing an even more significant part than it is today in maintaining this nation's economy and so both the well-being of the British people and the power and authority of Her Majesty's Government in the world.

12 The Role of the Large Tour Operator in the Development and Promotion of Tourism

BY A. J. BURKART

From a paper presented to the 22nd Congress of the International Association of Scientific Experts in Tourism (AIEST) in Istanbul, Turkey, between 3–9 September 1972 and published in *Méthodes de Recherches Touristiques et leur Application aux Pays et Régions en Voie de Développement*, Vol. 12 Publications de l'AIEST (Editions Gurten, Berne, 1972).

Introduction

The dramatic growth of tourist traffic to the Mediterranean countries of Europe is a major feature of the history of tourism in the last ten years. The coast of eastern Spain has been transformed from a region of fishing villages with some major ports into by far the largest holiday area of Europe; comparable developments have taken place on the Adriatic coast of Italy, and further afield the coasts of Greece and of its islands and of Cyprus have more recently entered the tourism 'league table'. In Spain, the Balearic Islands constitute the major resort area of Europe, and measured in terms of arrivals Palma is one of Europe's major international airports. A majority of tourists to Spain come from France and by car, but from other countries air travel is the principal method of transport, especially from the United Kingdom, from West Germany, and from Scandinavia. A major contributing factor to this growth of air travel holiday tourism has been the development of the inclusive tour, a method of packaging a holiday pioneered in the United Kingdom.

The experience of the United Kingdom illustrates this growth. For many years, both the number of holidays taken and the proportion of holidays taken abroad exhibited only slow expansion, but in recent years (even in a relatively unfavourable economic climate) growth has been resumed (*see* Table 12.1).

Thus, in absolute numbers and as a proportion of all holidays, holidays abroad by the British population are increasing.

For holidays of four nights or more, Spain is easily the most popular destination, and now accounts for a third of all such holidays (*see* Table 12.2). The remaining countries of Europe have individually accounted for less than 5 per cent of all holidays.

The mode of transport employed has moved heavily in favour of air transport: in 1960, only 40 per cent of holidays abroad used the air as the method of

Table 12.1

Holidays* taken by UK Residents, 1962–1971 (in millions)

Year	In Britain	Abroad	Total
1962	32	4	36
1963	31	5	36
1964	31	5	36
1965	30	5	35
1966	31	5,5	36·5
1967	30	5	35
1968	30	5	35
1969	30·5	5·75	36·25
1970	34·5	5·75	40·25
1971	34	7·25	41·25

Source: British Tourist Authority: *British National Travel Survey, 1962–1971.*
Note: *Four nights or more away from home.

Table 12.2

Destinations of Holidays Abroad of 4 nights or more
taken by UK Residents, 1967–1971 (%)

Destination	1967	1968	1969	1970	1971
Spain	24	29	32	30	34
France	13	10	9	11	10
Italy	14	10	10	10	8
Austria	7	7	6	8	7
Ireland	10	10	10	8	6
Switzerland	6	6	5	4	4
W. Germany	5	6	6	5	6
All Europe	92	90	90	88	89
All rest of world	6	7	8	7	6

Source: British Tourist Authority: *British National Travel Survey, 1967–1971.*

transport, but in 1971 this figure had risen to 67 per cent. In the same period, the proportion of holidays abroad employing some form of package arrangement had risen from 30 per cent in 1968 to 58 per cent in 1971. The increase in the popularity of Spain, the preference for air travel, and the increase in the numbers of holidays taken abroad are all to be explained as the effect of the development of the inclusive tour.

Part of the increase in absolute numbers of holidays abroad is accounted for by an increase in the number of additional holidays taken. This trend has had important effects on the seasonality of holiday traffic. The new availability of very cheap packages, mostly to the Western Mediterranean resorts in winter, has succeeded in extending the season for those resorts. It has also given a new meaning to the idea of a winter holiday, which now is as likely to be in Spain as in Switzerland; the ski resorts of Europe have now to compete with

Mediterranean resorts. The development of winter inclusive tours from the UK has reduced the peak/trough ratio from something over 1:20 in 1965 to about 1:5 in 1971. Visits to Spain in the first three months of 1971 were more than double the number in the same quarter of 1970.

The Inclusive Tour and the Industry

These recent and dramatic changes in the pattern of holiday tourism abroad by the British population are attributable to the vigorous growth of the demand for inclusive tours and to the emergence of a tour operating industry.

The principal feature of the inclusive tour in this context is that the tourist may buy for a single price a holiday much cheaper than would be attainable by the holidaymaker if he bought the components of his holiday separately and directly or from a retail travel agent. The low price of the package holiday or inclusive tour is made possible by reason of the lower unit costs obtainable both for the air travel and for the hotel stay, when the tour operator enters into long-term contracts for aircraft seats and hotel beds. This is achieved by time-chartering aircraft and making parallel contracts with hotels.

The principal in this is the tour operator. It is the tour operator who buys aircraft seats and hotel beds and from them and certain other facilities such as couriers or entertainment, he makes up the package. Historically, the tour operator has mostly emerged from retail travel agency, but today a clear distinction must be made between tour operator and travel agent. The latter, the retail travel agent, undertakes to sell the travel services of his principals, who will be airlines and other transport undertakings, hotel groups, shipping lines, and the providers of such ancillary services as travellers' cheques. For retailing these services the travel agent is rewarded by a commission from his principals. Prominent among the retail agent's principals is the tour operator. To perform his function of creating holiday packages, the tour operator needs considerable financial strength and the large tour operators are frequently owned or backed by large companies or groups with interests in many industries other than travel. Unlike the travel agent, the tour operator is a genuine manufacturer of a new kind of tourist product.

The inclusive tour is one of several devices which enable the tourist to enjoy the lower prices that result from the economies of chartering aircraft. These other arrangements must be distinguished from the inclusive tour. The affinity group charter organizer may charter an aircraft for the purpose of making cheap travel available to a closed group of travellers, e.g. the members of a club with an interest in something other than cheap travel. The affinity group organizer may or may not also offer to provide accommodation for the members of the group. The tour operator of inclusive tours by contrast sells his package, the inclusive tour, to the public at large, and his customers have nothing else in common than that they are all buying the same inclusive tour.

Tour operation depends for its success on the achieving of very high load factors for the aircraft and very high occupancy rates for the hotel. In this way unit costs can be kept sufficiently low to enable the tour operator to offer his package at a price which is often less than the cheapest available fare alone. For example, the lowest available scheduled international air fare to Palma from London in the summer of 1972 is an off-season midweek night tourist excursion return fare of £39·75. One of the largest tour operators in the UK offers eight days in Palma from £31 or fifteen days for £42, inclusive of the flight and hotel accommodation and some ancillary services.

These prices can only be reached by the high load factors and occupancy rates referred to above, and the tour operating industry's profit as a result is extremely volatile. A 5 per cent drop in load factor as compared with the budgeted load factor can turn a substantial profit into a considerable loss. The licensing authority in the United Kingdom, the Air Transport Licensing Board, which has the duty of issuing air service licences to airlines for inclusive tour purposes, has shown some anxiety over the financial stability of tour operators. In September 1971, the Board issued a statement drawing attention to the ease with which profits could be turned into losses (*see* Table 12.3).

Table 12.3

Tour Operators' Profits and Losses
(57 Tour Operators)

Year	Turnover £'000	+Profit/ — Loss £'000
1969	105,649	+1,573
1970	140,790	−1,621

Source: Air Transport Licensing Board.

In spite of a big increase in business, lower than budgeted load factors in 1970 turned an industry profit into a loss. Some commentators on the UK scene would hold that the Board itself must bear some part of the blame by granting virtually all the capacity applied for, which resulted in the capacity on offer being greatly in excess of the demand for it. (For a full discussion of tour construction, *see* Burkart, A. J.: 'Package Holidays by Air', *The Tourist Review*, No. 2, April/June 1971.)

The precarious profitability of tour operation, and the need for strong financial resources, have tended to bring about a large measure of concentration in the United Kingdom, with the bulk of the inclusive tour market being dominated by a small number of large operators. The applications to the Air Transport Licensing Board illustrate the point (*see* Table 12.4).

Applications for licences do not guarantee that the capacity applied for will actually be operated, but the picture is nevertheless clear; in 1971, judged by the applications for the following year, the first five tour operators accounted for almost 60 per cent of the market, and together with the next five, the first ten operators account for 75 per cent. This degree of concentration suggests

Table 12.4

Applications by Airlines for Licences for
Inclusive Tour Charters: Summer 1971 and 1972

| | Seats applied for | |
Tour Operator	1971	1972
Clarksons	745,418	735,026
Thomsons	336,659	476,632
Sunair	147,589	347,724
Horizon	318,805	327,839
Cosmos	204,975	306,180
Global	174,727	190,429
Blue Cars	158,263	137,962
Lunn-Poly	131,896	90,246
4S	41,089	79,658
Lyons	128,639	76,255
All operators	3,374,439	3,689,640

Source: Travelnews, 97, 16 September 1971.

the existence of barriers to entry or at least barriers to growth. One such barrier
would be the absence of adequate financial resources to withstand the volatility
of profits referred to above, and it may be noted that all the leading tour operators, with the exception of Horizon, are subsidiary companies of much larger
conglomerate companies.

The marketing resources of the large tour operator also probably constitute
a barrier to entry and certainly to growth. The tour operator is indeed a manufacturer of a tourist product, but he is also a marketing man. The growth of the
British tour operating industry has been achieved as a result of planned and
deliberate marketing.

Marketing

The tour operating industry recognized in its early days, even before the practice
of time-chartering had become common, that demand for a foreign holiday was
extremely price-elastic, and that the customers would flock to the tour operators
with the lowest prices (less than modern aircraft originally enabled the price to
be kept low and only with jet aircraft did time-chartering become the usual
practice for the larger operators).

Granted this price-elasticity of demand, the next step was to create a kind of
package that could be marketed as a mass market product. The solution to this
problem can be inferred from an inspection of tour operators' brochures. The
product has been standardized into a package consisting in essence of an attractive hotel in a sunny climate, possibly on a beach but if not certainly with a
swimming pool, the whole being visibly enjoyed by people with whom the
potential customer can easily identify himself or herself. The effect of this

standardization is to suggest that the purchaser of an inclusive tour is largely indifferent to the country in which his attractive hotel is located. The holiday at Cattolica appears not to be different from that at Benidorm; even the name of the country is barely mentioned.

This standardization has an important consequence for marketing. If a tour operator serves any large number of destinations – a big tour operator may list thirty or more – and if he were to attempt to market each individually, the level of marketing intensity for each destination would not approach the threshold level. But by standardizing his product he can market his name, his brand name, to a level well above the threshold. The instrument by which this is achieved is the tour operator's brochure – in effect his catalogue – which lists and illustrates his products, and invariably contains a booking form. Very large quantities of the brochure can be produced and the primary task of his promotion by advertising is to get the brochure in the hands of the public. The advertising in the mass media has the purpose of selling the brochure in the first place, and it is expected that the brochure itself will sell the holiday product.

In this brochure distribution, the retail travel agent has a central part to play by providing local access to the stock of brochures and subsequently by converting the customer's interest into a booking. Typically, 80 or 90 per cent of a large tour operator's bookings will come through retail travel agents. In the present state of the art there is little evidence of brand loyalty displayed by the retail travel agent, and a normal commission of 10 per cent is supplemented by a wide range of incentive bonuses aimed both at the manager or proprietor of the retail agency and at the counter clerk, in the shape of cash, free holidays, or even relatively expensive consumer goods.

The typical marketing campaign is thus a two-stage matter, the first objective being to obtain the widest possible distribution of the brochure, and the second to obtain bookings which result from the brochure distribution.

Two variations from the characteristic marketing pattern described above merit consideration. Firstly, the marketing of inclusive tours by mail order has been attempted in this country, notably by the *Reader's Digest*, but without establishing the success attained in West Germany by this method. In the United Kingdom, there appears to be a sufficient network of retail travel agent's outlets, numbering about 4,000, to make the use of mail order unattractive to the public. Nevertheless, a large tour operator may expect to effect some 10 per cent of his bookings directly by mail to his head office. Further, the large tour operators have a small number of branch offices open to the public (Horizon, for example, list fourteen such branch offices). Thirdly, one tour operator, Sunair, a recent recruit to the top five (*see* Table 12.4) does not advertise to the public but relies wholly on the retail agent and his ability to merchandise the Sunair brochure effectively. It is probably too early to assess the success of this departure from the typical marketing strategy.

As far as the United Kingdom is concerned, charter inclusive tour traffic is by far the fastest growing part of tourist flows to Western Europe (*see* Table 12.5).

Table 12.5

Annual Percentage Increases in Passenger
Air Traffic, UK to and from Western Europe

Year	By scheduled services	By charters
1964–1965	+ 8	+33
1965–1966	+10	+27
1966–1967	+13	+38
1967–1968	+ 4	+14
1968–1969	+ 6	+15
1969–1970	+10	+37
1970–1971	+ 7	+27

Source: British European Airways: *Report and Accounts*, 1964–1965 to 1970–1971.

By far the largest part of the last column covers charter inclusive tours, which exhibit a growth rate between three and four times faster than the growth of scheduled services in good years and in bad years alike.

Tour Operation and Tourist Authorities

That the growth of inclusive tours by charter is so dramatic suggests that the market for inclusive tours is very sensitive to the absolute level of fares and holidays pricing, as well as being acutely price-elastic. Certainly this is the view of leading tour operators, and the initial successes of very cheap winter IT [inclusive tour] prices confirm this. These latter developments have transformed the retail travel agency from a highly seasonal business into a year-round one. A similar year-round pattern is emerging in the hotel field in the principal destinations. From their viewpoint, this can be satisfactory too.

The high gearing of profits in tour operating to load factor makes tour operating very volatile. In turn, this volatility can be a barrier to growth. From the tourist authorities' point of view at the destination, this means that tourist arrivals may fluctuate sharply from year to year or from season to season. The basis of the winter growth is the assumption that the public will not substitute very cheap winter holidays for the traditional summer holidays. The tour operator expects to cover the bulk of his fixed costs in his summer traffic, and to operate during the winter to cover direct operating costs plus a modest contribution to overheads. If any considerable change occurred in the volume of summer traffic so that load factors fell, unit costs in the summer would rise and consequentially prices in the winter would be forced up. With the demand being so price-elastic, this could only result in fewer tourist arrivals. The great sensitivity of this market to price should engage the attention of tourist authorities everywhere in order to keep the cost component contributed by accommodation and other services as low as possible.

Tour operation has shown itself to be capable of generating very large volumes of tourist traffic. In countries where there is a substantial tour operating industry, as in the UK, the promotional role of the reception countries' tourist authority will change. If the argument above is correct, the traditional appeals of the tourist authorities are superfluous. The inclusive tour holidaymaker appears to be indifferent to his destination's nationality, and the 'Come to sunny Ruritania' approach is outmoded. The marketing of the principal inclusive tour destinations has passed from the tourist authorities, from the individual airlines and hotel companies to the tour operators. The role of the receiving countries' tourist authorities ceases to be directly promotional, and changes to a more subtle task, that of facilitating the construction of tours, of helping the travel trade in the generating country, and ensuring in the receiving country that tourist amenities including accommodation are available in the form required and at a price appropriate to the inclusive tour market. In the case of countries developing or initiating a tourist industry, the appreciation of the requirements of tour operators will enable an accelerated pattern of tourist arrivals, and there will be no need to persuade the public of the attractions of the country. The Ruritanian National Tourist Office need not sell Ruritania to the public of industrialized Western Europe; rather it will concentrate on selling Ruritania to the tour operator.

Conclusion

The tour operator thus emerges as the only true manufacturer of the tourist product. This product is the inclusive tour, packaged, standardized, quality controlled, and mass-produced. It can be sold at the level of the retail travel agent without the counter staff having to be highly trained in tourism. It can be marketed successfully in the tourist generating countries to a mass market just because it is standardized, packaged, and quality controlled, and is therefore susceptible to the same marketing techniques that are applied successfully to the marketing of consumer goods.

Finally, the recent development of inclusive tours in the winter indicates that the inclusive tour is the most effective way yet devised for extending the season. In a market where demand is so highly price-elastic, the very low prices available are the key factors in winter traffic. In the UK experience, it seems that the retired segment of the market is largely attracted to winter holidays by inclusive tours, a segment whose members are relatively poor with fixed incomes. The winter inclusive tour has thus achieved a downward penetration of the market. Nevertheless, if money incomes continue to rise, the use of the inclusive tour in the second-holiday market segment will grow increasingly in importance.

In the past ten years, European tourism has been transformed by the charter inclusive tour. There seems no reason why the growth of tour operation should be halted. Its effect has been to transfer the marketing function in tourism from the individual provider of tourist services to the tour operating sector. With this has come the industrialization of tourism – 'Le tourisme aérien intra-européen prend une nouvelle dimension et passe du stade artisanal au stade industriel' (R. Peladan: *Transports*, No. 150, March–April 1970).

Part VII
Marketing in Tourism

Introduction

One of the peculiarities of tourism is that the tourist product is a compound or amalgam of several components. A total journey, for example, may be made up of a flight by air, of use of accommodation, and of a number of other services. A crucial stage in the marketing in tourism is the correct formulation of the tourist product. Another peculiarity of tourism, which is not manifest even in the case of other services, is that the consumer actually 'consumes' the product under the supervision of the producer, an hotelier, an airline, or another supplier.

Medlik and Middleton examine in Chapter 13 the concept of the tourist product, and consider the applicability of consumer goods marketing principles and practices to the field of tourism. Having postulated the three main components of the tourist product amalgam – attractions, facilities, accessibility – their main concern is the implications of the true nature of the tourist product for the consumer, for the suppliers of tourist facilities, and for the tourist destination.

In Chapter 14 Burkart addresses himself to the problems raised by the invisible nature of, in this case, a travel product. He notes that in an industry in which firms cannot compete in pricing (airline fares are fixed for all airlines), and where all the firms are offering very similar products (as exemplified by a handful of aircraft types), the creation of an individual house style is a hallmark of competition by product differentiation. This differentiation extends significantly beyond the marketing of the product, to embrace the consumption stage and to maintain a recognizable identity towards the consumer at all times. Burkart also considers the alternative responsibilities for the house style in various types of organization.

13 *The Tourist Product and its Marketing Implications*

BY PROFESSOR S. MEDLIK AND V. T. C. MIDDLETON

From *International Tourism Quarterly*, No. 3 1973, Special Article No. 9 (Economist Intelligence Unit, London).

Marketing – Finding a Definition

Marketing is about markets and products and their relationships.

According to the British Institute of Marketing, 'marketing is the management function which organizes and directs all those business activities involved in assessing and converting customer purchasing power into effective demand for a specific product or service and in moving the product or service to the final consumer or user so as to achieve the profit target or other objectives set by the company'.

This view emphasizes that marketing:

1. co-ordinates all aspects of business (and not just a department);
2. means assessment and conversion of purchasing power into effective demand for the product or service (and not merely producing products or satisfying demand as it appears).

According to Krippendorf,[1] marketing in tourism means 'the systematic and co-ordinated execution of business policy by tourist undertakings, whether private or state-owned, at local, regional, national or international level, to achieve the optimal satisfaction of the needs of identifiable consumer groups, and in doing so to achieve an appropriate return'. Krippendorf stresses that marketing in tourism:

1. involves co-ordination of policies of several organizations at several levels (not just policies within an organization);
2. is concerned with the needs of identifiable consumer groups (not merely with the market at large).

Products, as discussed in this article, should be seen in relation to the customer's wants and expectations – if those wants and expectations are to be turned into effective demand and if they are to produce an appropriate return. Marketing, as expressed in these definitions, is both a management philosophy and a set of business techniques. The philosophy is dominant as it formulates and coordinates the whole approach of an enterprise or organization to its business.

[1] Krippendorf, J., *Marketing im Fremdenverkehr*, (Herbert Lang, Berne, 1971).

It is based on an understanding of the consumer and on gearing the product directly to his wants and needs. Marketing is thus much more than a modern refinement of the traditional approach to selling, and the tourist product is examined here in the context of consumer-orientated marketing.

What is a Tourist Product?

The concept of consumer orientation makes it necessary to examine the components of the tourist product from the consumer's point of view. As far as the tourist is concerned, the product he buys covers the complete experience from the time he leaves home to the time he returns to it. In other words, the product is not an airline seat, or an hotel bed, or relaxation on a sunny beach, but rather an amalgam of many components, or a 'package'. This package is most clearly seen in the case of the inclusive tour, in which the tour operator or other organizer brings all the elements of a holiday together, and offers them for sale at one inclusive price. However, 'all tourists buy packages whether or not they use travel agents'.[2]

In other words, all tourists buy, either separately, or as an inclusive tour, the various components of the tourist product. Either way, the end result of all these purchases is a 'package'. This view of the tourist product holds good whether a business trip, a holiday or, indeed, any other form of tourism, international or domestic, is under consideration. Airline seats or hotel beds may be individual products in the eyes of their producers, but they are merely elements or components of a total tourist product, which is a composite product.

We may postulate three main components of the tourist product amalgam:

1. attractions of the destination, including its image in the tourist's mind;
2. facilities at the destination: accommodation, catering, entertainment, and recreation;
3. accessibility of the destination.

The three basic elements

The *attractions* are those elements in the tourist product which determine the choice of the tourist to visit one destination rather than another. They may be site attractions, related to the natural or built environment, or attractions related to events. Site attractions are those where the place itself is the major inducement for the visit. In this category would be, for example, natural attractions such as the Alps, the Grand Canyon, or Niagara Falls, or built attractions, such as Disneyland. Event attractions are those where the event staged is a larger factor in the tourist's choice than the site, for example, the Oberammergau Passion Play, the Olympic Games, or a congress or exhibition. Sometimes the site and the event determine together the tourist's choice as is the case, for example, with the Salzburg or Edinburgh festivals.

[2] Jeffries, D., *Defining the Tourist Product – and its Significance in Tourism Marketing*, *The Tourist Review*, Vol. XVII, Number 1, January/March 1971.

The *facilities* are those elements in the tourist product which do not normally themselves provide the motivation for tourist flows but the absence of which may deter the tourist from travelling to enjoy the attractions. Absence of accommodation facilities would be an obvious deterrent to tourism. Similarly, an absence of sailing boats for hire in an area noted for sailing possibilities would be a deterrent to that type of tourism. The provision or the absence of caravan parks would again have an obvious influence on tourism to a destination. Facilities may form part of the attractions of a destination, but are rarely the sole reason for tourism to it; they may complement the attractions – a well-appointed hotel may enhance the attractiveness of a resort.

Accessibility is the third of the components of the tourist product and relates to the mode of transport to the destination chosen by the tourist. It is determined by the proximity of a destination to the tourist's place of residence and is best interpreted in terms of the time and the cost to reach the destination, i.e. as economic distance, rather than in terms of physical distance. For example, the link between aircraft technology and the development of tourism across the Atlantic has been a major factor in accessibility changes of tourist destinations in relation to generating centres of population.

Each destination has a particular product or products to offer, which is made up of attractions, facilities, and accessibility. Switzerland offers an environment of mountains and lakes, which may be used for skiing in winter and for walking, climbing, and relaxation in the summer. The French Riviera offers an environment of Mediterranean sea and sun. Blackpool offers an environment of breezy beaches and entertainment. In each of these destinations the tourist selects an activity or activities which he wishes to pursue, and the services which he uses during his stay. In this sense selecting the destination product is analogous to selecting consumer durables in a shop, to which the buyer goes to make his purchases. If the buyer has the articles delivered to his home, the delivery forms part of the purchase, for which he pays directly or indirectly. In an analogous way transport to a tourist destination is an integral part of the tourist product.

With these three basic elements of the tourist product or package – and it must be emphasized that all three are capable of considerable independent variation – it is possible to examine the implications of the tourist product for the consumer, the suppliers of facilities, and the destination.

Some Tourists are Indifferent to the Destinations

However, it must be stated at this point that many tourists appear to be increasingly indifferent to the destination they visit and that a particular type of tourist product may be increasingly provided by more than one destination. For example, a tourist product with sunbathing as the main attraction and activity and a stay in a modern hotel with a swimming pool is available in a number of resorts within similar distances from the same concentrations of population in generating countries. Destinations offering this product at similar prices are then readily interchangeable with others. The idea of the *unique selling proposition* of a product or a range of products is as relevant to tourism as it is to the marketing of any consumer goods.

What the Tourist Product means for the Consumer

From the marketing definitions discussed earlier, it can be deduced that the process of assessing consumer demands and the process of product formulation are opposite sides of the same coin. In the marketing of mass-produced consumer goods it is, of course, common practice to manufacture products specifically tailored to match consumer requirements; indeed, success in modern marketing is very much geared to the process of product innovation, which is therefore a matter for continuous heavy investment in research into both product development and consumer's requirements, tastes, and preferences.

In tourism it is not normally very easy to adjust the product or the packages available since this is a function of environmental attractions, facilities, and accessibility, and since it has implications for the permanent resident population of the destination. However, if the process is more difficult it is none the less still valid. As P. H. Kotler stated succinctly 'Marketing's short-term task may be to adjust customers' wants to existing goods, but its long-run task is to adjust the goods to the customers' wants'.[3]

Because the tourist product contains intangible elements and perceptions, as well as physical features, and is perceived as an experience, it is sometimes a relatively straightforward matter to engineer changes. Any particular destination may embody not one but several products; similarly any particular product may be provided by more than one destination. This flexibility in terms of alternative product possibilities gives tourist destinations considerable scope for altering their particular product amalgams over a short period of time, notwithstanding the fact that long-term changes in tourist products are likely to involve substantial investment in facilities. Bermuda provides an example of the extent to which product changes can be effected, without altering the physical facilities.

Before the war, Bermuda was a supplier of market garden produce to New York. When tariff barriers curtailed its market garden trade, Bermuda developed facilities and created an identity or image as a winter resort. The advent of long-range aircraft made the more certain sun of the Caribbean as easily and as cheaply reached as Bermuda and dealt a heavy blow to Bermuda as a winter resort. The island then refashioned the image of its product to become a summer resort. What has primarily been changed has been the image or identity of the island in the mind of the tourist rather than its basic physical plant, to match the skilfully identified new markets.

[3] Kotler, P. H., *Marketing Management-Analysis, Planning, Control* (Englewood Cliffs, N.J., 1967).

Market Research in Tourism

The relationship between the consumer and the product calls for a comment on market research in tourism. Market research is as much the basis of tourism marketing as it is for the marketing of any consumer product. If, for example, tourist flows can be analysed in terms of the products or packages bought, a very fruitful line of approach is opened up whereby broadly homogeneous market segments can be identified in terms of consumers' habits and attitudes in relation to the packages bought, and these can be matched with broadly homogeneous combinations of the tourist product elements or packages. This is just another way of saying that marketing involves 'assessing and converting customer purchasing power into effective demand for a specific product or service . . .' (*see* BIM definition of marketing quoted above).

What the Tourist Product means for Suppliers of Tourist Facilities

It is fundamental to the approach to the tourist product in this article that the suppliers of tourist facilities (hotels, restaurants, entertainments, and in this connection airlines and other transport operators) are supplying only components of the total package. This is not to suggest that there are necessarily automatic advantages in the vertical integration of such suppliers, but it does raise the question whether airlines are really in the business of selling identical seats in the air (a transport experience) and whether hotels are really in the business of offering multiples of identical beds in multiples of identical rooms (an accommodation experience). Are not both types of suppliers rather serving to facilitate what is seen by the consumer to be part of an overall tourist experience? If the latter is true, it follows that the interests of all suppliers of facilities would be more effectively served if they:

1. identified their respective roles in the tourist experience (i.e. the product amalgam), and
2. organized their respective marketing efforts accordingly, although not necessarily by pooling their funds and identities.

Misdirected Promotional Effort

This means co-ordination in market research, product formulation and development, as well as in product promotion. At present it appears that many suppliers of tourist facilities are sufficiently confident of their short-term future to engage in extensive publicity to promote their specific images and individual products. It is our view that much of this money is misdirected and that the level of demand depends on factors other than those which image advertising of an individual firm can affect. In other words, the advertising campaigns of many major organizations are based on a basic misunderstanding of the nature of the tourist product, and their role within it. When over 75 per cent of international tourism is for non-business purposes and when there is an ever-growing commitment of investment in tourism capacity, it would appear that the time is ripe for a major rethinking of the marketing approach by the major suppliers of tourist facilities. There are encouraging signs that this may already be happening. For example, hotels are linking with transport interests in the selling of cheap weekends in London and on the English south coast as packages. Airlines, in operating charter companies, are linking with accommodation, car hire, and entertainment interests, producing packages such as fly-drive schemes in Europe.

What the Tourist Product means for the Tourist Destination

In discussing the components of the tourist product earlier, the focus of the variables was on the destination. Since all tourists arrive somewhere to do something, the destinations concerned are the most important bases of the product 'package' which the consumer buys.

The elements of tourist products at the destination may be developed consciously to appeal to particular markets or they may develop without any conscious effort. In the former case certain features of the destination are selected and developed in the physical sense – promenades, swimming pools, parks, and large-scale indoor entertainment facilities are examples; they are also developed in the minds of potential tourists through the creation of a particular image of the destination by promotion. The conscious development of tourist product elements should be determined after a study of the potential market. When the elements of the tourist product develop without any conscious effort, the market tends to shape itself to the product.

If the analysis of product packages in this article is correct, it is clearly in the best interests of the destinations to seek to discover the 'package' or 'packages' with which they are concerned. Of course, in the past, when the numbers of tourists to a destination were small or when demand invariably exceeded supply, it was not necessary for destinations to assess the nature of their tourism flows. However, at the present time, and increasingly in the future, it is certain that tourism flows will reach saturation points in certain places, whilst other areas with a massive investment in tourism facilities will see their market demand diminish. In either case the analysis of tourism flows will be necessary and in our view this can be achieved most effectively by analysing the tourist packages and the market segments by whom they are bought.

An analysis of the product packages has other advantages. For example, it is possible to define accurately the capacity of each product. In an Alpine village, the capacity of the skiing 'package' can be easily calculated, for a village has only so many hotel beds, so much ski-lift capacity, so many car parking spaces. In the short run, the separate elements of the package may be frequently out of balance, but in the long run they must achieve broad harmony unless tourism flows are to be diverted elsewhere. Admittedly, the calculation of the capacity of natural resources to absorb tourism – how many skiers can a hectare of snow slopes accommodate, for example – is a less easy matter to define, but since this must be related to measurable facilities, it is surely appropriate to begin by assessing what is readily measurable.

It may be further argued that the analysis of tourist products based on destinations is an essential prerequisite to planning and development measures in relation to tourism. If, for example, it is considered that too many tourists to a particular destination are bringing in caravans as part of their particular package, it is a relatively simple matter to impose controls on the amount of space available for caravan parking, or on the minimum standards of facilities to be provided for caravan sites. Thus, given an appreciation of the total impact of tourism packages, a destination would be in a position to regulate by marketing and by planning procedures the total demand for tourist products and the volume of demand for each of the different 'packages' with which it is concerned. In other words, by quantifying the supply of facilities in relation to the demand for tourist products, destinations would be able to form judgements on total capacity and, perhaps even more importantly, be able to balance the various aspects (or packages) of demand in the interests of those who live at the destination.

The Tourist Product in a Marketing Perspective

In the western industrialized countries of Europe and North America, which generate the great majority of tourists, a conscious emphasis has been given to consumption – first, to consumable goods like food and drink and other day-to-day needs, and at a later stage to consumer durables like cars, refrigerators, and washing machines, and finally, to consumer services like entertainment and recreation. Tourism represents a prominent element in these consumer services and can be expected to follow a similar evolution as other economic activities serving the consumer. For most of them three phases may be distinguished.

THREE PHASES OF DEVELOPMENT –
The first phase is characterized by a shortage of available goods and services. Demand is in excess of supply. There is no sales problem: what is produced can be also sold. The main problem is to increase the output. There is a seller's market and production orientation – what is available to the consumer is determined by what the producer wants to sell and by his capacity to produce it.

The second phase comes when technical progress makes mass production possible; increased productivity leads to lower unit costs and lower prices. Concurrently, higher real incomes generate increasing purchasing power, but much supply may be in excess of demand. There is a buyer's market and sales orientation on the part of the producer – the increased output has to be sold, for continuous production is a condition of producing at all.

The third phase is characterized by further growth of output and of incomes producing the 'affluent society'. The need to secure continuous production leads to a recognition of the necessity to meet identifiable consumer needs. Selling alone may not be enough by itself. The buyer's market brings about a marketing orientation on the part of the producer; consumer needs become the starting point for determining what is produced.

Not all industries in all countries undergo these three phases consecutively and in step with each other. But the basic pattern has been from a seller's market and production orientation through a buyer's market and sales orientation to a buyer's market and marketing orientation. In the process, what is sold becomes defined in relation to those who buy it. In other words products come to match markets. The consumer's choice may become more limited, but he enjoys lower prices and defined standards of particular products which he may identify by brand names. Mass media inform him of the availability of the products, and distribution networks ensure that he can buy them in his district. Modern marketing is designed to achieve optimal satisfaction of the consumer and to do so at an appropriate return to the producer.

– APPLIED TO THE TOURIST PRODUCT

Until the 1950s much tourism was still in the first phase described earlier, characterized by shortages of transport and even more prominently of accommodation capacity. The introduction of the Boeing 747 aircraft and the creation of very large hotels are clear examples of the second phase in which overproduction of both airline and hotel capacities are real possibilities. Amsterdam, Brussels, and London hotels, which were until a few years ago in a seller's market, are in a buyer's market, as are many resort hotels. More recently the first signs of the application of the marketing concept in tourism have become apparent in the planning and execution of new resorts where consumer needs are reflected in the provision of facilities, which enter into the tourist product provided for a particular market or markets.

But the transition from selling to marketing is slow to achieve in its full implications. For example, as a result of the indiscriminate effects of the Hotel Development Incentives scheme in Britain in the period 1969–1973, the volume of higher-priced accommodation in London has produced a situation in which hotel groups are in a highly competitive market, which is causing some radical rethinking of the marketing approach – after the event. The shift from a seller's to a buyer's market in London (and in Liverpool and elsewhere) may be one of the most interesting aspects of tourism in Britain. But, hopefully, the lessons have been learnt; an adherence to the marketing concept calls for both a market assessment and for product formulation, before the product is launched.

Summary

A tourist product is an amalgam of tangible and intangible elements centred on a specific activity at a specific destination. It comprises and combines the actual and perceived attractions of a destination, the facilities, and the destination's accessibility, from which the tourist buys a combination of activities and arrangements. To the tourist a product is perceived as an 'experience'.

Product formulation in tourism marketing, as in the marketing of any products or services, is concerned with the consideration of demand and supply. In terms of the demand for products, product formulation involves analysing and assessing consumer requirements (existing and potential) and identifying homogeneous groups of potential purchasers for specific tourist products. In terms of supply, product formulation in tourism involves analysing and assessing the product elements, and identifying product amalgams from the range of possibilities available at any destination in relation to demand.

14 *Design as an Instrument of Competition*

BY A. J. BURKART

From The Design Oration given at the Royal Society of Arts on 22 November 1962 and published by the Society of Industrial Artists in the *SIA Journal*, No. 118, in December 1962.

Let me pose my first question. Why does BEA have a design policy? It does have such a policy, whether or not everyone in my audience will agree that it is a well-conducted one, at least I think we can fairly claim that we try. This will lead me to say something about the nature of BEA as a major European airline, and perhaps also something about the nature of the airline industry as a whole.

One of the most significant developments of the post-war world has been the astonishing and rapid growth of air transport, no less in Europe than throughout the rest of the world. I think it would have been a bold man indeed in 1946 who would have ventured to predict the volume of passenger and freight traffic that the world's airlines now carry. While still a stimulating and exciting experience, to travel by air is now something that will be well within the experience of almost everyone in this room tonight: to fly on business or to fly on holiday has now become an accepted and important part of modern life. Nor I suggest does the pace slacken. Each year more capacity is being offered by the airlines, and new places are being served by modern and up-to-date air services. It is true that at the moment the industry is going through a difficult phase; this is a phase of development certainly not a phase of contraction. Looking forward to the next five or ten years, already the aircraft manufacturing industry is talking about supersonic aircraft, and various plans are being laid, quite actively, to this end. While airlines as operators may currently have some doubts about the wisdom of rushing into supersonic aircraft, for economic reasons, I suppose it is true to say that within the next decade or so we shall certainly see passenger-carrying machines flying faster than the speed of sound. Thus, in something like twenty-five years, that is, this astonishingly fast-growing industry will have graduated from carrying passengers at 150 m.p.h. to something like ten times that speed or even more, perhaps between 1,500 and 2,000 m.p.h. It may be worthwhile to look at the experience of the airlines and to study the pattern of their growth so that lessons learnt by this industry can be applied in the future to other industries which may display such astonishingly rapid technological advance. I would like, therefore, for you to view the airline industry as a kind of guinea-pig on which we may carry out certain experiments and make certain hypotheses which will be relevant in the future to other industries.

The first point I want to make about the air transport industry in Europe is that it is intensely competitive. There are something like fifty or sixty airlines operating either directly within Europe or with services transitting most of the important cities of Europe. Make no mistake about it, air transport in the international field in Europe is one of the most hotly competitive industries today. This competition does not come merely as between airlines; above all it comes from the great growth of ownership of the private car. Any airline today not only faces its other airline competitors but also the use of the private car for transport, particularly for holiday transport. As if this were not enough, most European countries are also extensively developing other sorts of surface transport; there are the trans-Europe trains, the network of motorways and super-highways rapidly being developed over Europe, and we can see the nature of competition that an airline faces even if we look at this country. For example, between London and Manchester, not only do we operate as BEA very frequent services with very large aircraft – the Vanguard – but also the main railway line between London and Manchester is being electrified at a cost of many many millions of pounds and ultimately, presumably, the M1 motorway will be extended beyond Birmingham and Rugby to Manchester. Whatever we may think about this from the point of view of a logical transport policy for this country, for an airline it does mean that its business life is one of intense competition from other airlines and from all forms of surface transport.

It is from our recognition of this vigorously competitive European and United Kingdom market for air travel, that our need for maintaining and enhancing BEA's corporate identity springs. Moreover, the actual product which we deliver at the airport or at the town terminal is consumed over a considerable period of time.

This goes on in an industry where other airlines and other means of transport are competing vigorously and skilfully with us for a share of the travelling public. This is why we in BEA believe in the need to have a good clear coherent design policy which will establish BEA's corporate identity at every point at which a member of the travelling public comes into contact with the airline, when he is at the sales office, when he is at a travel agent, when he receives a letter from us, when he handles our ticket, when he boards our aircraft, and when he is being looked after on the aircraft: in all these situations it is of the greatest importance to us commercially and competitively that a passenger should readily be able to distinguish between BEA and some other airline. It is important that he should be able to recognize during the whole course of his journey that he is in the hands of the same airline, BEA. It is not too much to say that through all this diversity of place, time, situation, and language, the single unifying factor readily detectable to the passenger is the beacon of our familiar corporate identity and house style; it is because we are selling an intangible product, because we are delivering the product over a relatively long period, and because the customer has a good deal of time and the ability to change his mind even after the initial sale that we need to keep constantly before him a clear image of BEA as a solid, reliable, resourceful organization which has at its command the full ability and resources to deliver to him what he has bought on trust from us.

I now want to turn to the third part of my discussion. I should perhaps preface what I have to say by saying that I do not claim that the hypotheses that I shall shortly be advancing are in anything like incontrovertible form.

So far as I am aware there has been very little examination made of the kind of climate in industry in which a proper care for design arises. I cannot think readily of any study made of those firms which do practise a care for good design, nor of comparisons made between them and those which have less care for these matters. If a proper care for design is a good thing, as everyone here would agree, then why is this proper care for design a fairly rare occurrence? Why is it necessary for official and semi-official bodies to keep on urging it? Despite, no doubt, your occasional exasperation with your industrial clients, it is I think too naïve to attribute any shortfall in a proper care for design simply to the barbarity of the industrialist or the entrepreneur! Why then, and how then, do some industrial and commercial organizations pay attention to these matters while others do not? Why, if you like, do the wicked flourish or at least prosper not less than the good? This is the question I want to discuss. I do not pretend, I repeat, to know the real answers; all I can offer, perhaps, are the speculations of someone who is concerned in this matter from day to day.

Let me first of all define my field a little more closely. The English language, I fear, is lacking in a suitable word to embrace the whole spectrum of a company's visual presentation to its public, but it is in fact this whole visual presentation to the public that I wish to discuss. Design is perhaps almost too narrow a word, and the other words that are readily available, such as advertising, are also too narrow, but clearly the whole question of a company's visual presentation to its public is one, and I think one can undoubtedly construct a continuous spectrum to embrace this whole visual presentation. At the one end, perhaps, lies the whole complex of conventional advertising, on television, in the newspapers, on outdoor hoardings, in brochures and so on. Move along this spectrum, and we shall come to the narrow band of a simple house style stationery, vehicles, buildings, and their associated notices and signs: then, the packaging of the company's product, and finally the design of the product itself. We might indeed debate what should or should not find a place on this spectrum, and also we might debate the order in which the various items should be arranged, but I think it is nevertheless useful to envisage that such a spectrum can be constructed, and that incidentally conventional advertising must be part of it; indeed, conventional advertising is an important part of it because this is the medium of mass communication today which most large industrial or commercial organizations employ. Throughout the whole of this spectrum questions of design and some elements of a house style or a design policy will have their place as individual items somewhere along this spectrum, and earlier I tried to draw a picture of that spectrum as we see it in BEA. It is the whole question of this visible manifestation of a company to its public that I wish to discuss and when I talk about a proper care for design I mean a proper care for design in all these fields, in advertising no less than in stationery and in buildings, in notices and signs no less than in the product itself.

I have already indicated that in BEA we believe in a consistent and coherent design policy for competitive reasons. I now want to examine the nature of this competition that exists between airlines in the hope that examination of this in particular will throw light on the general case; I wish to use airline experience as the prototype for considering industry as a whole.

I think you will find the picture as painted to be generally recognizable, and at first sight it looks as though there might be some quite noticeable lack of competition in the airline industry. In fact, competition is intense not only between the parallel operators on any one route for the traffic that is already travelling by air, but also with the various surface carriers which operate over the same or similar routes. However, there has been in the past, at any rate, some misconception about this, and many people still suppose that the airlines enjoy a relatively non-competitive life. It is worth, therefore, having a look to see what sort of competition is possible: what kind of competition, for example, can one airline offer against another? I think there are four main sectors of competition for an airline. First of all in price, that is to say charging a different fare from its competitors. This is not practicable: fares are fixed for all airlines over a given route, at least so far as their scheduled services are concerned, so at once we must admit that one important sector of competition, that of price competition, is not applicable. Secondly, to a very large extent, the immediate transformation of price competition has also been eliminated. I refer, of course, to the standards of in-flight service. Competition in this sector has not been entirely eliminated, but such things as the general standards of the meals to be served, the distance between the seats within aircraft and so on, has been largely regulated, probably I think because these are in effect direct transformations of price. The third main area of competition for an airline is in its schedules, that is to say it can offer better times, superior equipment, and better times of departure and arrival as well as better speed than its competitors. Here certainly competition is intense, but there are various practical problems that arise for each and every airline in the integration of their fleet with a view to securing utilization.

If, generally speaking, the best departure times from most European capital cities is 10 o'clock in the morning, it would be quite impracticable for every airline to leave at that time; it would be impracticable probably partly for air traffic control reasons, and it would be extremely uneconomic for the airlines doing this. Each airline has to accept that some of its departures, for example, will not be ideal. But nevertheless there is intense competition between airlines on any particular route to try to ensure that their departure times, their speeds, are better than those of their competitors. The fourth sector of competition, I think we may call, generally speaking, the visual presentation of an airline to its public, for which of course a large part will be conventional advertising. I shall be returning to this in a moment.

The point I now want to make is that what has happened is that the area of competition still available to airlines has been carefully defined and regulated. The one thing that is absent, by and large, is competition in price, and with it, generally speaking, competition in standards of in-flight service. Internationally in the airline industry it is not possible for one airline unilaterally to reduce its prices, or substantially to alter its standards of service. Even if the industry were not regulated so closely as in fact it is, both internationally and domestically, the prices to be charged and the standards of service offered would probably tend to be very much the same between airlines by the facts of technological development. The difference between flying in one jet aircraft and another is not all that large; a small difference, of course, does exist. Moreover, because rights to fly between two points tend to be in the hands of the national carriers because they are the chosen instruments of their national governments, it will often happen that these two airlines – the two national carriers flying between any pair of points – will between them secure the lion's share of the traffic, the remainder being shared by a miscellany of other operators, often transit operators passing through the two pairs of points concerned. Not only price regulation has to some extent limited competition, but also the facts of technological development.

We cannot look at this in great detail, obviously, but I think that it will be clear to you from this description that competition between airlines has in fact been fairly strictly limited to non-price areas of an airline's activities. In this non-price area is to be found an airline's scheduling policies and also advertising as conventionally understood, but which I prefer to regard as part of the spectrum of visual presentation of an airline that I referred to earlier. Indeed, this visual presentation, including conventional advertising, is a major competitive weapon between airlines and an important marketing strategy – at least, it is so in default of widespread price competition. Also in this area of competition and as part of the visual presentation to the public, lies the architectural design of airline sales offices. I think we are probably all familiar with the imposing, sometimes even brash, airline offices grouped down a few major streets in the capitals of Europe – in Bond Street, Regent Street, and Piccadilly in London, the Via Bissolati and the Via Nazionale in Rome, the Champs-Elysées in Paris, and so on. In this area of competition, of course, lies a concern for house style. For airlines at least an interest in presentation to the public, advertising, design, architecture, is an important feature of competition, competition which is not possible in the broader area of price and in the services offered and in variations of the product. But do not think that competition does not exist; it exists most vigorously, and a feature of it is that the competition is on a narrower front than in the case of many other industries. No one walking down one of the airline streets, if I may call them that, would have any doubt at all that each airline is fiercely and strenuously competing with its principal rivals.

It is true to say that the airline industry is in fact concerned with design problems. Possibly you will feel that not all airlines successfully solve their design problems, but I think that you will probably agree with me that all airlines do have some sort of care for their house style, their corporate identity, the whole of their visual presentation to the public. Indeed, one of the features of life in large urban centres is the proliferation of airline insignia in the streets I have mentioned. Most airlines, again, take great pains to ensure that the markings of their aircraft form part of their general design policy, and that their advertising, and indeed all their visual presentation to the public, conforms to consistent and coherent standards. So that we can say, I think, fairly safely, that the airline industry is an industry which has a climate in which concern for design can grow and flourish. But it is also an industry where competition in price and substantial differentiation of products offered, has for a variety of reasons been ruled out.

I think my thesis is becoming clear to you now, but before I formally enunciate it, I think I should like to look at one or two other industries apparently displaying different tendencies. First of all I think I ought to find an industry making tangible products as distinct from a service industry or one where the product, as in the case of the oil companies, is actually very nearly intangible. Perhaps one should look here for an industry which has been frequently berated for its lack of interest in design. I suppose one thinks in this case of the pottery industry or the furniture industry; both have come in for their fair or unfair share of criticism for their lack of design consciousness.

I submit that in these industries we have a situation quite different from the one I have mentioned above. In the pottery industry or in the furniture industry we might first of all expect to find great design consciousness; after all design ought to be part of the product itself in this case. Both these industries are, to a large extent, bound to be influenced by current shifts in taste or, indeed, even current shifts in fashion, and yet curiously both have come in for a good deal of criticism in the past for their lack of design consciousness. Secondly, it is noteworthy that characteristically both these industries are made up of a large number of small or medium-sized firms. Thirdly, these firms produce widely differentiated products – there is nothing like standard chinaware or pottery, nothing like a standard chair. Further, as you might expect, there is a very wide variation in price as between different products and as between the products of different firms, and finally, perhaps as a consequence of this, their expenditure on visual presentation, on advertising and related matters, is comparatively modest. In other words, the pottery industry and the furniture industry display characteristics quite different from those of the airline industry, the major international oil companies or banking. They are in fact at the opposite end of the scale and they are remarkable because by and large they are alleged to display some lack of consciousness of design, though one would expect exactly the opposite in view of the very nature of their products.

Let me put my thesis now directly. I maintain that a proper care for, and an interest in, design matters will chiefly tend to be found in industries where competition, particularly price competition, has been limited, or is highly imperfect and oligopolistic. I would say that a multiplicity of small firms, each competing for a comparatively small share of the market with widely differentiated products, widely differentiated in price, does not seem to be conducive to development of advanced design policies. But where an industry achieves, *de facto* at least, a reasonably uniform price structure among a few large firms which dominate it, it seems to me almost as though price-fixing, regulation, or what you will, has frustrated an outlet for competitive effort, and that this competitive effort has expended itself among other things in design and the whole spectrum of visual presentation. I might almost venture the thesis that a firm's interest in design matters tends to be inversely proportional to the number and extent of the other competitive weapons, particularly price, which are available to it. It is almost as if the normal competitive urges have been sublimated into the field of design and of course into other fields closely related such as conventional advertising. Let me put the matter another way. Where a firm cannot compete directly by means of price you will find that the urge to compete finds an outlet in advanced and vigorous design policies, including in this the whole visual presentation comprised by house style, by packaging, by product design, and by conventional advertising. But where there are other means of competition readily available to the firm or to the industry then you will find that those weapons of competition, those instruments of competition, are in fact preferred by those firms and those industries to design. I think myself that the explanation of this fact lies partly at least in the nature and implications of a concern for good design. To embark on a programme of design is surely to undertake an investment. A design programme, whether product design or house style is surely nothing if it is not expected to last at least a decade or even longer. I suppose, for example, that the banks have had their characteristic house style for something like fifty or sixty years, and the big international oil companies for thirty or more. I am not thinking, of course, of individual items, but of a firm's conscious design programme and policy.

This is an investment, and indeed it is an investment to which, for balance sheet purposes, at least a large element of good-will might well be attached. There can, I think, be little doubt that the characteristic visual presentation of one of the major international oil companies is an investment in a real sense of the word. If, then, to embark on a design programme is to make an investment, one might expect that the conditions under which a firm is induced to make any medium- or long-term investment might be the same conditions in which a design investment might be made.

From a point of view of a firm if not of society as a whole, a highly competitive situation is fundamentally an unstable one; intensive competition, particularly intensive price competition, tends to inhibit long-term planning. It unsettles and disturbs managements, and although all this may be a good thing from the point of view of society, naturally the inclination of any firm is to try and reduce the instability which is associated with the vigorous activities of its competitors. Without reasonably stable conditions, planning and direction by management will be short term, liable to frequent changes, possibly even barely profitable, and certainly management in these circumstances will be deterred from making any investment other than short-term investment. This is, of course, a familiar enough picture. Even if society regards free competition or something like it as a good thing, it is only a good thing from society's point of view, presumably, because it disquiets individual firms and, as it were, keeps them on their toes. But as I have suggested, this feverish activity of competition, probably price competition, among large numbers of small or medium-sized firms is not likely to be a climate in which a proper care for good design will flourish. If design is to flourish and a design programme is to be regarded as an investment, then I think relatively stable conditions are essential. I think we shall often find this stability where there has been some kind of price regulation, or at any rate, for technological or other reasons, prices of individual firms tend to be the same as those of their competitors. We shall also find this stability when large numbers of small firms in an industry have merged into larger units. But it would be a great mistake to think that because part of the area of competition has been removed or has been neutralized, that for this reason the industry or firms concerned are any less competitive. The residual competition may be very fierce indeed as it is in the airline industry.

I do not pretend to have worked out all the implications of the hypothesis that I have presented for your consideration, namely that in the modern world design is one of the prime instruments of competition available to the industrialist, but at first sight I think this hypothesis does offer a kind of explanation of certain features of the world as designers know it.

For example, many of you may have been uneasy about what I said about the furniture and the pottery industries. Some of you may be saying, 'Ah yes, but there are many small potteries, and of course some not so small, in the industry, which are producing excellent work. How do you fit these into your thesis?' I think I would fit them in, frankly, by saying that in the much more cut-throat world of an industry consisting of comparatively large numbers of comparatively small or medium-sized firms, there will be some potteries which are too inefficient to compete on price; these, then, compete on design. They are, if you like, offering a better quality article at a higher price. Again, design is being used as an instrument of competition.

Let us look at another example. Why is it true by and large that, particularly in the house style sense, only the largest companies and organizations are concerned with the creation of a proper corporate identity, with the creation of a design policy for themselves? The answer too often given, of course, is the question begging one, prestige. But I suggest, perhaps, that the hypothesis that we have entertained does give a more satisfying answer. Big companies would not become so unless they had either neutralized or limited the competition that they faced, especially, perhaps, price competition. Hence it is precisely the big companies, unable or unwilling longer to compete in price, who seek alternative instruments of competition such as a care for the whole visual presentation of their corporation to the public, and indeed also conventional advertising.

Further, if we regard my hypothesis that a proper care for design is an alternative strategy to competition in price, it does perhaps point a way of estimating what a design programme is worth to a company. This, after all, is an important question. If it is proposed to invest, say, £10,000 in any one year in some part of a design programme, it should not be too difficult for a firm to make estimates about the value of this kind of programme in investment terms; after all, in practice, firms are constantly making judgements of this kind, and

I believe that once design matters are seen in the light of being instruments of competition, judging the worth of a design programme should not be too unfamiliar an experience. Or to look at the matter in a slightly different way, if to embark on a design programme is to undertake an investment of a certain amount, it really should not be too difficult for a firm to specify the kind of yield it expects to get from that investment. This, after all, is a day-to-day judgement that any management has to make constantly.

In concluding, I would repeat the warning that I gave earlier. I have attempted to do no more than to say something about the world of design as it looks to a person working in industry in a field where his work impinges on the whole question of design. My hypothesis is unproven, and I have presented it to stimulate thought and if the members of your Society care either to prove or disprove my hypothesis, or perhaps even start an investigation into the incidence of a proper care for good design in industry as a whole, then perhaps I may be well content.

Part VIII
Planning and Development

Introduction

The growth of tourism demand (and also of recreation demand) has led to an awareness of the need to manage that demand, for without management fragile tourist attractions may risk destruction. Many of these fragile attractions are historic sites, others are areas of natural beauty. The problem is not merely one of preventing saturation; the modern tourist is certainly gregarious by choice, and tourist facilities provided must recognize this fact. The tourist (except perhaps for an educated minority) likes being in a crowd of his fellows, he wants the company and he perhaps even seeks the congestion of large numbers. The problem of management is thus how to provide the gregarious experience in fragile attractions, not how to substitute privacy for the crowd.

McCaskey discusses in Chapter 15 the experience of Colonial Williamsburg in the United States. The principal aims of this famous creation are educational, but as often happens demand to visit this unique attraction was outstripping conventional techniques for managing it. There was very little comparable experience in the USA or elsewhere to guide the organization, and the solutions to the day-to-day problems were arrived at by trial and error. Any organization responsible for an historic site will want to consider Colonial Williamsburg's claim to have adapted to the impact of large numbers and at the same time to have enhanced the quality of the visitor's experience of it.

The Donegal project, reported by McCarthy and Dower in Chapter 16, is a classic example of a logical and systematic approach to tourism development. In making plans for the development of Donegal for tourist and recreational use, the authors lay stress on the need to evaluate the capacity of the attraction (for example, a beach) in relation to the existing demand and in relation to the desired level of future demand. This approach has been adopted too infrequently in the past, and failure to attempt an adequate estimate of capacity has been responsible for some of the worst effects of tourists' demands on the environment. No activity of man can be entirely free of environmental effect, but McCarthy and Dower offer a significant approach to estimating that effect and for displaying the policy options entailed.

15 Conservation of Historic Areas – Management Techniques for Tourism in the USA

BY T. G. MCCASKEY

From a paper presented at a Conference on Tourism and the Environment organized by the British Tourist Authority in London on 11 November 1971.

My assignment is to discuss the management controls which made it possible for a continuous experience of high quality to be maintained at Colonial Williamsburg. This outdoor museum, one of the largest in America, has been a major travel destination for over forty years, and while we are a new historic preservation, as compared with some of yours, we have developed a few innovative ideas for controlling the flow of tourism. These may be of interest to you, even though they come from a former hot-bed of revolution.

What is Colonial Williamsburg

Your first question may well be 'what is Colonial Williamsburg?', and I would answer that it is a very small city in the State of Virginia which in the eighteenth century was the capital of the British Colony of Virginia. At that time its boundaries included eight of our present states. Williamsburg was a typical English city and the centre of cultural and social life of the Colony. It was the place where many of America's early leaders lived and worked to found a new nation. Among them were George Washington, Thomas Jefferson, Patrick Henry, Peyton Randolph, and William Byrd. Its heydey was from 1699 until 1780, at which time the capital was moved westward to Richmond.

One hundred and fifty years later, Mr John D. Rockefeller Jr. visited the sleepy remains of Williamsburg and envisioned them to be a window on the past, where Americans might personally experience something of the time when the basic precepts of our nation were conceived. To date approximately £35,800,000 have been spent in the preservation, restoration, and reconstruction of some five hundred buildings, gardens, and greens of this city. Just prior to the start of this work in 1926, Williamsburg was a run-down community, with only its remaining original buildings to comfort its decline from glory. Many former gracious old structures survived without benefit of paint or care. As one native put it, 'we were too poor to paint, and too proud to whitewash'.

Williamsburg Since 1930

Millions of people have visited Williamsburg during its four decades as a travel attraction. They came partly because of its educational and cultural values, but also for its resort facilities and the pleasure of just being in a place which is different from other vacation destinations. Sir Winston Churchill, visiting Williamsburg many times during and after the last war, called it as English as nearly any town in the British Empire.

The colonial capital is now an old city within a new city. The historic area is a mile long, containing many buildings of every size and nature, which have been preserved after meticulous historical and archaeological research. Authenticity has been the watchword of the Williamsburg restoration, and much of our documentary research was done here in England. One of our most priceless discoveries was made in the Bodleian Library at Oxford in 1930. This was a large copper engraving which disclosed precise drawings of the principal public buildings in Williamsburg, some of which had been destroyed by fire.

We have preserved eighty-eight original eighteenth-century structures and reconstructed hundreds more; we have restored eighty-five colonial gardens with only authentic plants of the eighteenth century; we have revived sixteen colonial crafts seldom seen anywhere in America today; and brought together one of the outstanding collections of British and American antiques. Music, games, the foods of two hundred years ago plus many of the daily events of those times all serve now to create an illusion of the past in Williamsburg.

We have tried to emulate our forebears from England, Scotland, Ireland, and Wales by maintaining in our restored village something for the whole man, body and mind and spirit. The men of the eighteenth century in Europe, and also in the American colonies, were confirmed naturalists, alert environmentalists. The woodlands, their gardens and fields, the streams and ponds were, as you know, of paramount interest to them. Today 60 per cent of our travel show is free, with no tickets required for wandering at will through pleasant gardens, craft shops, public buildings and past fascinating outdoor craft demonstrations. Our historic area is an open, lived-in city, without barriers or entrance gates, except those to shut off gasoline-powered vehicles.

In fact, the principal streets are closed to cars and buses. This is an aesthetic benefit first, and second a means of controlling the flow of visitors and their automobiles. Without this closure plan, which went into effect about seven years ago, our colonial atmosphere would have vanished into the confusion of uncontrolled tourism. Such massification can and does kill travel destinations. As it is, visitors can walk the stately Duke of Gloucester Street, using either its varied sidewalks or the street itself, with care only for the occasional carriage or other horse-drawn vehicles. Of course, there are numerous bicycles and tandems.

Significance of the Project

The Colonial Williamsburg Foundation has 3,000 employees dedicated to providing a believable experience in American heritage. Its operation is not motivated by profit, but the extensive visitor facilities in the outer city are very profitable. Here there are rooms to sleep 7,500 persons per night and restaurants and every service to take care of other visitor needs. These have produced substantial income each year for the private operators, for the City and the State of Virginia.

In the outdoor museum field of tourism, the presence of a calm and peaceful atmosphere is necessary. A purposefully created cocoon must offer relief from daily pressures and tensions while an aura of another time, another place is evoked. Strikingly different smells, sounds, and sights all help to build a total picture for the visitor's experience. But most important is a natural, believable environment which Williamsburg tries to reproduce.

The quality controls decided upon by our founder, Mr John D. Rockefeller Jr., resulted in a lasting experience for millions who have visited Williamsburg. The effect has been to enrich both city and the local environment. We attempt to follow closely the philosophy of our founder which calls for operating well above the average standards. This was his life-long formula for success, and it has guided us in developing management techniques in one of America's oldest outdoor museums.

L. P. Jacks, the well-known British philosopher and first editor of *Hibbert's Journal*, once wrote that 'survival of a nation depends on the use of its leisure'. When the Williamsburg motto, that the future may learn from the past, is added to that wisdom, we must conclude that a proper use of leisure is to employ it for the advancement of the national understanding.

We believe that anything worth preserving is worth protecting. Since the beginning of our project in 1928, we have taken all possible measures to guard it. This has not been a deterrent to its growth nor its impact on the economy. To the contrary, it has made sustained growth possible and has heightened the impact through a high standard of presentation.

The Quality Controls

The volume of visitation has grown in Williamsburg about 6 per cent per year over the past fifteen years, and the problem of keeping the experience good has increased proportionally. New limits are set and then surpassed. As they are exceeded, old methods of interpretation and presentation have been upgraded, and former procedures for controlling the flow through our village altered.

Like other business operations we have had to anticipate demand. We have two motivations. The first is to produce sufficient income to support the project, using a taxable department to generate a cash flow which is used to aid the educational, tax-free company. The second is to provide controls which will maintain the quality level of our product. We have found it necessary to stay one step ahead of the co-existing problems and opportunities offered by tourism. This constantly calls for advance thinking and planning, a type of research which we feel is equally important as the historical planning which created the restoration.

Many of our problems were new to the American travel industry, and as a result we were forced to experiment, using trial and error to find correct solutions. Among these experiments were our central information and visitor processing stations, an early trial in managing crowds. When Colonial Williamsburg had been a tourist destination for only sixteen years, we began to realize that as the number of visitors increased, the satisfactions were decreasing. This was because our old system of guiding small groups through the town was being overwhelmed.

Our initial answer to this problem came in 1948 and took the form of a Reception Centre placed between the two existing hotels. It was strictly a temporary structure, a demountable concrete slab warehouse, which was brought in for the experiment. Here we tried our first 'processing' of the visitor, using specially designed brochures and maps, plus a twenty-minute slide presentation to show the recommended highlights of Williamsburg. It worked very well and visitors were not only willing to be processed, but anxious to have a briefing which condensed their visit into a comprehensive audio-visual capsule.

The next experiment was a shuttle system using a rented transit bus to learn if we could remove automobiles from the historic area and thereby preserve its colonial atmosphere. We were also testing to determine if this would make it possible to process more visitors in an organized way during their average stay of two and a half days, without detracting from enjoyment of the city.

We now have twenty-four of these buses, all non-diesels, circling around the perimeter of the old city, stopping near all places of interest. They operate without charge on a five-minute headway the year round. In one year they handle over six million riders, all of whom are absolutely delighted with this free transportation service, tailored to their needs and also to the objectives of the Colonial Williamsburg Foundation. These buses serve to separate the visitors from their automobiles, an essential procedure, since 92 per cent of them arrive by private car.

Another result of early experiments was the building of a very large and efficient Information Centre to keep ahead of increasing numbers of people. It was scientifically designed to 'keeping the marbles rolling downhill', to quote its builder. It was constructed on the outskirts of the historic area, at a place where the incoming highways meet. At this new centre we put into effect the things learned at the old experimental building. This included a one-way flow of visitors from the centre's two ample parking lots, through the indoctrination process, past the ticket booth, into one of two theatres which operate alternately, and then down the escalators into the waiting shuttle buses.

Incidentally, the interiors of these very unusual motion picture theatres were designed to give viewers an intimate relationship with the screen. We use a very large screen and a colour film presentation instead of the former slide show. It does not indicate how or what to see in Williamsburg, but instead, it sets the mood for a visit into another time. In so doing, it re-creates the life of our eighteenth-century village and depicts people of that time, their gardens, customs, games, and amusements along with their problems and challenges. This film provides life of colonial days and plants it in the visitor's mind prior to their tour of Williamsburg. When they actually visit the historic places and buildings, the mind's eye provides authentic action at each scene.

The Summer Peak Problem

During July and August, when visitation is at a peak, an auxiliary Information Centre operates on the South side of town, with its own theatre, a large parking lot, and other facilities which duplicate the North side Centre.

Thus we have settled on a processing plant and a private transportation system to help handle our overcrowding success problem. What else can we do, and what can you do, to deal with this common problem?

For one thing, we at Williamsburg have extended the number of exhibitions in the historic area during the summer peak. Additional craft shops and outdoor demonstrations, and four additional colonial exhibition buildings have recently been opened. As demand grows, the visiting hours run longer, both indoors and out, and interpretation devices change with the flow in visitation.

Special events are major attractors for Williamsburg and are valuable control tools. Among these are a permanent Fife and Drum Corps and a Colonial Militia Company who march and drill, play eighteenth-century instruments, and fire ancient weapons. Their activities are increased during peak weeks. Extra runs by carriages, wagons, and carts provide the auto-free streets with vehicles of the colonial period. Added concerts, plays, and entertainments of colonial vintage are also performed.

Various techniques to keep the summer waiting lines from becoming irksome have been introduced. Among these are costumed musicians and attendants entertaining those waiting to enter; lines run through gardens and in the shade wherever possible; escorts are stationed in each room rather than conducting building tours.

Other Management Controls

A more recent discipline for the peak periods, whether they occur in the spring, summer or fall, involves the restriction of group tours. Many travel attractions in America and in Europe depend on group tours for much of their income, and groups often receive preferential treatment. The Colonial Williamsburg Foundation is a non-profit operation, with educational commitments which we take more seriously than mass income. We feel that we cannot afford uncontrolled group business which brings with it some of the most serious peak visitation problems.

When I visit some of Europe's most historic and meaningful travel attractions and find them totally overwhelmed by bus groups, I wonder if these destinations can afford this mass visitation pattern much longer.

Another control, resulting in greater charm and more believable atmosphere, was the adoption of a life-tenancy programme by our Foundation. By this, the old families of Williamsburg were given life rights in their restored homes after Colonial Williamsburg bought them and the preservation work was completed. This was on a rent- and tax-free basis, and it greatly encouraged local co-operation in the project. All the buildings in Williamsburg's historic area are fully used, lived in daily by people of this century, who conform to the customs of another. They are people living between two centuries and adding life to our outdoor museum.

In order to keep the image of restored Williamsburg before the public, we have a programme of publicity, promotion, and travel advertising. This is particularly active in the fall and spring seasons. However, it is almost abandoned in the summer for control purposes.

This is a self-imposed discipline which we work hard to maintain, even to the point of asking our friends in the newspaper, magazine, and broadcast fields to forget about Williamsburg from June to September.

Incidentally, our advertising and publicity avoids the approach which would indicate that Williamsburg has anything in common with the amusement or theme park presentations. We make no excuse about Williamsburg's being a cultural experience, but stress it as an extremely enjoyable and worthwhile learning activity.

One of the most vital management controls at Colonial Williamsburg occurs during the off season. During the three months of winter, our escorts, hostesses, and all persons who interpret Colonial Williamsburg, engage in an extensive training programme. This not only keeps them busy in the lean months, but also provides them with new information and greater stimulation for the job at hand. Each interpreter is required to have 264 hours in an on-job training programme each year.

We believe wholeheartedly in a face-to-face dialogue with the visitors. Interpretation of our outdoor museum is done by people in the dress of colonial days, and many of them are engaged in the crafts and arts of the eighteenth century as they make their presentations. Our hosts and hostesses are not allowed to remain at the same building for more than two days consecutively. They are rotated often so as to retain sparkle and enthusiasm in their presentations.

Each year, in various seasons, we take in-depth surveys of visitor reactions to determine satisfactions or dissatisfactions with the experience in Williamsburg. This is not a questionnaire left in hotel rooms, but a personal interview on the streets of the historic area. Several thousand persons are thus brought into our thinking and planning process each year.

Visitors are amazed that they do not find the usual litter and the defacement of buildings, fences, washrooms, etc. in Colonial Williamsburg. Our discipline to combat these problems is very simple. We refer to it as the 'Cathedral Theory', which depends on maintaining a pristine appearance as a pyschological defence against littering and defacement. This may be a simple procedure, but it is also a costly one. However, in the long run it is less expensive to avoid these things than to repair or replace properties.

Colonial Williamsburg is also surrounded by an extensive green belt which totals three thousand acres of desirable, valuable land. Shielding the eighteenth-century area from most of the twentieth-century intrusions, this protective zone was acquired throughout the development period. Strict zoning laws have also been valuable protection aids.

The restoration of Historic Williamsburg transformed a tired, down-at-the-heels village into a protected beauty spot. It greatly enhanced the environment for residents and visitors alike, and offers an example of how historic areas and tourism work together for the good of the community. Such places contribute flavour for tourism, providing 'difference', which is a priceless element capable of motivating the desire to travel. In turn, tourism will enhance and perpetuate historic areas by making them economically viable.

Historic attractions enable visitors to get more than an empty wallet from tourism, giving them something meaningful for their time, trouble, and expense. Modern techniques of interpretation based on solid historical research are the touchstone for making history play a full role in world travel.

The Results

This recitation should give you an idea of what Colonial Williamsburg is all about and why we have adopted some unusual controls. But the question might be asked, what has all this done for us? In response, I ask you to remember Williamsburg, Virginia of 1920, before its restoration, by-passed by westward expansion, tired, and drab. Its population was only 1,000 persons and the economy was equally small. Williamsburg continued chiefly because two public institutions were located there, the College of William and Mary, founded by Royal Charter in 1693, and the Eastern State Hospital for the Insane.

Preservation and tourism combined to bring it back to full life. Today the area population is twenty times its former size, and almost all of its people labour in the fields of tourism. A whole new economy, built around the care and feeding of visitors, has transformed a sleepy village of the nineteen-twenties into a prosperous and beautiful centre of arts, crafts, heritage, and culture. Williamsburg has become an international destination, known by tourists and scholars as a year-round attraction with a wide range of interests.

Approximately one million visitors, each of whom spends about twenty pounds on a two-day stay, contribute an estimated £20·5 million to the Williamsburg area annually. Visitors on their way to and from Williamsburg are said to spend an equal amount in the State of Virginia during their journey of several days.

Therefore, we estimate that its economic impact is £41 million annually, attributable to one small town, an historic attraction known as Colonial

Williamsburg. State officials have estimated that the tax revenues resulting from the Williamsburg visitation alone could have made its preservation an economically feasible undertaking.

We have learned that many people, who are more cursed than blessed by new-found leisure, are looking for quality experiences on their holidays. Many seek new dimensions and more meaning for their lives in the hectic, harried society of this century. They are looking for just such places as Williamsburg to escape from the mediocrity and the mass-produced stimuli of today. They are looking in America, in Germany, Japan, and equally or perhaps even more so in Great Britain.

In Summary

The Colonial Williamsburg historic preservation achieves five general objectives:

1. It teaches history and illustrates heritage;
2. It demonstrates a different life style which can be enlightening to our society;
3. It offers beauty in a controlled environment under responsible management;
4. It promotes respect for the land and also for the environment;
5. Williamsburg helps to inspire hope for the future, particularly among the younger generation.

As the shock of rapid change arises in tempo, historic places with an environment of quiet and order, of beauty and good taste, which maintain high standards of quality will be of increasing importance to the world's tourist structure. Through a self-imposed discipline, by individuals like yourselves, to maintain the high standards required for a meaningful travel experience, our industry will make a lasting contribution to society.

The United Kingdom has excellent national organizations to guide and aid in the development of tourism, such as the Authority under which this meeting is called. But there is probably plenty of room for private initiative and for action at the city and county levels. It is here that historic tourism can mean the most, for it thrives best on effective measures of control where the sites are located.

The travel industry of the world today is concerned over a wide variety of pollutions which plague it. Crowding, noise, litter, overbuilding, foul odours, ugly sights, oil spills, impure air, and polluted water are all symptoms of an illness which directly results in a decrease of aesthetic and economic values of tourism. We are searching for the solutions to these problems. I know of no better place to start than by protecting and improving the quality of the travel experience with as much zeal as is put into the pursuit of profit. We should realize that declining standards are the basic ailment. These must be raised if we are to restore the quality and vitality of our travel industry. Working together, I feel certain that we can find answers for all our 'sliding down' problems.

You have heard what we are doing in Virginia, and some of these techniques can be applied to your problems. However, some of them cannot for each attraction is a separate thing. It is up to every individual area to work out basic quality controls, which will be ideally suited to its problems. These must be chosen well so as to protect the travel destination and also the total environment. The time to start is now, for we must live with conditions which we either create or allow, for the remainder of our lives.

16 *Planning for Conservation and Development – an Exercise in the Process of Decision-making*

BY P. E. MCCARTHY AND M. DOWER

From the *Journal of the Town Planning Institute*, Volume 53, No. 3, (Town Planning Institute, London, March 1967).

Introduction

The project from which this article springs is based in Ireland. But we believe it has a much wider significance as a contribution to a theme of growing moment in every western country – the development of tourism and leisure opportunities, coupled with the conservation of natural resources.

Almost every country is seeing dramatic growth and change in the pattern of leisure and recreation among its own people. Almost every country is seeking to increase the number of visitors from abroad. At the same time, country after country is showing more and more active concern with the conservation of its scenic and cultural heritage, a heritage threatened not only by the general pace of development but notably by the very leisure, tourism, and recreation for which it is the prime resource.

The paradox and link between development and conservation, between visitors and resources, between access and beauty, are seen very clearly in both North America and Europe. In the United States, growing controversy centres on the amount and type of recreation facility which should be provided in the National Parks. In Britain, the National Park Authorities struggle to keep in balance their two objects, the protection of natural beauty and the encouragement of public access.

The struggle for the countryside, in fact, is becoming everywhere more complex. The tourist, the farmer, the sportsman, and the resident himself all claim title to its use. Each has his own activity for which he can make a good case. Each, if given the chance, would exclude one or all of the others.

In this circumstance, the emotion of a Ruskin or William Morris, even the insight of a Thoreau, are not enough. The system of taking decisions must match the new complexity and scale of pressures. Who shall determine the manner and method? In the western world, it is not clear that this can be done by either Government alone or private enterprise alone. Each has a large, but not a complete, stake.

Thus much of the resources, both of land and of enterprise, lie in private hands. But large-scale private development may demand public investment in support services on the same large scale. One thousand new hotel beds may imply heavy public cost in new water, sewerage, and road systems, and may place heavy new pressures upon beaches and park lands which the public bodies maintain. Yet the public authority may feel that these costs and pressures are not balanced by the benefits of new income for its ratepayers.

Reconciling development and conservation thus depends upon a skilful sorting out of goals and values, both public and private. The tool increasingly used in many countries to do this is the physical development or land use plan. But the nature of this plan is critical. Too often it is a rigid statement of views by the public authority, reflecting their goals only, responsive neither to the legitimate values of the private land-owner or the citizen, nor to the fact of rapid change and wide range of opportunity.

As we see it, a planning system concerned to reconcile development and conservation must have a framework to bring together all parties, public and private, concerned with both themes. Notably, this must include the public bodies who are responsible for spending public money and for protecting such public values as the scenic heritage; the commercial interests whose concern is to exploit resources and promote development; and the private groups who seek to protect private rights or minority values. This bringing together of people demands a common language or understanding of problems; and a process for resolving differences and making decisions.

The planning system must also be flexible in time and in scale. There is no absolute or all-time best use of a resource or a piece of land. The pattern of demand changes over the years. A beach once used only by local people may prove, with changing access patterns, to be a regional asset of the first importance. It must be possible to make and remake decisions – but to do so within a system that shows up clearly the consequences of considered changes by measuring them against standards of performance and in terms of benefit and cost. It was the object of the Irish project to formulate such a system.

The Project in Ireland

Ireland has a magnificent heritage of scenery, historic sites, and wild life – a heritage virtually unaffected by industrialization. With a population that has fallen from 9 million in 1840 to about 3 million now, it has not suffered the pressures of spoliation which have afflicted both America and much of Europe. But the Irish Government is keen to boost income from tourism, as part of its general drive to improve Ireland's economy. They know that their main tourist asset is the scenic and cultural heritage; and they realize that this heritage must be protected as development grows.

To this end, the Government in 1963 passed the Local Government (Planning and Development) Act, which for the first time required local authorities in Ireland to prepare development plans. To assist the authorities in carrying out this new and unfamiliar function, the Minister for Local Government set up the National Institute for Physical Planning and Construction Research. This Institute is assisted by experts supplied by the United Nations Special Fund. One of the first projects was the launching of a model amenity-tourism study for the beautiful county of Donegal (*see* Figure 16.1), by a team including

Figure 16.1 Location of Donegal

officers of the National Institute and of Donegal County Council, together with ourselves as United Nations Advisers.

The object of the Donegal exercise was not so much to produce a plan for the county as to create a thought process which could be pursued by all the local planning authorities in Ireland. These authorities are multi-purpose bodies, responsible *inter alia* for the roads, water, and sewerage services, and public housing in their areas. The planning function is new to them, and very few of them have qualified planning staff. It was therefore necessary to create a thought process which could be used at once by small and untrained staffs but which could grow in sophistication as their information and expertise increased.

At the same time, Ireland has many other bodies, public and private, involved in her general process of development; a rapidly growing tourist industry based almost wholly upon private enterprise but assisted by a central Tourist Board; and a small number of amenity and other heritage-protecting bodies who are able and willing to help the conservation effort. It was therefore vital to involve them not only in the plan-making process but also in whatever system of decision-making was to be proposed.

The Thought Process

After some trial and error, a simple six-step thought process was evolved on these lines:

1. Survey of amenity and tourism resources
2. Survey of client groups
3. Measurement of capacity
4. Statement of options
5. Amenity budget
6. Policy implications.

The first two steps are traditional surveys, carried out by the planning staff with information and help from other bodies. That of resources covers a fairly wide range, including the broad patterns of land use and landscape character; the main scenic resources; the potential for shooting, fishing, hill-walking, pony trekking, and water sports; man-made recreational facilities such as golf courses; the cultural, historical, and scientific heritage; communications; and the accommodation and services which the county could offer to the tourist. The only unfamiliar thing here was the use of a comprehensive survey data sheet, showing all the resource items for which field survey was needed on a standard sheet which could be readily used as an office record.

The form of the survey of client groups was dictated by the material available, which was more national than local in application. It did permit reasonably accurate estimates of the numbers of visitors in each of several national groups coming to the county; the season in which they came; their length of stay and expenditure. Information on the occupancy of hotels and other accommodation permitted a rough estimate of where the visitors stayed within the county. The numbers of local people present and likely to be using leisure resources was also calculated.

Capacity – The Key

The third step in the thought process is the critical one. When the resources and the clients have been surveyed, one must find a way to compare them directly with each other, in order

(a) to see how far the resources are, or are not, adequate for the present use of the clients;
(b) to judge what surplus resources there are which might entertain or serve more people and what new resources would be needed if more people came; and
(c) to ensure that the resources are not damaged by an excessive growth in the number and activity of people.

The last point is critical when one is dealing with conservation and development. On the one hand, amenity resources must be protected: on the other, tourism and recreation must be encouraged. A way must be found to balance goals of conservation with goals of development.

The key to this problem is the idea of capacity. Each resource – hotels, beaches, golf courses, cafés, water supplies, roads and so on – has a measurable capacity in terms of people. The capacity of each resource must be kept in balance with the people using it. If the people exceed the capacity, the result may be discomfort, danger or damage to the resource.

The theme, in fact, is not unlike the Buchanan formula for towns – that a given area of countryside has a measurable capacity to take people: this capacity cannot be exceeded without congestion and damage to the resources unless the capacity is increased by physical works. Such works might include provision of access to beaches or improved anti-pollution measures on reservoirs used for sport.

In order to measure capacity, and so to compare resources and clients directly, we pursued a simple sequence of thought. First, we divided the county into 'planning areas', each of such a size that the people living within or visiting it could be expected to have the bulk of their activity, and hence of their demand upon resources, within that area. This was necessary because the measurement of capacity cannot usefully be done at county scale: a beach at one end of Donegal could not be regarded as useful to a tourist 50 miles away at the other end of the county.

Then we identified a 'resource base', i.e. those resources which were critical to the development of tourism and recreation. Ten resource items were chosen: night accommodation (non-casual); night accommodation (casual); day resources; wet-weather facilities; meal facilities; evening facilities; water supply; sewerage; road capacity; and public transport. These explain themselves, except for the two types of night accommodation. 'Casual' includes caravan and camp sites plus youth hostels, since these tend to serve a different type of visitor from the 'non-casual' (hotel, guesthouse, and other types).

We then assessed the 'existing capacity' of the surveyed resource in each of the ten categories for each planning area. This was a straightforward matter for most categories, the basis being the beds or bed-spaces in night accommodation; seats in wet-weather, meal and evening facilities, and in public transport; gallons a day in water supply and sewerage schemes; and passenger car units per day of 'tolerable capacity' on main roads, estimated on formulae similar to those in the *US Highway Manual*. The one category on which existing capacity was not so readily estimated was day resources. This includes natural resources such as beaches and mountains; items of heritage such as historic sites and nature reserves; as well as man-made day facilities such as golf courses. Day resources are thus the meeting point of conservation and development. For them, the estimate of capacity must serve not only to show how much of the resource is needed by a given number of people, but also how many people the resource can take without physical or ecological damage to the resource and without change to the character which people expect the area to have, unless that change is deliberate.

Capacity of Day Resources

We therefore made a provisional estimate (informed guess, if you like) of the capacity of each type of day resource to take people at any one time in the context of Donegal. This is a quiet and remote county, with slim resources. The county council cannot devote much manpower or money to maintenance; nor do visitors expect to find Coney Island or Brighton densities on the beaches. The capacity estimates were therefore set at a level calculated to minimize the risk of physical or ecological damage; and to match the sense of quietness and remoteness which people might seek in Donegal.

The estimates of notional capacity include low basic marks for all enclosed rural land (5 people per square mile), rough or hill land (1 person per square mile), coast and lake-shore (40 people per mile): plus additional marks for specific activities such as shooting, fishing, and hill walking, or for special qualities of attraction and accessibility. To give one example, an attractive and accessible beach, one mile long, might be marked as having the following capacity:

Basic mark for coast	40 people
Attractive and accessible coast	+200
Beach	+200
	440 people

This total estimated capacity of 440 people to the mile of beach can be used as a guide to the number of people who might be happily occupied on the beach without crowding; to the level of human use beyond which physical or ecological damage might occur to the beach or its surroundings; and to the scale of roads, car parks, etc., which would go with or provide access to the beach.

The next step is to estimate the demand that the people present in each planning area at any one time place upon the resources which make up the resource base of that area. To do this, we split the people into three main groups, each with a different pattern of demand upon resources:

(*a*) night visitors
(*b*) day visitors
(*c*) local people

and we then estimated what that demand might be. Again, for some resources this was easy. For example, for water supply, the following basic formula was well established in the county:

$$\text{Demand for water} = 70a + 10b + 100c \text{ gallons a day}$$

i.e. 70 gallons a day would be needed for each night visitor present, 10 for each day visitor, 100 for each local resident (including industrial and agricultural as well as domestic consumption).

But for some resources, new formulae had to be evolved. Thus we estimated the demand for day resources as follows:

$$\text{Demand for day resources} = \tfrac{5}{4}(a + b + \tfrac{c}{4}) \text{ people-units}$$

i.e. the total day resources should be sufficient to entertain all the night visitors, all the day visitors, and up to one-quarter of the local population (e.g. children on holiday) at any one time, plus a one-quarter margin to allow for a bad match between the types of resource available and the desire of people to use them.

These calculations of demand for each resource allowed us to express a 'necessary capacity' for these resources arising from a given number and mix of clients. This necessary capacity could then be directly compared with the existing capacity to show how far that existing capacity was adequate for present demand or what surpluses or shortfalls there might be.

A graphic example of this comparison is shown in Figure 16.2, which shows

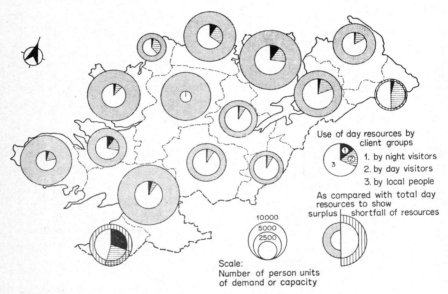

Figure 16.2 Comparison of existing capacity of day resources with current use

the existing capacity of one resource category, day resources, compared with the use of those resources by clients at present. Each circle refers to one planning area. Several striking things at once emerge:

(a) the strong dominance of the coastal areas in existing resource capacity (as shown in most cases by the outer circles);

(b) the uneven pattern of use or demand upon these resources, strongest in the east of the county (as shown by the three-part circles);

(c) the large part which the local population play in this demand (as shown by the white part of the three-part circles);

(*d*) the fact that two planning areas at the north-east and south-west corners of the county have a shortfall in resource capacity, i.e. demand is already above the level estimated as consistent with character and avoidance of damage. This is confirmed by actual experience in these areas;

(*e*) all the other planning areas have a (generally handsome) surplus of day resources not now used.

In a county of such marked scenic and cultural heritage, known for its beauty and quietness, the presence of this surplus of day resources (largely, in fact, natural resources) is the main reassurance that further development can be made compatible with conservation. If the existing capacity were already exhausted (as may well be the case in large parts of, say, the Lake District National Park in Britain), one would know that further development could not take place without either accepting over-use and hence damage to the natural resources or changing the character of the county by the introduction of man-made day resources such as holiday camps.

Statement of Options

The estimates of capacity, no longer merely qualitative but based on direct and refinable measurements, thus become the ground for the consideration of future policy. This is approached, as the fourth main step in the thought process, by the statement of options.

No county has a single, all-time, obvious course of development. There are always choices, each reflecting a different set of goals or values. To weigh the choices against each other, it is necessary to pose them as distinct options. Each option is a simplified goal or aim, different from the other options. This does not mean that only one goal or aim can be pursued at the same time, or that one option could not complement or follow the other. It is simply a method of showing the implications of various possible policies, in such a way that one can judge their relative merits and see whether they could be usefully applied together; in sequence; or as alternatives.

Each option must take into account both development and conservation. This is done by arguing straight on from the earlier steps in the thought process, with its emphasis on clients and resources. Each option has an element of both, by answering two questions:

1. How might a group, or groups, of clients grow or change?
2. If so, how might their growth or change be disposed to have the best impact on resources?

Each option is based, in fact, upon either a notional change in client groups and their effect on resources, or a notional change in impact on resources and its implications for change in client groups. Each option chosen must be relevant and reasonable for the county, based upon appraisal of its resources and of its present or potential clients.

In the Donegal exercise, the options chosen for analysis were:

1. An increase in 'holidaymakers', i.e. those staying for the bulk of their holiday at one place in the county, made up in terms of national groups and types of people according to the share which the county might reasonably expect of the increases in holidaymakers foreseen by the Irish Tourist Board.
2. An increase in 'tourists', i.e. those moving through or within the county on tour, with their make-up estimated as for holidaymakers but distinguished from holidaymakers because of their different pattern of pressure on resources. Both 'tourists' and 'holidaymakers' fall within the general group of night visitors.
3. An increase in day visitors from outside the county, mostly coming across the international border from Northern Ireland.
4. An increase in all three groups at the same time. (No increase in the other main client group, local population, was projected in Donegal at this stage because the other sections of the Development Plan were not at that time available.)

The 'client mix' implied by each option was based on the projection of estimates up to 1985. But this date was not taken as binding for the reason that one element of choice, or of response to circumstances, will be to go faster or slower than a given projection. We decided it was more realistic to talk about units of clients, growth by one unit being a notional target, than to set a number-at-a-given-date as a target.

Each option became expressed as an increase in clients of a given mix, by units of a given size. Thus the unit in the first option might be 1,000 people, all holidaymakers: that for the fourth option might also be 1,000 people, of which 500 would be holidaymakers, 200 tourists, 300 day visitors. No limit was placed on the speed of development; and each option was taken, for purpose of analysis, up to the point where all the day resources (here taken as the major limiting factor, for reasons stated above) would be fully used.

Once each option was expressed as a client mix in stated units, the impact of each such unit upon resources could be assessed. It was easy to calculate how much of each resource in the resource base would be required by each unit in that mix, using the formulae for necessary capacity described earlier. This new necessary capacity could then be compared with the existing capacity to see what new shortfalls were created and what surplus capacity remained.

Amenity Budget

Most of the material was thus ready for the final stage in the analysis, the preparation of the amenity budget. This was seen not only as a straight capital budget in the traditional sense, with financial costs and benefits set out and compared; but also as a chance to take stock of non-financial resources, notably those limited and perishable natural resources which formed the character and prime asset of the county. The amenity budget is in fact the point at which all the foregoing analysis crystallizes into a single statement.

The basic tool used for this purpose was a budget diagram, of which Figure 16.3 is an example. It shows the impact of Option I (increase in the night visitors) upon the resources of one planning area in Donegal. The main elements in it are as follows:

1. The total number of clients present in 1964, represented by column *D* up to the first strong horizontal line.
2. Ten columns, from *E* to *Q*, representing the resource base.
3. The present use of these resources, shown by the strong horizontal line marked 1964, which is also the base line for the options.
4. The upward extension of column *D* showing the possible future growth of clients by units of 1000 up to the line labelled 'ultimate', which represents the full use of day resources in column *J*.
5. The boxes at the base of the diagram show the amount of each resource which is needed by each unit of 1000 clients; and also the cost of providing the unit of resource if this is necessary.
6. The white columns above the 1964 line in columns *J* to *Q* shows the surplus existing capacity in these resources, scaled by the unit size mentioned above.
7. Thus the horizontal line opposite each unit number (+1, +2, etc.) shows the extent to which each unit of increase in clients will eat into surplus resources (white columns) or create shortfalls (vertical hatching). These shortfalls represent the need for new investment, assessed according to the unit costs shown below. (The upper part of column *J* is shown hatched because beyond a certain point investment, e.g. in access roads, is needed to realize the capacity of the day resources.)
8. The combined costs of making good all shortfalls can then be calculated for each unit of increase in clients. These combined costs are shown in column *R*.
9. These total costs can then be compared with the benefits shown in columns *S*, *T*, and *U*, which represent:
   S Total client expenditure: this is the estimated annual expenditure represented by each unit of clients in column *D*.
   T Employment in tourism: this is an estimate of the number of people directly employed in tourism during the summer as a result of the presence of each unit of clients in column *D*.
   U Rateable value: this is an estimate of the total rateable value of properties wholly used for tourism by each unit of clients in column *D*. It is based upon average rateable values per bed in hotels and guesthouses and per seat in evening facilities.

In columns *R* and *S*, the actual amounts of total cost and total client expenditure involved by each unit of increase in clients are shown. This represents the first step toward a direct cost-benefit analysis. This analysis can show at once not

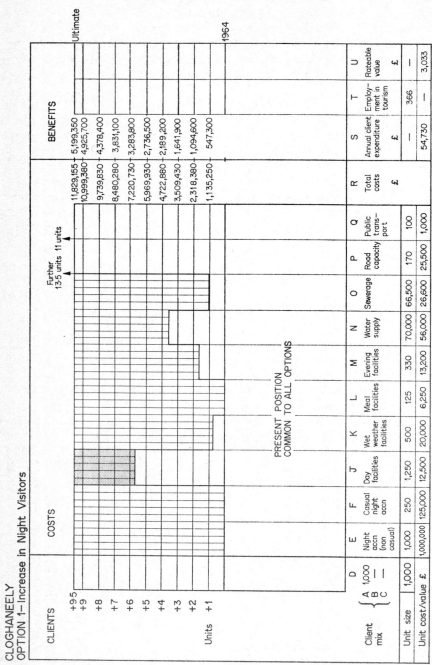

Figure 16.3 Example of a budget summary

only the scale of the cost or benefit, but also the incidence of it – for example to public bodies where road or water supply investment is needed, to private enterprise largely where hotel investment is involved. However, we emphasize that the budget diagram is a neutral document. It does not make decisions: it merely shows, in a clear and comparative way, the implications of a given course of action.

Plan-budget Process

We envisage that one such diagram would be prepared for each option in each planning area. This would, of course, be only part of a complete plan-budget process. Clearly the main strategic options would be formulated at county scale. It would then be necessary to express and examine them at each planning area; and then to proceed to more exact physical and financial appraisal at the scale of the individual resource. We therefore posed a formal plan-budget process, illustrated in Figure 16.4. This process is suitable not only for the preparation

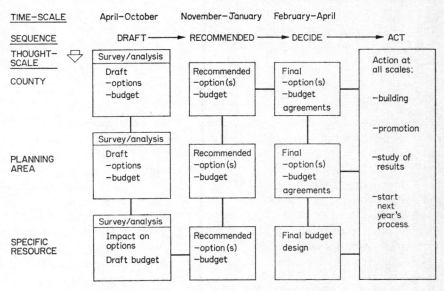

Figure 16.4 Annual plan – budget process

of the initial plan and its regular review; but also for the preparation of annual budgets. There are three levels in the process – county, planning area, individual resource. The plan-budget process moves from one level to the next during the sequence of thought.

For the initial plan or review, the process starts with the full stages of survey and analysis stated earlier at county scale. The draft options are stated for the county; and a tentative budget is proposed, mainly in the sense of the capital which the county feel that they and other bodies might make available. These options and draft budget are examined at planning area scale, and a set of budget diagrams are produced on the lines shown in Figure 16.3. A plan is then prepared to show the possible impact of each option on the specific resources of the planning area. If necessary, detailed study is done at resource scale to decide what this impact might be and what consequent costs might occur.

It may be very clear from this study of specific resources that one option would be preferred. The recommendation might therefore come from the level of a specific resource to the planning area. From the planning area then comes a recommended option and budget to be put together at county level with the recommendations from other planning areas. At the county level, the sets of material from the planning areas are put together to form recommended options and budget, upon which final decisions are then made. These final decisions form the basis not only for the county council's own action but also for discussion and agreement with other bodies who may be involved. This is the moment when contact between public and private bodies is most forcefully needed.

When the decisions and agreements have been reached, their implications for each planning area are expressed. This is then reflected in the final budgets and design briefs for each resource. Action then follows at all three levels, not only in the form of building and promotion, but also in on-going study which can provide a continuous checking and refinement of the decisions which have been made.

Annual Budgeting

To assist the annual budgeting, the process is repeated each year following the approval of the initial development plan, and follows the same series of steps. Thus each year it is necessary to check at county scale the impact of previous decisions, and of any other changes that have occurred in the resources or the clients and hence in the options which are available; and to state draft options and budgets for that year. A check is then made of similar changes at the planning area scale, and draft planning area. Any changes in the capacity or usage of specific resources are then noted and the implications of the proposed options in terms of cost are calculated.

Recommendations are then made for specific changes in resources, and hence for options and budgets for each planning area; and these options and budgets are brought together at county scale. The county can then decide the final options and budget for that year, and possibly the draft options and budgets for an on-going period of five years, at the county scale; and make agreements with other bodies accordingly. These decisions and agreements for action are expressed at planning area scale, and design work on specific resources is put in hand. Action is then pursued at all scales, including a start on the plan-budget process for the following year.

The process is deliberately a merry-go-round, with the end of each year's work being simply the start of the next. Planning is a continuous process, depending upon the constant refinement of information and constant checking

of decisions as the years go by. Planners often take years to gather the information that will satisfy their desire for accuracy. But the world will not wait for
years; and many a chance may be lost or resource destroyed while the search
for fact is being carried out.

The plan-budget process allows for action to start with tentative information.
But it also provides for the checking and improvement of this information which
must be done if large-scale action is to be safely launched. Annual planning
and budgeting with careful back-checking and feed-back will make the budget
process a more and more accurate tool for making decisions. Using it in this
manner will soon eliminate a large portion of the guess-work in both the public
and private pursuit of conservation and development.

Policy Implications

Most of the policy implications arising from the Donegal study were straightforward and predictable. The most important of these were the emphasis upon
the need for constant refinement of information over the years; for careful
relating of the amenity-tourism material to other sections of the County Development Plan and to the more local plans for towns in the county; and for the
protection of the county's heritage and resources either because they are already
in use or because they are the raw material for future development.

But the most profound implication which emerges quite clearly from the study,
indeed from the very premises set out in the introduction to this article, is the
need not only for a thought process which can involve all the many interested
bodies, public and private – but also for an organizational focus for those
interests.

The amenity-tourism study has convinced us that there must be, at county
scale, an organization capable:

(*a*) of ensuring the collection and collation of information, and its gradual
refinement over the years;

(*b*) of ensuring a steady progress on the preparation of the County Development Plan and of local studies;

(*c*) of co-ordinating the protection of amenity and tourism resources; and

(*d*) of ensuring the co-ordination of action and investment programmes by
the whole range of bodies, public and private, involved in conservation
and development.

The last of these points is perhaps the most important. Conservation and
development, like urban renewal in America, need co-ordination of action and
investment by multiple interests. There must be an acceptable focus for both
strategic and annual agreements, if necessary of formal or contractual type,
between these interests.

For example, an important (and possibly a dominant) element of investment
in a tourism plan may be new hotels, built by private enterprise. The building of
hotels may demand new public investment in water supplies, sewerage schemes,

and roads. The private interests will wish to be assured that these services will be created: the public interests will need to be satisfied that the hotels will be built to justify their investment. Each side may therefore seek formal agreement from the other, and from any other parties involved.

This implies the creation of a new body, or the extension of some existing body, at county scale, and consisting of representatives of the county planning authority, other public bodies concerned with amenity and tourism, and private enterprise interests.

This body would have a liaison rather than executive function, but would have the main responsibility for pushing forward the full range of programmes necessary for the coherent pursuit of policies for the development and conservation in the county.

We further believe that this county body must be complemented by a similar, though less powerful body, in each planning area. This would be responsible for the collecting of necessary information in the planning area, and for focusing interest and enterprise relevant to conservation and development within that area. It might take the form of a formalized and strengthened local development association.

Conclusion

We believe that the success of either conservation or development objectives depends upon striking a balance between them. This balance must recognize the effect which actions taken by either the public or the private sector will have on the well-being of people and of their heritage and resources. The thought process described in this article is therefore designed to do five things: to gather the material needed for the process of decision-making in this field; to measure the capacity of the raw and processed resources; to state the relationships between the human, physical, and economic components involved; to set a clear process that permits regular overview to the public and private actors in both conservation and development; and to create a focus for comparison, compromise, and choice by all parties. We very much hope that other people may take whatever opportunity they have to use and improve upon these ideas.

Part IX
Tourism Policies

Introduction

By its nature, tourism is a visible, recognizable phenomenon, which not infrequently arouses a degree of xenophobia in the populations of the resort areas. Something can be done to mitigate this hostility if the resident population knows and approves the government's policy on tourism. Few governments have had the vision, courage, and the ability to think through a policy for tourism; by 1974, five years after the Development of Tourism Act, the United Kingdom still lacked a policy for tourism. For the commercial sector (hotels, airlines, tour operators, and others), the absence of a policy means lack of guidance and uncertainty; for the official tourist organization it may mean misdirected effort.

Eden's address in Chapter 17 is remarkable for being the nearest thing to a policy guidance that the UK has seen. It is as relevant today as it was on the day of its delivery. Eden attempts to position tourism within his Government's overall objectives, examines the position of tourism within regional policies, and delineates the respective roles of government, of the public sector (tourist boards, local authorities), and of the commercial sector in the development of tourism. He makes no easy assumption that tourism is either wholly good or wholly bad, and his successors in office might well re-read this address, even if their approach to tourism may be different from his.

The man in the street does not recognize New York, Paris or London as tourist resorts, a role they have always played, and as resorts they extend well beyond Fifth Avenue, the Champs-Elysée or Buckingham Palace. From time to time, tourism becomes a political issue, and this has occurred in London again in the early 1970s.

Maison's article in Chapter 18 makes a comparison of the organization, policy, and impact of tourism between the UK, the Netherlands, France, and Greece. Maison correctly identifies the importance of metropolitan tourism although it is not new; visitors flocked to London before Bournemouth or Blackpool were built. But comparative studies of this kind are few and this one should assist in the resolution of the approach of cities to tourism. The article is concerned in the main with international tourism and with the response of four cities to the challenge of tourism.

The text of Eden's speech was issued in May 1971 as a DTI Press Notice, and is reproduced with the kind permission of the Controller of Her Majesty's Stationery Office. We are also grateful to the Greater London Council for permission to reprint Maison's article.

17 Tourism and the Government

BY SIR JOHN EDEN

An opening address to the one-day conference on The Nature and Future of the English Holiday Market, organized by the English Tourist Board at Coventry on 17 May 1971.

In a modern state Government policies in many fields affect tourism both directly and indirectly. It is natural that those who are engaged in the industry whether as local authorities or as members of the commercial interests concerned, should want to know where the Government stands.

One of the great advantages of having a new Government – from time to time, that is; we mustn't make a habit of it! – is that, coming fresh to office, it is in a marvellous position to take a long hard look at all existing Government activities and expenditure. Some of the activities may no longer be appropriate; some areas on which money has been spent may no longer need support. In other cases the activities or the financial support may be directed towards objectives which need to be reviewed or revised.

So when I took on my present responsibilities I asked myself three, questions:

Why had successive administrations put public money into the support of tourism?

Were there good reasons for continuing expenditure from public funds in the interests of this sector of our economic life?

If so, were the present objectives the right ones?

The answer to my first question was fairly straightforward. Successive administrations had backed tourism because of the importance of its foreign currency earnings to our balance of payments. Substantial Government funds have been provided for overseas promotion with the objective of achieving the maximum growth in earnings, and maximum benefit to the balance of payments from this source.

But as time went by it became apparent that something more was needed. It was not enough just to encourage visitors to our shores. We had to be sure that, once here, adequate accommodation was available for them. So Government financial assistance was extended for this purpose by means of the Hotel Development Incentives Scheme.

The impact of this policy has profoundly affected the thinking of all who are engaged in tourism in this country. Many places which traditionally receive few overseas visitors have been anxious to secure the kind of facilities which they believe will attract them. For tourism success has been measured in terms of the proportion of foreign visitors secured.

This remains a yardstick of the very greatest importance. We must continue to increase our earnings from foreign visitors; and we must see to it that the success we have had so far is sustained by a much wider spread of these visitors over the country as a whole. These objectives will most certainly still have our active support. And by support I mean cash.

The UK Government puts more into overseas promotion for tourism than any of our competitors. This year we plan to give the BTA a grant in aid of £3·5 million.

This has been a sound investment which has so far yielded a handsome dividend. But we must not relax our efforts. We have grown used in the past few years to an ever-increasing flow of visitors from overseas. Last year the total reached the record of 6¾ million – more than double the 1964 figure of 3¼ million. And in the first three months of this year the total has been 600,000 more than in the first three months of any previous year.

The March figures actually show a drop compared with those of March 1970. This is mainly due to special factors – our Easter visitors last year appeared in the March figures; this year they will be in those for April. But this 'hiccough' should at least jolt us into the realization that we cannot take anything for granted. To continue to increase our overseas earnings from tourism means more hard work, both here and abroad.

But important though all this undoubtedly is, the tourists' contribution to our balance of payments should not be the only objective of our tourism policy.

When I moved on to my second and third questions, and considered the justification for continuing expenditure of public funds on tourism, it became clear that our objectives needed to be reviewed and broadened. As a result of concentrating so much effort and attention on our balance of payment problems we have come close to ignoring other no less vital aspects of the tourism scene. For example, tourism can be a factor of major significance in evening up the balance between the major industrial areas and the rest of the country. Of course it needs imagination and drive but the scope for tourism in this country is enormous. It provides a form of economic activity which can be successfully introduced in areas which are totally unsuited to industrial development and it helps bring the wealth earned in one part of the country to be spent in another.

In failing over past years to realize the importance of tourism to our regional policies the full value of the domestic tourist market has been overlooked. The home holidaymakers are the backbone of the holiday industry in this country. It is their expenditure which helps to bring prosperity to areas which otherwise might never know it. We realize that when people go abroad for their holiday the host country benefits from the money they spend there. But we have not sufficiently recognized the value to us here of the holidaymaker who stays at home. By moving on holiday from one part of this country to another they help to spread our resources and in this way make a valuable contribution to the battle against both inflation and regional unemployment problems.

In many parts of the country, I know, great effort is made to meet the needs of the home holidaymaker. Nowadays that means increasing flexibility and variety and a readiness to adopt changing requirements. But overall, this has tended to take second place to the pursuit of the overseas visitor. There are no doubt good reasons for this – their higher expenditure per head being one factor – but we need to keep things more in balance. Perhaps the main reason for this rather unenthusiastic response to the demands of a growing home holiday market is that too many have failed to appreciate its importance.

It has not been given the degree of priority it deserves.

Our own understanding of this was amply demonstrated during the passage through Parliament of the Development of Tourism Bill, when we took the lead in creating the English Tourist Board. The Board has a special responsibility for encouraging the expansion of the home market; and I am sure that this will be carried out in a way which will have regard to the economic requirements of the regions.

Our new proposals to offer £1 million to help tourist projects in development areas in Great Britain announced by the Chancellor last October springs directly from the wider objectives which we have set ourselves. For the first time we shall be offering a wide range of projects which help to provide attractions for tourists. For the first time this will be done on a selective basis. The funds available are limited – and rightly so. We do not aim to help all tourist projects in these areas; we do not even aim to help most tourist projects. The new measures are designed for the special case. They provide a means of triggering off development where tourist potential is not fully realized. As such they should encourage market research both by Tourist Boards and by the tourist industry aimed at finding out what the tourist of the future really wants. The benefits of this work will not be limited to the areas directly concerned. The techniques will be able to be applied to other parts of the country and to areas where tourism is already an important economic activity.

In addition we have arranged for hotels started in Development Areas since 31 March this year to be eligible for Local Employment Act assistance. As long as these projects create fifty or more new jobs they may apply for loans and grants of up to 35 per cent of their cost. There is already a scheme to help smaller tourist accommodation projects which is operated by the Development Commission. So altogether we are offering help to a wide range of Development Area tourist schemes.

I have often been asked why these measures of assistance have been limited to the Development Areas when so many of our holiday areas lie elsewhere. I entirely accept that a large number of our resorts and of the areas where there is tourist potential are not within the Development Areas. But some of the growth points are in these areas and it is an essential part of the Government's overall policy that development here should get priority.

It has been suggested to me that we ought to designate special Tourist Development Areas and give them special assistance. But it would be inconsistent with our immediate objectives now to extend the limited funds now available to help tourist projects to parts of the country outside the present designated areas. There is another reason why I think it would be wrong to create Tourism Development Areas. Some people, when using this phrase, have in mind areas of potential development. I know that over the next few years our Tourist Boards will be examining the country's tourist potential in detail. But I doubt very much whether they will find this potential tidily arranged within definite boundaries. Would anybody here today be prepared to stand up and say that his part of the country had no tourist potential? Another interpretation of the TDA concept is an area in which the tourist business is in decline. There are likely to be several different reasons for changes in the ability to attract tourists. New social patterns, changes in fashion, the effects of industrial development and other economic and geographical factors. I have a strong suspicion that such an attempt by Government to influence market forces could well do more harm than good. The right way to encourage existing tourist areas to make the best use of their potential is by helping them to *market* their wares more effectively. By creating more business, efficient marketing can encourage further investment. I am very glad that in the paper before this Conference the English Tourist Board have laid so much stress on the importance of an effective marketing strategy.

We want to see a flourishing tourist industry in all parts of England, both in the present tourist areas and elsewhere. To achieve this we must certainly encourage the improvement of existing facilities and the development of new ones. But excessive reliance on Government grants is not the right way to go about it. Our policy for this as for other sectors of the economy is to create conditions in which the industry can on its own develop healthy growth and expansion.

We have already taken some very important steps in this direction. SET [Selective Employment Tax][1] – long source of complaint from the hotel industry – is to be halved – and it is not only hotels that will benefit. Holiday attractions and other services for tourists will also benefit from the effects. And this is true also of the general reductions in taxation which the Chancellor has announced.

Another system which will be particularly helpful is the new system of depreciation allowances for plant and equipment for which, unlike investment grants, the service industries are eligible. There are two points I should like to mention in this connection. These allowances will do a lot to encourage modernization of holiday accommodation. But more than this, they are evidence of the Government's determination to end the discrimination against the service sector. And that is what matters to the people who plan to invest in tourism.

Given the right conditions, it is a sound principle that tourist facilities should meet normal commercial criteria. Where there are no direct earnings the investment should be able to be justified on the expected indirect earnings. Holidays

[1] Abolished completely since. [Eds.]

and travel bring many real benefits but that does not mean that holiday facilities should be provided as a social service. Tourism is business – or rather a variety of businesses – and it must be left as free as possible to respond both to the pressures and the requirements of the commercial environment in which it has to operate.

I have talked a lot about objectives and I have done so deliberately. If any public money is to be spent on furthering tourism, it is right that the Government should set out the objectives which the expenditure is designed to secure.

But having done that, it is clearly important that the Government should not try to spell out their detailed interpretation. Since taking over my responsibilities I have had a good deal of advice about how I should carry them out. I have been told, for example, to encourage a particular type of tourist area, to concentrate on bus tours, or to see that we have more dolphinaria. But that is not the job of Government. I know that in some countries the Government lays down a rigid blue print for tourist development: a piece of coast here is to be rid of mosquitoes and developed with twenty-five hotels and ten car parks; a mountain area there is to become a ski resort. This is all very well for countries whose tourist product is different from ours; where stretches of the country, unused by the local inhabitants, are given over exclusively to tourism. But this would not be appropriate in our case. We have quite different and a wholly unique product to sell. Unlike many other countries we have a strong home market and our overseas visitors come to see how we live as much as to see what the country is like. The development of tourism cannot be separated out as though it were a specialist function on its own. It is an integral and an essential part of development as a whole, contributing to the life and character of each particular locality from which it in turn derives so much of its own personality.

And so I shall not try to do the job of the English Tourist Board, of local planning authorities or of the tourist trades. But I would ask those of you who will be shouldering these tasks to bear in mind the objectives which we have been discussing today. We most certainly must not – and will not – forget our overseas visitors. But the time has come for a completely new approach to the home market – we are not second-class holidaymakers. If we concentrate on establishing the characteristics of the home market and catering for its needs we shall provide a basis for growth not only in existing tourist areas but in many parts of the country where the economic benefits of tourism offer real hope.

18 International Tourism in Four European Countries

From *GLC Intelligence Unit Quarterly Bulletin*, No. 24, September 1973.

L'activité touristique dans le monde connait l'un des taux d'expansion les plus élevés et les plus soutenus.

Atelier Parisien d'Urbanisme (1971a)[1]

The Growth in International Tourism

International tourism has been one of the fastest growing industries in the world. On the basis of statistics from the Organization for Economic Co-operation and Development, the British Tourist Authority (1971a) has estimated that international tourist journeys throughout the world grew from 71 million in 1960 to 181 million in 1971, representing an annual increase of approximately 9 per cent.

Tourism is the main sector of the economy in some countries, providing the major source of finance for development, whereas in others tourism plays a vital role in the balance of payments position. 'Tourists will be welcomed in almost all countries, socialist or capitalist, as the inadvertent financiers of development plans ... They will assimilate and destroy local cultures; they will cause roads to be constructed and settlement patterns to be re-orientated.' (Cosgrove and Jackson, 1972).

The growth of tourist numbers[2] and revenue in certain countries is shown in Table 18.1. It must be remembered that, when comparing one country's performance with another's or when compiling global trends, different indicators may be used in different countries, such as numbers of visitors, expenditure or numbers of nights spent, and these may be incompatible.

The growth of international tourism anticipated in the future is expected to be considerable, although there may be fluctuations, as in the past, because of changes in fashion, political unrest, restrictions on foreign exchange allowances, and government activities in promotion and development. In the words of the OECD (1967):

---

[1] Details of all references are given on pages 201–2.

[2] The Tourism Committee of the OECD defines a foreign tourist as any person visiting a country, other than that in which he usually resides, for a period of at least twenty-four hours. Migrant workers, immigrants, and travellers passing through without stopping are specifically excluded (Organization for Economic Co-operation and Development, 1971).

'It is reasonable to foresee that by means of the steady growth of such features of modern life such as the paid vacation, the long week-end, the fashion for more than one holiday and inexpensive charter flights, both new economic and social groups and new areas of the world can be increasingly brought into the international tourist trade on a vast scale.'

What has caused this recent surge in international tourism and what factors influence the tourist's choice of destination? As Armstrong (1972) states:

'There is undoubtedly a duality of motivation explaining international tourist demand. One set of essentially socio-economic factors explains the *propensity* of individuals to become international tourists, for example population characteristics, disposable income, and leisure time. Another set explains the *distribution* of these tourists between different destinations and concerns the relative characteristics and appeal of the recipient countries, such as climate, holiday costs, ease of communication with generating countries, etc.'

Four variables are particularly important in determining the rate of growth of international tourism: the growth of leisure time, personal wealth, personal mobility, and technical advance, with aircraft economics and charter growth being particularly influential. 'It has been possible this year to cross the Atlantic for £25 in spite of inflation. The lowest fare in 1950 was £125. This represents as large a revolution as the reduction in journey time from 5 days to 5 hours' (Lickorish, 1971).

Perhaps the most comprehensive list of factors influencing the growth of tourism comes from Louis Erdi (1970) of the Swiss Federal University:

1. Greater affluence and more leisure for an increasing number of people, particularly in the developed countries.
2. The emancipation of the young, and the relatively high wages they possess (when they have no family responsibilities), enabling them to travel.
3. Transport facilities, especially air, are very much better and cheaper, and there is a high rate of car ownership.
4. An enormous growth in international business, necessitating travel.
5. Package tours allow people unused to making their own arrangements to travel with an easy mind, and are good value because of bulk buying of transport and hotel accommodation.
6. Relief from adverse climatic conditions in the home country may be found abroad.
7. Travel has become a status symbol.
8. Conferences and business meetings are proliferating.
9. Better education has interested a large sector of the public in cultural tourism.
10. World exhibitions and trade fairs have become very popular.
11. Publicity becomes more and more aggressive, whetting the appetite of even the most timid.

12. Ideological pressure groups (political, cultural, scientific, etc.) hold more and more annual rallies.

There are three main types of international tourism: metropolitan tourism, based on historical, cultural, entertainment, and shopping attractions; rural/coastal/countryside tourism, based mainly on sun, sea, and scenery; and specialized tourism, such as winter sports, health spas, etc. These three types overlap to some extent but this article is mainly concerned with the first type, namely metropolitan tourism. The countries selected for study were Great Britain, France, the Netherlands, and Greece. Availability of data and the possibility of interviewing or contacting the relevant national tourist organizations were the main reasons for selecting these countries. In all four countries the pre-eminence of the main city and its environs (i.e. the day-trip zone) as destinations for international tourists often generates similar problems. Great Britain, and in particular London, are treated in greater depth, although many of the problems encountered in London are common to other centres receiving large numbers of tourists. In general the accounts given here are purely descriptive and detailed comparisons are not made.

Table 18.1

Index of visitor arrivals and expenditure, 1970

Country	Arrivals 1964 = 100	Revenue (excluding fares) 1964 = 100
UK*	207	195
Spain*	208	179
Austria†	144	199
Netherlands†	136	174
France*	134	148
West Germany†	126	149
Italy*	122	158
Switzerland†	117	151
Europe (OECD members)	150	161
World	158	169

* Arrivals recorded at national frontiers.
† Arrivals recorded in registered accommodation.
Source: British Tourist Authority (1972).

Great Britain

As Table 18.1 shows, the number of overseas[3] tourists coming to Britain and the income Britain derives from tourism have both been growing, not only in line with strong global trends, but also in relative terms. Recently the rate of growth

[3] 'Overseas' is used rather than 'international' in Britain, since Commonwealth citizens and holders of British passports living abroad are added to 'foreign' visitors in totals for overseas tourism. In other countries, international tourists and foreign tourists are synonymous.

has been spectacular. Britain has changed from being an international back-water as far as tourism was concerned: 200 thousand visitors came in 1945; 7¼ million came in 1972.

Why has Britain shown such a good record? It seems that the 1967 devaluation gave Britain a marked advantage during a period when traditional tourist countries such as France and Italy were suffering a reaction from rising prices. 'Studies by the IMF (International Monetary Fund) and the OECD suggest that in a relatively high cost country like Britain, a change in exchange rates should have a major impact – and this has certainly been borne out by the tourist influx since 1967' (London Tourist Board, 1972). Additionally, there has been an international craze for all things British, from pop to pubs, actively encouraged by promotional literature, particularly appealing to the younger groups. With these factors of devaluation and anglophilia, there exist, of course, the basic attractions of Britain, namely its history, culture, shopping, and 'friendly people' (*see* Table 18.2), as shown from various British Tourist Authority nationality surveys.

THE DESTINATIONS OF OVERSEAS VISITORS

Information on the numbers of international tourists visiting different parts of Great Britain has to be drawn from many, often incompatible, sources. The International Passenger Survey[4] (IPS) included questions on regional distribution only between 1964 and 1966, and in 1971. The questions referred to numbers of visits to, rather than nights spent in, localities. Sir George Young's analysis of the IPS data for 1965 and 1966 (Young, 1970) showed that of the overseas non-business visitors staying in one locality (in Sir George Young's words, 'terminal visitors') 74 per cent chose London. The geographical distribution of overseas businessmen shows even more concentration: 85 per cent of 'terminal' businessmen stayed in London.

A further source of information is the British Tourist Authority's nationality surveys. These again concentrate on visits rather than overnight stays. London was the most popular destination for non-business visitors: the survey revealed that 86 per cent had either stayed in or visited London; next came Stratford upon Avon (22 per cent) followed by Oxford (21 per cent).

Studies made by the hotel industry also provide information on the geographical distribution of tourists. In a recent publication the Hotels and Catering Economic Development Committee (HCEDC, 1972) estimated that 60 per cent of all overseas non-business bednights in 1969 were spent in London. The dominance of the capital is even more marked for business and conference visitors as 81 per cent of their bednights were spent in London.

The Scottish Tourist Board (1972) estimated that 800 thousand overseas visitors went to Scotland in 1971. A report by the HCEDC (1972) estimated that

[4] Conducted by the Department of Trade and Industry, this survey is based on a large sample of passengers interviewed at most airports and seaports throughout the year. The main questions concern numbers, mode of travel, area of origin, purpose of visit, and length of stay.

Table 18.2

Attractive Features mentioned by Non-business Visitors (percentages)

Nationality	London as a whole	Landscape and countryside	People	Castles/ architecture	Language	Museums	Prices	Entertainment	Culture
Belgian	23	32	23	18	16	12	–	–	–
French	17	20	25	13	17	6	3	–	55
Dutch	43	52	32	14	10	8	4	3	10
United States	16	23	31	30	–	13	–	–	–
Canadian	19	–	27	33	–	12	–	–	–
Swiss	37	32	21	8	11	20	24	11	–
Spanish	17	20	23	19	–	–	–	–	–
Swedish	21	25	60	–	21	–	–	8	35
Norwegian	27	–	25	–	12	–	–	17	31

Source: British Tourist Authority nationality surveys 1966 to 1971 (unpublished).
Note: The percentages shown do not add to 100 since visitors could mention more than one feature

overseas tourists spent 1·7 million nights (2·2 per cent of the British total) in Wales in 1969. These figures show that only a relatively small proportion of overseas tourists visit Scotland or Wales.

The feature that is consistent throughout this assortment of data is the concentration of overseas visitors staying in or visiting the capital. The causes for this concentration on London are not hard to find. In the BTA nationality surveys questions were asked about the 'most attractive features of the trip' (*see* Table 18.2) and 'the activities undertaken'. London contains the nation's most famous historical treasures, museums, art galleries, and shops, as well as possessing most of the business headquarters. It is clear that these attractions strongly affect the geographical distribution of tourists. The location and usage of airports and seaports, with their concentration in the south-east, and the distribution of hotel accommodation (particularly large, new, modern accommodation most in demand by overseas tourists and their tour operators) both reinforce the advantage of London and the south-east as being the primary area for receiving and accommodating the overseas tourist.

Another reason for the geographical distribution of overseas visitors may be due to the low percentage of visitors bringing their own cars.[5] Apart from the relatively small percentage driving and hiring cars, overseas visitors, many of whom make long journeys from the United States or Commonwealth countries, rely on coaches or public transport or car journeys with friends and relations. This relative lack of car usage limits Britain's development as a touring country.

As recent new hotel developments depend on high occupancy rates for profitability, many have located in London. The availability of modern hotel accommodation in London encourages tourists and tour operators to arrange holidays there rather than in other parts of Britain.

THE PROBLEMS GENERATED BY OVERSEAS TOURISTS

The basic problems arise from the large numbers of tourists staying in and visiting London, especially in the months of June, July, and August when 40 per cent of the annual total of foreign visitors arrive. Many of the current problems in London are well known. They may be divided into three groups: (i) the provision and location of suitable accommodation; (ii) the popularity of certain traditionally famous places; and (iii) the specialized needs of the business and conference visitor.

(i) *Accommodation needs*

To accommodate the great influx of overseas visitors, a hotel boom has been generated. The government's hotel incentive scheme (Development of Tourism Act, 1969) was an additional stimulus to development. Hotel building in London has accelerated sharply from 1968 onwards. The main planning problems have been discussed in GLC publications such as the Green Paper *Tourism and hotels*

---

[5] *See* the summary report on the survey of overseas motorists to Britain 1969 by the British Tourist Authority (1970) which estimated that 11 per cent of non-business arrivals came by car. (The figure for Italy was 76 per cent and for West Germany 88 per cent.)

in London (Greater London Council, 1971) and *Tourism in London – towards a short-term plan* (Greater London Council, 1973) and may be summarized as follows:

Aesthetic: Many new hotels are larger than those built previously, owing to (*a*) the high price of land which necessitates high rise and (*b*) economies of scale in the hotel industry generally. Their size, shape, and materials give rise to problems in areas of architectural interest.

Locational: New hotels tend to cluster round the West End, Heathrow Airport, or the major lines of communication between them, such as the Cromwell Road and the M4. The locational and aesthetic problems are related when one considers that large parts of the central area are conservation areas.

Residential accommodation: The shortage of residential accommodation is exacerbated by the creeping conversion of residential premises to hotel use.

Employment: Low-paid workers in central London hotels have difficulty in finding accommodation nearby.

Traffic congestion: Local traffic congestion is often caused by taxis and coaches arriving at hotels for conferences, and by on-street coach parking.

At least one-third of all visitors to Britain are estimated to be between the ages of 16 and 24 (in 1972 this represented some 2 million people). The growth in youth tourism has been felt more in London than elsewhere because of active promotion and current enthusiasm in the young for English clothes, music, and 'culture' in general. The recent growth of this sector, and its concentration in London, has led to difficulties, particularly in the provision of suitably cheap accommodation in a capital city of high land prices and acute land shortage. These and other problems have been considered in a report to the English Tourist Board by the Young Tourism Study Group (1972).

(ii) *Congestion at tourist attractions*
The popularity of the traditional sites causes problems because of the numbers gathering at them at certain times of the year. London's historical, cultural, entertainment, and artistic amenities are in the greatest demand among tourists. One of the most extreme manifestations of this is the Changing of the Guard, which can be seen satisfactorily by 4,000 people, yet on peak days some 9,000 or 10,000 go to Buckingham Palace in the hope of seeing it. Westminster Abbey had 4 million visitors in 1969 of whom 80 per cent were estimated to be non-British (Binder, Hamlyn, Fry & Co., 1971). Data over a number of years on the impact of the overseas visitors on particular attractions are hard to obtain. In most cases it is impossible to separate the overseas visitors from local visitors and even to define a visitor is difficult unless a ticket or a turnstile is used.

Little is known about the capacity of most tourist attractions, the scale of the problem and the contribution of overseas visitors to congestion. Ideas of capacity have physical, psychological, and other aspects which are often difficult to quantify or express. The solution to such problems can be sought in improved circulation and site management. Planning involves itself more directly in the preservation, conservation, and enhancement of key buildings and surrounding areas. If overseas visitors continue to come at the same times of the year and to visit the existing key attractions to the same extent, a point may be reached where conditions at some basic attractions will deter the overseas visitor from coming to London, and once London is deleted from his itinerary he is more likely to choose to visit some other country than to explore other less well-known parts of Britain.

Since many visitors to London stay in hotels (concentrated particularly in Westminster) and do not use cars, there is the problem of congestion caused by coaches both near the principal attractions and near hotels. Although the problem may be eased by traffic management schemes, by altering schedules, by licensing or by greater parking provision, the difficulties lie in the fact that the hotels and main attractions tend to be concentrated in just a few areas in London.

(iii) *Facilities for business and conference visitors*
Business visitors account for just under 20 per cent of all overseas visitors to Great Britain. The growth rate is dependent to some degree on the rate of growth of Britain's exports and overseas business. Entry into the European Economic Community is likely to accelerate the growth of business visits. Sir George Young (1970) forecast 2·13 million business visitors in 1975 and nearly 4 million in 1980. As 90 per cent of business visitors arrive by air on scheduled flights, the location of airports (particularly Heathrow) and of business activity are the main factors controlling the distribution of business visitors. The other important characteristics of overseas business visitors are their high usage of hotels and their more even distribution throughout the year since visits of this kind are not normally influenced by season.

The conference visitor also represents a potentially great source of growth. In 1972 there were an estimated 650 international meetings held in Britain (the majority in London) attended by some 300,000 delegates (British Tourist Authority, 1973). Any demand forecasts must take into account supply constraints, important being the present lack of a large purpose-built conference centre in Britain. Existing facilities include university accommodation, multi-use buildings such as the Royal Festival Hall and the Royal Albert Hall, and the conference rooms provided in many of the new hotels. With its entertainment and tourist facilities (increasingly more important as delegates combine business with pleasure), its nodal position in air travel and its modern hotels, London has great potential. There is some demand for a large purpose-built conference centre but problems arise in balancing resource allocation between the specialized needs of the business visitor, and the needs and wishes of the residents. Safavi's study (1971) of US convention centres shows most centres need to be subsidized.

THE ORGANIZATIONAL RESPONSE

There is no Ministry of Tourism in Britain, nor any single agency soley respon-sible for planning the growth and development of overseas tourism. Responsi-bilities are shared by the Department of the Environment, the Department of Trade and Industry, the British Tourist Authority, and the regional tourist boards.

Apart from the establishment of the present structure of tourist organizations, and financial inducements for hotel development in the Development Areas (English Tourist Board, 1972*a*), the most significant government influence has been through the Hotel Development Incentive Scheme operated under the Development of Tourism Act, 1969. The provision for assistance to the hotel industry under this Act was a grant of 20 per cent of the expenditure, or £1,000 for each letting room, whichever was the less, for new developments or exten-sions. To be eligible for a grant, work was to have begun not earlier than 1 April 1968 and not later than 31 March 1973. These incentives helped start a rush of activity in hotel development, although not all was directly due to this scheme. The growth in overseas visitors and the attraction of hotel investment compared with other types of development were further reinforcing factors. Owing to the dependence of the hotel industry's profitability on occupancy rates, and with occupancy rates being highest in London,[6] the boom in new hotels, particularly larger and more expensive ones, has been heavily concentrated in the capital.[7] Of large hotels with over 200 rooms under construction or planned in England by January 1973, 27 were in London, 5 in the rest of the south-east and 22 else-where (English Tourist Board, 1973). While large hotels remain heavily con-centrated in the three central Boroughs of Camden, Westminster, and Ken-sington and Chelsea (84 per cent of the total), some new hotels have been built near Heathrow Airport and in other parts of London (*see* Table 18.3).

In planning terms, many of the problems and subsequent policies have been the result of trying to fit the specialized needs of the rapidly growing tourist population with the land and other requirements of the resident population. Hotels are not allowed to prejudice the conservation of the housing stock, and should be located if possible outside traditional central London locations, in areas with good transport facilities and where they contribute to urban renewal. However, most hotel developers are cautious in their locational requirements and often have very rigid financial specifications to be met which allow them little chance of being 'experimental' in location under present conditions. (An example of a hotel scheme outside the traditional hotel areas is the new Tower Hotel, which forms a part of the St Katharine Docks redevelopment scheme.)

SUMMARY

Tourism is a complex subject of study involving many agencies, both public and private, in Britain. It is often split between domestic and overseas tourists and

[6] The English Tourist Board conducts a monthly survey of hotel occupancy by size and area. *See* also London Tourist Board (1973).

[7] *See* English Tourist Board (1972*b*). Greater London had 47·5 per cent of the bedrooms applied for under the grant system and 56 per cent of the proposed capital expenditure.

Table 18.3

Distribution of Large Hotels (200+ rooms) in Greater London

Area	February 1971			March 1972			January 1973		
	No. of hotels	*No. of rooms*	*% rooms*	*No. of hotels*	*No. of rooms*	*% rooms*	*No. of hotels*	*No. of rooms*	*% rooms*
Westminster	29	11,928	57·5	36	13,925	60·9	42	15,741	51·9
Camden	11	3,855	18·6	11	4,039	17·7	11	3,914	12·9
Kensington and Chelsea	7	2,410	11·6	7	2,466	10·8	11	5,659	18·7
Central area total	47	18,193	87·7	54	20,430	89·4	64	25,314	83·5
Heathrow (Hillingdon and Hounslow)	5	2,128	10·3	4	1,826	8·0	7	3,591	11·8
Others	1	435	2·1	2	603	2·6	5	1,424	4·7
Greater London total	53	20,756	100	60	22,859	100	76	30,329	100

Source: Data supplied by the London Tourist Board

these groups can be sub-divided according to the purpose of the visit into holiday, business, conference, and other visitors. The many agencies involved make planning for the overseas tourist in Britain a difficult exercise in co-ordination. Overseas tourism is often studied as one aspect of subjects such as housing, leisure and recreation, transport and communication, etc. but is rarely studied on its own. This makes planning for tourism difficult to execute.

The many different types of tourism all generate problems and have differing costs and benefits. For instance, the business and conference visitors are relatively high spenders, use hotels more and show a better distribution over the whole year than holiday visitors. Yet this category of visitor shows more marked concentration in London (Hotel and Catering Economic Development Committee, 1972). The young tourist is a relatively low spender, with difficult accommodation requirements, yet he may represent an important future 'market'.

There is no national framework in which local planning authorities can measure individual applications for tourist facilities such as marinas and hotels. It is difficult to determine the weighting to be given to such schemes when the needs of resident and visitor have to be balanced. There are also the additional problems of who is to pay for and provide facilities such as low cost accommodation in central London, a large purpose-built international conference centre, a meeting place for young tourists or similar projects, which are often non-profit making in immediate economic terms yet are essential to the further development of the tourist industry. This lack of context and lack of commitment makes it politically difficult for local authorities to subsidize projects for overseas visitors from local revenues.

The growth expected in the future is considerable. Nearly 12 million overseas visitors are expected by 1975 (British Tourist Authority, 1971b) and Sir George Young (1970) envisages 17 million by 1980. The tourist authorities are trying to encourage overseas visitors to come at less popular times of the year and to visit other parts of Great Britain. Yet certain characteristics of the overseas visitor may change in the future and this will probably limit the amount of dispersal into other regions: an increase in package tourists and airborne travellers based on London's large and recently expanded hotel stock and a declining length of stay[8] will lessen the chances of visiting less well-known areas. In addition, an increasing proportion of overseas visitors will stay in hotels in the future (Hotel and Catering Economic Development Committee, 1972). As many of the large new hotels most likely to be used by package tourists have been built in London and the south-east, one is left to choose between the alternatives of (i) a greater commitment in planning policy to provide for an assumed

[8] From IPS data it can be seen that the average length of stay has dropped from 18·2 to 14 days between 1965 and 1970, a trend that is expected to continue as communications, particularly by air, become easier and, in real terms, cheaper and as people prefer a 'grand tour' and greater choice. In addition, as international tourism penetrates deeper into lower social classes, so budget-watching becomes more important. A reinforcing tendency is to take more shorter holidays rather than one main one. Length of stay varies greatly according to purpose of visit and area of origin.

geographical distribution of the future growth in numbers (HCEDC, 1972) or (ii) a situation in which the conditions experienced by overseas visitors are such that there is a great reduction in the numbers of visitors.

The Netherlands

The Netherlands was chosen for study as it is a densely populated country with a strong growth in foreign tourism, concentrated in one city, Amsterdam, features that show some similarity to Britain. In 1971 approximately 2½ million foreign visitors went to Holland, and the number of nights spent by foreign tourists in Dutch hotels totalled 5·8 million.

THE DESTINATIONS OF FOREIGN TOURISTS

In examining foreign tourism in Holland, the facts that the country is small and that it is the nearest coastline for the populous Ruhr conurbation are significant. Holland faces, on a smaller scale, the same concentration of tourists in one city as Britain. From the comprehensive statistical source, the Statistiek Vreemdelingenverkeer (Tourist Traffic Statistics) (Centraal Bureau voor de Statistiek, 1972), it is seen that in 1970 just under 50 per cent of foreign visitors nights spent in hotels were spent in Amsterdam (*see* Table 18.4), a share that has slightly increased over the last decade. With its historic seventeenth-century

Table 18.4

Regional Distribution of Visitor-Nights in the Netherlands (percentages)

Region	1959	1965	1970
Amsterdam/Rotterdam*	46·2	48·0	49·6
North sea coast	25·2	22·9	21·6
Veluwe and Veluwerand	2·8	3·0	3·0
Utrecht and Heuveirug	1·2	1·0	1·0
Het Gooi	1·0	0·8	0·8
Zuid-Limburg	1·6	1·6	1·0
Rest of Netherlands	22·0	16·2	17·7
Total	100·0	100·0	100·0

* The majority of these visits were to Amsterdam.
Source: Centraal Bureau voor de Statistiek (1972).

core, its canals, museums, art galleries, night clubs, and restaurants, Amsterdam attracts many of Holland's visitors. Its nodal position in European sea, rail, road, and air communications make it easy for tourists to travel to and from the Netherlands. Proximity to picturesque villages such as Marken and Hoorn and to the tulip fields helps reinforce the attraction of Amsterdam to the tourist. In 1970, 81 per cent of Americans, over 90 per cent of Japanese, and 46 per cent of English and Scottish visitors who stayed in hotels in the Netherlands stayed in Amsterdam (*see* Table 18.5).

Table 18.5

The Proportion of Foreign Tourists visiting Amsterdam/Rotterdam
(percentages)

Country of origin	1960	1970
Belgium/Luxembourg	37·6	38·9
France	51·2	50·2
Switzerland	55·1	58·8
West Germany*	20·8	13·2
Sweden	48·3	50·6
England and Scotland	49·8	46·2
United States	75·3	81·3
Total foreign visitors	46·3	49·6

* West Germans, particularly those from the Ruhr, use the Dutch coastal resorts heavily in summer as this is their nearest coastline.

Source: Centraal Bureau voor de Statistiek [5](1972).

THE PROBLEMS GENERATED

When comparing the planning problems generated by foreign tourism in Amsterdam with those of London, the difference in size and scale must be remembered. In 1971 Greater Amsterdam's population was 1·03 million; Greater London's was 7·45 million. The concentration of hotel nights in the city and the relatively high occupancy rate (70 per cent) in Amsterdam's existing hotels (more than double that of hotels in the provinces) led to developers choosing Amsterdam for new hotel construction. In 1968 Amsterdam had 12,500 hotel beds; this total had increased to 15,000 by 1970, and is expected to increase to 20,000 beds by 1973. The requirements of modern hotels in terms of size, location, and materials have led to difficulties in making them compatible with the intimate scale of the seventeenth century central area (similar problems arise in conservation areas in London). However, some hotels, such as the Pulitzer, have been well integrated into this historic core by conversion of existing buildings. An area has been designated in the south of the city for large-scale buildings including hotels (the Esso Motor Hotel and the Alpha are here) and this has been successful because it is not far removed from the central area or from Schiphol Airport. Plans for a hotel in the large public housing sector to the south-east of the city have never materialized. Two particular examples of problems arising from new hotel development are, first, the Okura, a Japanese-owned tower hotel which intruded into Berlage's area of architectural interest, and second, a hotel project in Weesperzijde which was cancelled because of a public outcry that, in view of the chronic housing shortage, housing should be built instead. Amsterdam has similar problems to London with coach traffic congestion (near the Central Station), the shortage of lower- or medium-priced tourist accommodation suitable particularly for the very great increases in numbers of young visitors, and in the compatibility of new hotel development with aesthetically and historically sensitive areas. The problem of 'creeping conversion' of property from residential to hotel use does not arise in Amsterdam as all tourist accommodation is licensed.

THE PLANNING RESPONSE

In Amsterdam itself no definite policies for hotels have been established by the city planning authority, although the city planners have agreed with developers on a maximum height of five storeys in the central area. A positive attitude is taken towards the growing needs of young tourists since they are thought to represent a potentially important future market and because the city council feels that the country has a tradition of tolerance to maintain. The city council has established a camping site with toilet and washing facilities for those with sleeping bags in the Vondelpark, despite some public opposition. One million guilders has been allocated for youth tourism projects by the city council. In addition the municipality and the Dutch Tourist Board have 2,000 beds available for people who cannot afford or cannot find a commercial hotel.

The Ministry of Economic Affairs is committed to expanding tourism for political, economic, cultural, and social reasons (Quaedvlieg, 1970; 1971). One key policy has been to stimulate tourist and hotel growth in the less well-known regions. Since 1969, for regions with deficient hotel resources, it has been possible to obtain state help with capital works for hotel projects of 200 rooms or more. Certain help in providing infrastructure is available from the central government for tourist development. The government has announced its intention of imposing a 20 per cent levy on the construction costs of new hotels built within the Randstad.[9] Thus, regional incentives and a deterrent cost in building hotels in regions under pressure, may provide a better distribution of hotels and tourist numbers. This Dutch levy represents a far stronger locational control on new hotel building than the weak British incentives to build in the Development Areas under the Development of Tourism Act 1969.[10]

The Netherlands has developed considerable facilities (in particular those that are purpose-built) for the competitive international conference and exhibition markets. The Congresgebouw in The Hague has facilities for 9,000 delegates and cost £8·4 million. With the international congress and exhibition centre (The Rai) in Amsterdam and Rotterdam's congress centre, the Netherlands has three fully operational purpose-built conference centres, and is in a position to benefit from the high spending and anticipated fast growth of this sector of tourism.

France

France has traditionally been a tourist nation, characterized by strong organizational control and a very wide range of attractions that have recently become

[9] In 1973 hotel developers will have to go at least 8 km outside the city in order to be considered for planning permission for certain types of development.

[10] Section 11 of the Development of Tourism Act (1969) sets out the rate of grant. This will be 20 per cent of the eligible expenditure (25 per cent in the development areas) with a ceiling in the case of new hotels and qualifying extensions to existing hotels of £1,000 (£1,250 in the development areas) for each new or additional letting bedroom provided.

increasingly popular with greater promotion and development. In 1971 approximately 14 million foreign tourists visited France. Although the growth in tourist numbers and expenditure has been moderate over the decade, the 'events' of 1968 caused a sharp drop in the previous rate of growth, indicating the sensitivity of tourist flows to adverse political events. The Bank of France's tourist balance sheet showed a positive balance of $11·4 million in 1966 and a negative balance of $144 million in 1968. Devaluation of the franc, better promotion and tourist development as well as relative political stability have all helped in producing positive accounts since then.

THE DESTINATIONS OF FOREIGN TOURISTS

The Commissariat du Tourisme, a government body, publishes monthly reports giving the number of arrivals and nights spent by travellers in hotel accommodation in regional capitals, in towns of more than 50,000 inhabitants, in mountain districts, spas, coastal resorts, and winter sports areas. The pre-eminence of Paris as the major tourist attraction is clear. Paris takes 60 per cent of foreign visitor nights and 57 per cent of nights in registered hotel accommodation.[11] With its history, atmosphere, reputation, monuments, shops, and fashion houses, Paris is the premier attraction for the great majority of foreign tourists. In 1970 Paris and the Mediterranean were the most popular regions of France: for instance, two-thirds of all British tourists visited Paris at some time during their stay. Nearly half a million American visitors, over a quarter of a million West Germans, and over 220 thousand British stayed in registered tourist accommodation in Paris in 1969.

THE PROBLEMS GENERATED AND PLANNING RESPONSE

To the French planners, both national and local, the main obstacle to the future growth in the number of tourists is the poor quality, quantity, and structure of hotels. In 1967, for instance, over half (58 per cent) of the registered tourist hotel rooms in Paris had been constructed before 1918, and the average size of all hotels was only 44 rooms. Insufficient and unsatisfactory hotel accommodation was seen as the major barrier to the expansion of Paris's role as an international tourist city. Using 1959 = 100 as a base index, Paris's hotel capacity had actually decreased to 96·6 by 1966. The need for large purpose-built modern hotels was clear, particularly as standards of comfort were rising generally and this type of accommodation was in any case required for the business sector. In the 6th National Plan (1971–75), France's hotel stock was to increase by 50–60,000 rooms of which 8–10,000 were programmed for Paris. The government assisted the hotel building programme by providing subsidies and low interest loans to French firms building *de luxe* hotels in Paris, so that by 1973, according to government planners, 6,000 international class hotel

---

[11] These figures underestimate the total position. For instance, 140,000 camped in the Bois du Boulogne in 1970, 88 per cent of these being foreign visitors. Many visitors stay with friends and relatives or in non-registered accommodation. The grand total of tourists visiting Paris is over 10 million each year.

rooms in nine new hotels will have been added to the 2,900 existing in 1970. Air France have calculated the need for an additional 6,000 new hotel rooms per annum in Paris in the near future (Atelier Parisien d'Urbanisme, 1971*a*). Before the Hiltons at the Eiffel Tower and Orly, there had been no large hotel construction in Paris and its region since the George V opened in 1935. Despite relatively high occupancy rates in Paris hotels, site and financial problems have led to targets not being reached. Hotels are found in certain urban renewal schemes such as Les Halles, Maine Montparnasse, and Issy les Moulineaux but, as with London, there remains a concentration of registered hotels especially in the west and centre. Five arrondisements have half the total registered hotel rooms of the city (18th, 11th, 20th, 15th, and 17th) and a greater share of the larger and more modern hotels. The development of Roissy Airport and the urban motorway programme may help to spread the distribution of hotels more evenly throughout the city.

The attempts to insert large hotels into the existing urban fabric of Paris have caused problems. For example, the 1,000-room Hotel Vandamme Montparnasse intrudes disturbingly into the area around Les Invalides. Like London, Paris is faced with the limited architectural scope and quality of many new hotels which tend to be located in attractive areas close to the most fashionable parts of the city. Large new hotels may well contribute to the destruction of the very things tourists enjoy.

Like London and Amsterdam, Paris faces difficulties in catering for the young tourist. In a recent survey (Atelier Parisien d'Urbanisme, 1971*b*) at certain traditional tourist attractions 50 per cent of the respondents were under 25 years of age. Despite high usage of hostel, lycée, and university accommodation, as well as the camping areas around Paris (Bois de Boulogne, Champigny, Doudan), insufficient provision is made. In 1970 Foyer International d'Accueil had to refuse 84,000 written requests for accommodation.

Paris, like London, is wilting under the tourist pressure at certain sites. In 1970 the total number of visitors to the Eiffel Tower was 2·8 million, to the Louvre 1·2 million, and at Notre Dame 0·2 million (Atelier Parisien d'Urbanisme, 1971*a*). Although improved circulation and site management offers some scope for accommodating increased numbers, there is a real danger that unless acceptable secondary attractions are provided, visitors will not come to Paris because of the intolerable conditions. The new 'tourist' car park opposite Notre Dame is an example of the efforts being made to 'manage' these sites.

For business and conference visitors, Paris is a major international centre. Air France have recently found that in winter and spring 56 per cent of their passengers gave business as the principal purpose of their visit (Atelier Parisien d'Urbanisme, 1971*b*). The high spending power of this class of tourist and their usage of hotels in relatively slack periods of the year have been major reasons why this sector is keenly sought. As with London, the chief problem has been the lack of large purpose-built conference centres. A further problem has been providing suitable and sufficient accommodation, especially in the spring (the fashion season) and autumn. The Centre International de Paris at Port Maillot, with a total capacity of 8,000, a 1,000-room hotel, shopping facilities, a business centre, and an air terminal, due to open in 1974, is expected to improve Paris's position in this very competitive market.

NATIONAL PLANNING RESPONSE

Organizationally, as mentioned, the government agency responsible for the promotion and co-ordination of tourism in France is the Commissariat du Tourisme which has great interest in developing tourism in the regions. This Commissariat forms part of the interministerial council for tourism, a liaison group of relevant government departments. An advisory body at the national level, the higher council for tourism, has nine specialized commissions dealing with such matters as the preservation of the tourist heritage, finance, the hotel industry, and 'social' tourism.

The most dramatic evidence of government action lies in the strong measures contained in the National Plans to remedy depopulation and to help depressed regions. The 5th Plan (1966–70) promoted very expensive regional tourist projects for six areas including Languedoc-Roussillon, Provence, Aquitaine, and Corsica, all providing for the 'sun–sea–scenery' type of tourism. The Languedoc-Roussillon scheme represents a public–private sector partnership for the development of 25,000 hectares, involving state expenditure of 700 million francs over 10 years, resulting in six tourist units (the first of which is La Grande Motte) with an estimated capacity of 700 to 800 thousand tourists a year and providing employment for some 20 to 30 thousand local inhabitants.[12] The investment in mountain areas proposed in the 6th Plan's 'plan de neige' is another example of the large scale commitment of the French Government to developing tourism.

How far decentralization is helped by the high percentage of people arriving in France by car (thus tending to be more mobile), by promotional efforts or by the natural attractions of regions outside Paris which are becoming more accessible and attractive, is difficult to say. However, the government's activity and major projects will certainly afford a better distribution of foreign visitors in the future.

Greece

Greece was examined as an example of a country mainly concerned with the 'sun–sea–scenery' type of tourism, with strong historical and cultural attractions, and also because it has a concentration of tourist activity in the capital city.

In Greece, the growth of tourism has been considerable, with the numbers of foreign tourists increasing from just under 1 million in 1967 to $2\frac{1}{2}$ million in 1972, a projected $4\frac{1}{2}$ million in 1975, and 8 million in 1980 (personal communication from G. Apseridis, 1972). In the government's five-year plans, the number of hotel beds increased from 75,000 in 1967 to 135,000 in 1972. According to the next 5-year plan (1973–77) it is hoped to provide a further 150,000 beds by 1976.

[12] For further reading *see* Racine (1969), Raynaud (1969), and Souchon (1969).

It was difficult to obtain facts about the regional distribution of foreign tourists within Greece, although it is clear that metropolitan Athens, with its $2\frac{1}{2}$ million people, still represents a strong magnet, particularly for first-time visitors. There are tight building restrictions in the historic core of the city, as 'monument' areas are strictly safe-guarded. The government foresee the maximum desirable amount of tourist accommodation in Athens itself being provided by 1976. Hotel development will continue, however, in the south-east (Gulf of Euboea) and south-west (Saronic Gulf). Both these areas have the advantages of good and improving links with metropolitan Athens, an attractive coastline, and continuing, sunshine; they are also near internationally known attractions such as Delphi and Sounion.

PLANNING RESPONSE

With a more centralized government than many nations, and with very great potential for development, the Greek national tourist office has been extremely active. In 1956 the first signs of the possible scale of growth were seen, but the twin problems of a chronic shortage of suitable accommodation and an initial slowness of private enterprise to come forward led to government hotel development in areas such as Lesbos, Kerkira, and Rhodes, which acted as a pace-setter and was then sold off. The first systematic look at tourism was in the 1968–72 five-year programme, when the hotel building programme was stepped up. The government operates a hotel grant scheme for new developments, with initially low interest rates and with higher grants to remote areas.

Government activities now comprise national and local planning and the provision of infrastructure, rather than the actual building of new hotels. The government has been engaged in very strong promotion and advertising, in the improvements to harbours, ports and in the construction of marinas and roads as well as the usual utility services. Further intentions in the next five-year plan include increased emphasis on winter sports, camping activities linked with the road programme (anticipating far more car-based visitors), and the development of spas.

To help develop other regions and to spread the economic benefits of tourism more widely, as well as to relieve Athens itself, the Greek government has planned to promote six 'priority regions'[13] for tourist development, using both public and private funds. These have been chosen on the basis of a realistic appraisal of potential accommodation provision and the existence of a suitable airport.

Like many nations, Greece has been paying attention to extending the tourist season to ensure a more balanced flow, a fuller use of facilities and to counteract seasonal unemployment. The government's promotional literature is helped by climatic and scenic advantages, and winter tourism is seen as a very important growth sector, especially for Crete and Rhodes.

One feature in Greece, as with many 'sun–sea' tourist countries, is the possibility

[13] These are: Olympus and Athens coast, Halkidike; South Evia, Saronic coast; Rhodes; the Greater Thessalonika region; Western Peloponnese; Crete.

of creating new tourist complexes to aid the 'decentralization' of foreign tourists. Although the national tourist office does not normally allow more than ten hotels in one new area, the scale of projects such as the development of Varkiza (with 2,000 tourist beds to be provided in three years under the usual format of government plan and private money) and Vouliagmeni both on the Attica Coast south-east of Athens, allows quick development, in tandem with the build-up of infrastructure, to help spread the revenue from tourism.

General Conclusions

In certain countries, 'urban' or 'metropolitan' tourism has been growing and is expected to continue to grow at a fast rate. In many Western European countries the major cities have been the receivers of many international tourists as a result of their historical and cultural attractions, shopping, entertainments and well-developed accommodation and transport facilities. International businessmen and, to a lesser extent, conference visitors choose large and attractive cities, because of good airport connections and because of the location of business facilities and suitable accommodation.

In some major cities such as London, Amsterdam, and Paris, the rapid increase in tourist numbers has led to potential conflict between the resident and the visitor, especially as it is in these areas that demands for more space for residents and visitors alike are most pressing. The need for hotels and conference centres, the competition between tourists and residents for transport, entertainments and other facilities, and the congestion caused at major sites of interest are areas of friction politically, socially, and economically.

With the projected large future increases in numbers of international tourists, certain cities see that a ceiling will shortly be reached, or has already been reached, for the numbers and facilities that can be located in or near city centres. As Ian Murray (1972) picturesquely observes 'What worries the GLC and, to an even greater extent, the London Tourist Board, is the feeling that in the capital we are rapidly reaching the point where that old economic maxim the law of diminishing returns begins to bite. In other words, there is a strict limit to the number of Americans who can be crammed into one ancient monument without suffocating the former and wrecking the latter.' The situation is exacerbated by lack of information about 'capacity' and how over-crowding affects 'visitor satisfaction'.

With the existing problems and conflicts in certain cities and with the large increases in numbers projected, many authorities at the local, regional, and national levels are attempting to plan tourism firstly by decentralizing visitors and spreading the benefits of tourism to less well-known areas, and secondly by attempting to obtain a better seasonal distribution of tourist arrivals. However, it seems that quick and dramatic results usually stem from the 'sun–sea–scenery' type of tourism, as seen in Greece and Mediterranean France, rather than from the tourism patterns of such countries as Britain and the Netherlands. Languedoc and Varkiza are good examples of the rapid build-up of tourist complexes. The 'plan de neige' in France is another. The tendency for more and shorter holidays may well bring about better yearly distributions but the present constraints of school, university, and 'works' holidays are still strong.

Much more research is needed in this field. Key questions that need to be answered include: What is the relationship between the supply of facilities and demand? Do tourists precede or follow investment? What is the relationship between promotion, visitor numbers, and their distribution? How can attractive and alternative tourist facilities be created from new or from underdeveloped 'potential' in order to relieve over-congested areas? What are the deterrent effects of congestion: can it 'force' decentralization or will it lead to a loss of visitors to a country as a result of intolerable conditions? How far can the development of facilities for domestic tourists and leisure seekers be combined with the expanding international market?

Tourism is a volatile and fickle activity as Ireland, Israel, and Uganda know to their cost. Planning for the tourist often involves the co-operation and co-ordination of many agencies, and despite active promotion and development, political and economic factors (devaluation or revaluation, currency restrictions, etc.) can clearly upset careful plans. In the highly competitive tourist industry, inadequate or intolerable conditions will lead to the loss of both potential revenue and the less tangible benefits of tourism both to the country and to the regions within it which could have benefited from this potential.

References

Atelier Parisien d'Urbanisme (1971*a*). La situation du tourisme parisien. *Paris Projet*, no. 6, pp. 66–75.

Atelier Parisien d'Urbanisme (1971*b*). Les visiteurs de Paris. *Paris Projet*, no. 6, pp. 76–81.

Armstrong, C. W. G. (1972). International tourism: coming or going: the methodological problems of forecasting. *Futures*, vol. 4, no. 2, pp. 115–125.

Binder, Hamlyn, Fry & Co. (Management Consultants) (1971). *The impact of tourists on Westminster Abbey.* 11 pp. (Available from the Dean of Westminster.)

British Tourist Authority (1970). *Summary report on the survey of overseas motorists to Britain 1969.* BTA, 12 pp.

British Tourist Authority (1971*a*). *Research Newsletter, no. 3*, Autumn 1971, p. iii.

British Tourist Authority (1971*b*). *Research Newsletter, no. 1*, May 1971, p. iii.

British Tourist Authority (1972). *Research Newsletter, no. 4*, Spring 1972, p. ii.

British Tourist Authority (1973). *Research Newsletter, no. 8*, Spring 1973, p. ii.

Centraal Bureau voor de Statistiek (1972). *Statistiek vreemdelingenverkeer 1970.* The Hague, 48 pp.

Cosgrove, I. and Jackson, R. (1972). *The geography of recreation and leisure.* (1st ed.). Hutchinson, University Press, p. 42.

Development of Tourism Act (1969). HMSO.

English Tourist Board (1972*a*). *Tourist projects in England's development areas – new opportunities for tourism and how the Financial Support Scheme works.* ETB, 11 pp.

English Tourist Board (1972*b*). *Annual report for the year ended 31 March 1972.* ETB, 50 pp.

English Tourist Board (1973). *New hotels in England.* ETB, p. 5.

Erdi, L. (1970). Hotels. *Architects Journal Information Library Technical Study,* no. 1, pp. 1053–1522.

Greater London Council (1971). *Tourism and hotels in London: a paper for discussion.* GLC, 41 pp.

Greater London Council (1973). *Tourism in London: towards a short term plan.* GLC, 55 pp.

Hotel and Catering Economic Development Committee (1972). *Hotel prospects to 1980.* National Economic Development Office. 2 vols.

Lickorish, L. J. (1971). *Tourism forecasts for the next decade.* British Tourist Authority, 11 pp. (Paper presented to the conference on tourism and the environment, London, November 1971.)

London Tourist Board (1972). *9th annual report for the year ended 31 March 1972.* LTB, p. 4.

London Tourist Board (1973). *10th annual report for the year ended 31 March 1973.* LTB, p. 16.

Murray, I. (1972). Standing room only. *Observer,* 22 April, p. 15.

Organization for Economic Co-operation and Development (1967). Proceedings of the conference on tourism development and economic growth, Estoril, 1966. In: *Tourism development and economic growth,* Paris, OECD.

Organization for Economic Co-operation and Development (1971). *International tourism and tourism policy in OECD member countries.* Paris, OECD, 161 pp.

Quaedvlieg, A. H. W. (1970). La politique touristique au pays bas (1). *Revue de Tourisme,* no. 4, pp. 150–152.

Quaedvlieg, A. H. W. (1971). La politique touristique au pays bas (2). *Revue de Tourisme,* no. 1, pp. 21–28.

Racine, P. (1969). Mission Interministérielle pour l'Aménagement du Littoral Languedoc-Roussillon (1). In: *Multidisciplinary aspects of regional development.* Paris, OECD, pp. 51–60.

Raynaud, P. (1969). Mission Interministérielle pour l'Aménagement du Littoral Languedoc-Roussillon (2). In: *Multidisciplinary aspects of regional development.* Paris, OECD, pp. 61–67.

Safavi, F. (1971). A cost-benefit model for convention centres. *Annals of Regional Science,* December 1971, vol. 5, part 2, pp. 17–37.

Scottish Tourist Board (1972). *3rd annual report for the year 1 April 1971 to 31 March 1972.* STB, p. 12.

Souchon, M-F. (1969). La compagnie nationale d'aménagement de la région du Bas Rhone-Languedoc. *Cahiers de l'Institute d'Etudes Politiques de Grenoble,* Cujas.

Young, Sir George (1970). *Accommodation services in Britain 1970–80.* New University Education, 771 pp.

Young Tourism Study Group (1972). *Young tourists in England: report to the English Tourist Board.* ETB, 58 pp.

Part X
The Future of Tourism

Introduction

In looking into the future we have selected two very different approaches. One is a wide-ranging bird's-eye-view of tourism with particular reference to developing countries. The other is concerned with forecasting as a key area in the planning activity of an international airline.

The World Bank Sector Working Paper describes the growth of tourism throughout the world, the various factors which have affected this growth, and the prospects for developing countries to benefit from tourism. Its primary focus is on holiday travel since business travel is relatively non-responsive to an expansion of facilities and is, therefore, of less interest for the operation of the Bank. The Paper, of which our selected contribution is an extract, also recounts the role of the World Bank Group in encouraging the establishment and extension of the tourist industry in developing countries and outlines its plans for the future.

Newman's paper begins by examining the relationship between a number of economic, social, and demographic variables, and various aspects of the airline product on the one hand, and international air travel on the other. The trend forecasts for travel are then checked with propensities to travel and with growth cycles for other industries. The three independent projections which mutually support and reinforce one another, produce an optimistic long-term outlook for the airline industry.

19 *Tourism and Developing Countries*

BY WORLD BANK

From *Tourism – Sector Working Paper* (World Bank, Washington, 1972).

Recent Growth Trends of International Tourism

Since the early 1950s international tourism[1] has grown rapidly, particularly after the liberalization of foreign exchange and travel restrictions which characterized the years following World War II. In the early 1960s international tourism, which in Europe had been mainly limited to neighbouring countries, spread more widely and developing countries began to benefit increasingly from its growth. From 1950 to 1970 international visitor arrivals (including vacationers[2], business, and other visitors) in all countries grew from 25 million to 168 million, an average yearly growth rate of 10 per cent, while international tourism receipts rose from $2·1 billion to $17·4 billion, 11 per cent per year. In some of the developing countries much higher growth rates have been recorded in recent years as these more distant destinations have become increasingly accessible with the expansion of air transport.

There are three major tourist generating areas: North America (United States and Canada), Western Europe, and Japan. About three quarters of all international visitor arrivals, including the great majority of arrivals in developing countries, are accounted for by twelve countries – United States, Canada, United Kingdom, France, Germany, Sweden, Denmark, Belgium, Netherlands, Switzerland, Austria, and Italy. Until 1967, foreign travel from Japan was severely limited but with the easing of restrictions in subsequent years, foreign holiday travel particularly has grown very fast.

Factors Affecting Vacation Travel

Only a few countries have tried to analyse the factors affecting the various types of tourist demand and this only in recent years. The studies, usually based on sample surveys, indicate that levels of income, income distribution, educational levels, social structure, changing vacation habits, the degree of

[1] An international tourist, as defined by the United Nations and the International Union of Official Travel Organization, is a person who visits a country other than that of permanent residence for at least twenty-four hours, whatever his motive for travel.

[2] A vacationer, whether international or domestic, is defined by major European tourist services as staying away from home for at least four nights on any one trip and may in some instances include tourists travelling for a combination of business and pleasure. An excursionist is a person who stays in any one destination for less than twenty-four hours.

urbanization and geographical location, are the main determinants of the growth of vacation travel.

The proportion of the population in the more developed countries which travel on vacation, both at home and abroad, varies. The correlation between per capita Gross National Product (GNP) and vacation travel is not very close. In the US, with the highest per capita GNP, the proportion of the population travelling on vacation is considerably lower than in some European countries, and countries with similar per capita GNPs within the same region vary considerably in their travel patterns. In some highly industrialized countries like Great Britain and the nations of Scandinavia the proportion of the population travelling on vacation has reached 60 per cent and more of the adult population and this proportion is unlikely to rise much further. In many others, however, including such major tourism generating countries as the US, Germany, and France, it is only around 40 per cent. There appears to be a large potential for further growth in vacation travel.

The extent of foreign travel depends in part on income levels, levels of education, etc., but it is also heavily dependent on the size of the country of origin and its geographic location. A European vacationer is much more likely to cross an international frontier than a North American vacationer though the latter may travel a longer distance. Even in Europe, however, the bulk of vacation travel is domestic.

Although statistical data are incomplete, the broad pattern of present and prospective vacation travel is fairly clear. The bulk of vacation travel is over relatively short distances within and between the developed countries. Over somewhat longer distances there are substantial numbers of vacationers from the US and Canada visiting Mexico and the Caribbean and larger numbers from Western Europe visiting the Mediterranean. The figures of inter-regional vacation travellers provide a reasonable estimate of orders of magnitude. As a proportion of all vacation travel, inter-regional travel is small, and within the absolute total of such travel the share of the US is large (almost 60 per cent). The majority (52 per cent) of US travellers leaving North America visit Western Europe.

Analysis of the European travel market indicates that for the next decade an increase of some 40 million in the number of vacationers (approximately a 45 per cent increase over present levels) can reasonably be expected. A similar relative increase, if not higher, is likely for the US and Japan. Only a part of this growth will result in foreign travel and only a fraction in long-distance travel; it can be assumed that those already travelling will tend to go further afield in the future while newcomers to the travel market may seek their first experience in domestic tourism.

The costs of transport are a key element in determining tourist flows. In almost all tourist generating countries the private car ranks first as a means of transport and is likely to gain further ground. Rail travel, once the most important mode of transport in tourism, is steadily declining; its share in European travel is hardly more than 30 per cent and in the US much less. With declining tariffs (at least in real terms) and better and faster service, air transportation, while still used by only 6 to 10 per cent of all vacationers, shows the fastest relative growth. The growth of air charters especially has made possible rapid increases in traffic from North America to Europe, from northern Europe to the Mediterranean – e.g. Majorca and Tunisia – and on a more limited scale from Europe to more distant destinations such as Kenya, Thailand, Ceylon, and the Caribbean.

Long distance travel by air, which is virtually the only mode of travel to the more distant developing countries from the major tourist generating centres, will continue to account for a relatively small share of total tourism travel in the foreseeable future. Nevertheless, considering the likely growth of income in the main tourist generating countries and the rising proportion of the population earning higher incomes and enjoying higher levels of education, the absolute number of vacationers travelling long distances by air should increase very considerably in the next decade.

Likely Future Tourist Flows to Developing Countries

The factors which influence demand point to the likely development of tourism by areas of destination. The bulk of vacation travel will continue to be within and between the developed countries but there will be large increases in flows of visitors to the developing countries in the Mediterranean Basin and to Mexico and the Caribbean. These countries will include:

Mediterranean Basin: Spain, Yugoslavia, Greece, Morocco, Algeria, Tunisia, Egypt, Israel, Lebanon, Syria, Turkey, and Cyprus. The growth of tourism in some of these countries (Egypt, Syria, Israel, and Lebanon) has been hampered by the political situation.
The Caribbean: most of the Caribbean islands; Central American countries and Mexico; as well as Columbia and Venezuela in South America.

From studies made of the European market, and from data available on the United States, rough orders of magnitude can be given of the likely potential increase in vacation visitor flows to these two regions over the next decade. For the Mediterranean this figure would be about ten million additional visits, nearly doubling the 1968 total and for the Caribbean and Mexico an additional three to four million, compared with about three million in recent years.

For long distance travel, the areas of greater interest among developing countries are likely to be Eastern Africa (Kenya, Tanzania, Uganda, and Ethiopia) and South East Asia (Iran, Afghanistan, India, Ceylon, Nepal, Thailand, Indonesia, and Singapore). In these countries multi-destination circuits have developed, for example through Eastern Africa, South and East Asia, and the Pacific. With appropriate air fares and increased facilities such circuits might also be developed further in Western Africa and South America.

The magnitude of the likely visitor flows to each of the more distant destinations is difficult to predict. They are competing destinations and much will depend on the success of each in providing tourist facilities of the right type and at the right price. Overall, the growth in long-distance vacation travel is likely to be fast, but in absolute terms will probably not exceed two to three million additional vacation travellers over the next decade – approximately doubling the levels of recent years.

Regional tourism can also be expected to expand. The greatest growth is likely from Japan to nearby destinations such as Korea and the Republic of China, but more distant destinations – Thailand, Singapore, and Indonesia – will also benefit from the fast growth of the Japanese market. Other areas of regional tourism will continue to be in South America, between Argentina and Brazil and from these two countries to Paraguay, Uruguay, and Chile; in southern Africa, from South Africa to Lesotho, Swaziland, Malawi, Malagasy, and Mauritius; and in the South Pacific, from Australia and New Zealand to Fiji, New Caledonia, and Tahiti. A number of these countries will also be the destination of visitors from distant countries but in relatively small numbers.

Patterns of Tourism Expenditure

As a rule of thumb, vacationers are likely to spend an amount equivalent to one month's income per family on annual leave, although this varies according to the living standards, not only from country to country but also wiⳑ..n each country. Generally speaking, tourists will respond to price incentives. They have demonstrated strong price consciousness not only about accommodation and other services offered but also in choosing modes of transport and travel distances. Changes in tariffs have quite often resulted in considerable redirection of tourist flows. Moreover, changes in relative air fares have meant increasing price competition even between regional destinations such as Western Europe and the Caribbean where price levels had until recently been relatively independent. This empirical evidence that demand for vacation travel, both domestic and foreign, is strongly price-elastic has been confirmed by the limited amount of serious research carried out to date. The studies also suggest that expenditures on long-distance foreign travel are highly income-elastic.

A tourist's daily expenditure may vary from a very low amount (i.e. when camping and visiting friends and relatives) to large sums for luxury vacations. Tour operators, especially in Europe, exercise a certain price leadership in their market which indicates at what prices supply can be offered. For example, European tour operators at the present time regard a daily expenditure of about $9·00 for full board as a ceiling price, which will be exceeded only in exceptional cases. The individual tourist very often orients himself by comparing prices of total holiday packages (including transportation) offered by tour operators and therefore will not easily be prepared to spend more. With long-distance travel, not only do travel expenses increase but daily expenditure also tends to go up, since most vacationers prepared to travel long distances are likely to demand relatively high standards of accommodation. This, of course, limits the number of potential tourists.

The data on average daily expenditure by foreign tourists reflect the differences in the types of market for different developing countries. Mediterranean destinations such as Spain, Yugoslavia, Greece, and Tunisia appeal to a broad spectrum of middle-income tourists. In these markets the role of tour operators organizing package tours and budget holidays is very significant. This is also increasingly true of such distant destinations as Kenya, Ceylon, and Thailand. On the other hand, travel on the part of relatively well-to-do vacationers or business travellers and those who combine business and vacation travel predominates in most other distant destinations. Vacation travel to most Caribbean islands (other than Puerto Rico and the US Virgin Islands) has until recently been dominated by relatively high-income North Americans – most individual vacationers – at least during the main winter season.

Excluding travel costs, normally from 60 to 75 per cent of tourists' expenditures goes on food and accommodation. The balance is spent on excursions, entertainment, and shopping. In some tourist destinations shopping accounts for a much larger part of expenditures – notably in Hong Kong and Singapore, both internationally famous duty-free ports – but in virtually all destinations tourists buy souvenirs and local crafts, thus providing an addition to exports which might not otherwise occur. Travel costs as part of the total cost of the holiday vary greatly according to distance and mode of transport. For long-distance destinations by air, travel costs can amount to 50 to 60 per cent of total costs.

In the light of the patterns of tourism expenditure which have been described, it is clear that in a number of countries a really significant expansion in demand can be achieved only by increasing the supply of moderately priced accommodations, particularly if suitable arrangements can be reached with tour operators and airlines to reduce the costs of air travel. Some countries, distant from the main centres of tourism generation, might be better advised to concentrate on the high-income part of the tourist market.

Seasonality

School holiday patterns, industrial vacation customs, and climatic and geographic factors in both tourist generating and receiving countries cause most vacation tourism to be highly seasonal. There is, however, a growing trend to two or more holidays in some of the most highly developed countries, particularly where winters are very severe such as the Scandinavian countries, Canada, and the northern United States. This mitigates to some extent the seasonal peaks in some tourist destinations such as Majorca, Mexico, and some Caribbean and Pacific islands. Business travel has little relation to seasons and to a limited extent offsets variations in vacation travel. Other travellers, whose motivation might be for personal reasons, may travel at any time.

The possibilities of offsetting fluctuations in business and holiday travel are quite limited. Tourism facilities for vacation travel are often not suitable for business travel. City hotels usually show their lowest utilization during the peak holiday season and holiday resorts experience rather slack business during the rest of the year. Apart from the attempts to stagger school holidays, which have not been notably successful, there have been other attempts to lessen seasonality. The most promising seem to be in the creation of new demand, such as convention business and in price policies that induce tourism through preferential tariffs in the off-peak season. However, there are limits to price elasticity and also to the number of conventions to be arranged. Seasonality can never be fully balanced out. This is most important in planning tourism facilities since a project must be designed for specific occupancy rates.

The following yearly bed occupancy rates can reasonably be expected:

(a) *Business Travel* – 60 to 90 per cent; there is a tendency for declining utilization of business accommodation with the shortening of the work week.

(b) *Vacation Travel* – 20 to 60 per cent and higher, if the climate is very favourable in the tourist receiving country. Mediterranean resort hotels usually have occupancy levels between 30 and 45 per cent; in a few exceptional cases this may go as high as 60 per cent. In some of the Caribbean and Mexican resort hotels as well as some East African and South Sea resorts which cater mainly to vacation travellers, occupancy rates may go up as high as 80 and 90 per cent. This, however, is only possible with a very select clientele whose holidays are not tied to any particular time of the year.

Tourism Facilities

Tourism facilities do not consist only of accommodation like hotels and boarding houses. They include also recreational and sports facilities of great variety and, of course, all the necessary infrastructure like transportation and utilities. In countries of cultural interest, historical monuments may also be regarded as part of tourism infrastructure, and the preservation, restoration, or better accessibility of these monuments may be critical for the future of the sector in these countries.

The composition of superstructure, mainly accommodation, has undergone considerable changes in the last twenty years. New types of accommodation, particularly holiday villages suitable for family-type tourists, condominiums and apartment houses, private villas and camping facilities, have proved successful and to some degree are replacing traditional hotels and boarding houses. These changes reflect changes in demand with new, often younger, groups entering the international travel market and also new approaches to the problem of providing facilities in a very competitive industry with a highly seasonal demand.

It is typical of the tourism industry that individual units are of rather moderate size. Hotels in general range from 150 to 500 beds, while holiday villages may offer as many as 1,000 beds. Considering an average investment per bed to be in the range of $5,000 to $10,000 depending on quality and location, the total investment required for each unit could be in the order of less than $1 million up to $5 million and more. There are, of course, exceptions whenever the implementation of a whole complex is being considered; this type of development provides potential economies in construction and in marketing which are likely to be particularly significant in some less-developed countries.

In almost any developing country a need exists for some basic tourist facilities to accommodate business travellers. In these cases individual investments will be of relatively moderate size. By comparison, the supply of accommodation needed to meet demand for vacation tourism will call for relatively large investments in the regions likely to attract the largest tourist flows (i.e. the Mediterranean Basin and the Caribbean area) and for rather sizeable investments even in those not close to the major tourist generating areas (e.g. Bali).

Financial Aspects of Investment in Accommodation

Although international experience indicates that over the longer term well-conceived investments in tourism accommodation facilities show satisfactory financial rates of return, the supply of accommodation has often failed to increase in line with the growth of demand. In many countries starting the development of tourism, it has been difficult to interest the private sector to invest in hotels and other forms of accommodation. Apart from lack of experience in the sector, two features of hotel investment in particular seem to account for the reluctance of investors: (*a*) the fact that relatively large amounts of capital have to be tied up in fixed assets over a long period (up to 20–25 years) with all the risks of changes in market conditions, the political and social framework, etc., involved; and (*b*) the strongly seasonal demand which is particularly pronounced in resort areas. This gives rise to concern that it will not prove feasible to achieve sufficiently high occupancy rates to make satisfactory profits. All the more so since, contrary to a widely held impression, only a small proportion of hotel operating costs – the equivalent of 15 to 25 per cent of total sales – are variable in the short term. With fixed costs relatively high, there is little flexibility to adjust to low seasonal demand.

Many governments in both developed and developing countries have attempted to overcome this reluctance of private investors to finance hotels and other forms of accommodation through a variety of incentive schemes. These include providing cheap or free land, equipment grants, exemption from import duties, liberal depreciation allowances and tax holidays, loan guarantees, long-term government loans and interest rate subsidies. The different incentives are being provided in varying combinations. In some cases they are made to apply to investments in all new accommodation, in others they are used selectively in an attempt to direct investment to certain areas or for accommodation serving a specific market. In the Mediterranean Basin equipment grants and interest rate subsidies are the most common subsidy schemes in effect at the present time, while in other parts of the world, notably the Caribbean, tax holidays and tax exemptions are the most widely used incentives.

Planning for the Tourism Sector

In the majority of developing countries tourism has only recently attracted the attention of government as a sector warranting special economic policies and institutions. Too frequently, expertise in this sector is not presently available in government. Often and despite a sizeable flow, the private sector as well as the public lacks the know-how that would maximize benefits from tourism. Although training programmes are increasingly available from different institutions and the United Nations Development Programme (UNDP), the International Labour Organization (ILO) and various bilateral programmes have already made a significant contribution, the need for training and technical assistance in tourism will remain a constraint on the growth of the sector in developing countries for some time to come.

The need for an improvement in planning techniques for the sector is being increasingly recognized. Lack of expertise in market analysis, in construction techniques for hotels and other accommodation and tourist facilities, in appropriate financing for the sector, in tourism infrastructure requirements, in promotion techniques, and in means to reduce the adverse effects of seasonality, can lead either to over- or under-investment in supply of accommodation, as well as to inappropriate construction in relation to the market. Furthermore, the tourism sector can develop adequately only when given an appropriate government and semi-government institutional framework. In many countries such a framework does not exist and tourism is quite inadequately represented in high policy-making bodies where decisions are made on such topics as aviation policy and exchange rate policy which are critical for the industry. A major task of governments that have an important or potentially important tourism sector is to design and implement an integrated development plan for that sector. Many governments require outside assistance in formulating such a plan.

Foreign Exchange and Employment Effects of Tourism in Developing Countries

For a number of developing countries tourism has become a leading foreign exchange earner. In many cases gross tourism receipts amount to more than 20 per cent of the total value of merchandise exports and in some – Spain, Lebanon, Mexico, and many Caribbean islands – tourism has become the most important export of goods and services. Between 1960 and 1968, while exports from developing countries (other than oil exports) rose by 7·6 per cent a year, receipts from tourism increased at an annual rate of 11 per cent. In view of the dubious world market prospects of many primary products and the uncertainty about the extent to which the industrialized countries will permit increased imports of manufactured goods from developing countries, this trend may continue and the dependence on tourism by many of these countries may well tend to increase in the years to come. In any event, it provides for many a useful element in diversifying their sources of foreign exchange earnings and, for some, one of the very few export opportunities available.

The net, as a percentage of gross, foreign exchange earnings of tourism by developing countries vary considerably but tend to be high relative to many other exports. The countries fall roughly into three groups. Tourist facilities in such major tourist destinations as Mexico, Yugoslavia, and Spain are constructed, equipped, and supplied largely from local resources and staffed by local labour. Many of them are locally owned and operated. The net foreign exchange receipts are in excess of 85 per cent of the gross foreign exchange earnings of these countries. At the other extreme are some of the islands in the Caribbean and the Pacific and some of the relatively undeveloped countries of Africa. In many of them, operating supplies such as many foods and beverages come from abroad; specialized management, equipment, and a major part of construction materials have to be imported; and ownership of tourist facilities is often foreign. Even for these countries the net foreign exchange earnings are estimated to be seldom less than 45 per cent of gross receipts. In most other developing countries which are less heavily dependent on imports, net foreign exchange receipts from tourism range from 60 to 80 per cent of gross earnings.

Available data indicate that even for many developing countries where tourism has become a leading foreign exchange earner, the sector's output constitutes a relatively small portion of the GNP and employs directly only a small part of the labour force. It is often claimed that tourism is relatively labour-intensive but the available evidence is not conclusive on this point. Studies in Mexico and Kenya suggest that the relative amount of employment generated for each unit of capital invested has tended to be higher in tourism than in most other private sector activities. However, similar studies in Yugoslavia and Israel, carried out by the United Nations Conference on Trade and Development (UNCTAD) Secretariat, were far less conclusive. Since tourism can often be developed in the less-developed regions of a country, it may become a significant factor in redressing regional imbalances in employment and income. The extent to which this may be so will vary greatly from country to country. In some of the least-developed countries the rapid growth of tourism may even lead to the creation of acute economic and social disparities between the areas where tourism has its most direct impact on money incomes and employment and the rest of the economy.

Some Social Effects on Tourism Development

The rapid development of international tourism in some of the developing countries has given rise to social problems which must be of concern to governments and outside bodies. One such problem is the attitude of the local population to tourists and their reaction to the tourists' requirements for accommodation and service, which by local standards are luxurious. Another problem may arise from foreign ownership and management of tourist facilities and the feeling that indigenous people perform only menial tasks. Tourism may be regarded as a threat to the indigenous culture and mores, and there is a real possibility of a serious deterioration in standards of local arts and crafts as efforts are made to expand output to meet the tourists' demands. Not infrequently, resort development has resulted in local people being denied access to their own beaches. All these factors can give rise to serious problems in the reception of tourists and to demands for limitations on the flow of visitors. A further problem may be the demonstration effect of foreign visitor standards on the consumption expenditure patterns of the local population, and the dissatisfaction which can result if new wants cannot be satisfied.

While these possible negative effects of international tourism cannot be ignored, positive effects may be the increase in international contacts and in cultural exchanges which occur. The demonstration effect may also provide a stimulus to effort on the part of the population of the receiving country, while the growth of tourist traffic may open up needed economic opportunities.

The balance between the negative and the positive effects of international tourism varies in different countries. The effects are complex and little work has so far been done to try to assess the full impact of tourism development in particular destinations. By careful planning and regulation, the negative effects can be mitigated and it is important that the responsible public authorities should take this into account in formulating development policies and programmes for the sector.

20 *Forecasting at Pan Am*

BY G. NEWMAN

From an address presented at the Forecasting Seminar of the European Travel Commission in London in January 1971.

Forecasting is a key area in Pan Am's planning activity. The long-term forecasts (the subject of this paper) are the basis of our Ten Year Planning Horizon, Three Year Profit Plan, and the annual budgets. What will be described in some detail is the Total Market Traffic Forecast by major geographical area. For the Ten Year Planning Horizon, Pan Am's market shares in each area are estimated, producing a Pan Am passenger and passenger mile forecast. For the Three Year Profit Plan and the annual budgets these are further broken down by month, by route, and by flight number. Combined with yields, they produce a passenger revenue forecast. Combined with seat factors and unit costs, expenses are projected. Needless to say, this is an oversimplified and schematic description, but perhaps sufficient to outline the framework within which our traffic forecasts are used. There are many other uses, of course, from fleet planning to personnel planning.

The traffic forecasts consist essentially of an elaborate quantification of educated guesses. This is stated neither proudly nor apologetically. Complete mathematical models have been tried and found inconclusive. There are good reasons for this.

First, the industry's history is relatively short. Secondly, even this short history is far from a smooth progression of events, with relatively homogeneous periods broken first by the war, then by the introduction of the jets. Third, even within these periods there has been a large number of one-time disturbances (wars, strikes, rate changes – just to name a few) that significantly distort the basic trend. Fourth, the period ahead contains not only similar, as yet unknown and unpredictable disturbances (the word used to indicate deviations from the normal pattern, not necessarily negative), but also known factors, such as the introduction of SST [supersonic transport] service for which there have been no precedents and thus history is no guide. Finally, and perhaps most importantly, a mathematical formula based on past data can, at best, accurately project the historical trend. The art in forecasting international air travel is exactly in predicting the turning point in this historical growth pattern.

Thus, instead of making one more attempt at a purely mathematical solution (which even Professor Wheatcroft, having six months to do his study for IATA, found unsatisfactory), it seemed more fruitful to use the available time to expand, define, and estimate the factors that contribute to changes in the demand. The usual forecast of one market (total air travel) by three or four components was expanded to a forecast of three markets (pleasure travel – US residents, pleasure travel – foreign residents, and business travel) by fourteen components. Each component is forecast for nine geographical areas and two periods so that behind the aggregate forecast there are 252 separate estimates. Some are simple and straightforward, such as the population increase, although even in this case the projected shift in the age distribution was checked for its effect on the travel market. Others, such as the income effect, required extensive preliminary research, similar to what Mr Wheatcraft did on the fare effect. While he used, along with other forecasters, a single coefficient for the income effect, we have developed one for each area, each income bracket, and each time period as there is great variation among countries, income groups and over time.

The fact that judgment played a considerable role in arriving at some of the estimates does not mean that statistical analysis was not used to the extent possible at the component level.

As an example, let us look at the most important variable, income. Experience shows that doing the guessing at the most detailed level possible, using whatever data is available, results in more accurate aggregates than estimating directly these aggregates by hunches.

Income and Foreign Travel

Family income and the frequency of foreign air travel are highly correlated as one would expect.

Table 20.1

Income and Foreign Travel

	Transatlantic Trips		
Income	*Total*	*Pleasure*	*Business*
Under $5,000	4·5	4	0·5
$5,000–$10,000	9	8	1
$10,000–$15,000	20	15	5
$15,000–$20,000	47	28	19
$20,000–$25,000	108	65	43
$25,000–$50,000	253	145	108
Over $50,000	753	390	363

(Interestingly, business travel goes up with income even more sharply than pleasure travel. One probable reason for the frequency of pleasure travel not being even higher in the top income group is that business trips in many of these cases serve a dual purpose. To put it another way, people in these brackets are the most successful in combining business with pleasure. It is noteworthy that while in the lowest bracket there are eight pleasure trips for every business trip, with increasing income the ratio goes steadily down to almost one to one in the highest bracket.) That more income means more foreign trips is obvious. What is not so obvious is the difference the income level makes in determining *how many more* trips.

A 10 per cent increase in pay received by 1,000 upper middle income families ($10,000 in today's dollar) of the 1960s produced 3 foreign trips. A 10 per cent increase received by 1,000 upper middle income families of the 1980s (earning $20,000 in today's dollar) will produce 27 additional foreign trips.

Thus, the same per cent increase at twice the income level can mean nine times as many extra trips, attributable to the raise. There are two reasons for this. First, the same percent increase at a higher income means more dollars which, even at constant fares, buy more trips. Secondly, at a higher income level there are fewer competing claims on the increment, the necessities and even semi-luxuries having been taken care of.

To really understand and appreciate the income effect, we have to touch on what economists call 'income elasticity'. It is a multiplier that expresses the relationship between the growth of income and, in our case, the growth of international air travel. If it is 2·2, which we estimate it to be, then every 1 per cent increase in income triggers a 2·2 per cent increase in the number of trips. This 2·2 multiplied by a, say, 2·5 per cent rise in income gives us a 5·5 per cent 'income effect'. By 'income' we refer to family income in constant dollar. (The use of disposable income would be preferable, but it is not as readily available. Also, the distribution of the income gains by income group, to the extent they are uneven, should ideally be taken into account.)

Income elasticity varies greatly by income group.

Table 20.2

Income Elasticity

Income, $000	Up to 5	5–10	10–15	15–20	20–25	25–50	50 and over
Elasticity	0·7	1·4	2·1	3·7	3·4	1·5	1·1

The 2·2, as we can see, is an average of all these elasticities; more precisely, an average weighted by the income distribution of the travelling population. Income elasticity will increase in the next two or three decades, to 2·4 by 1975, as the majority of the population (and of the travelling population) moves towards and into the brackets ($15,000 to $25,000) in which elasticity is the highest, i.e. where rising income produces the largest number of incremental trips. It will not be before the end of the century that the majority will move on from these brackets to those where income elasticity is lower; only then will the average elasticity begin to fall.

The reason for the declining rate of elasticity in the highest income groups is that by the time people earn $25,000 or $50,000 a year, they apparently travel as much as they care to and are practically immune to any further inducements, including more income.

It is interesting to look at the propensity to travel by income group over time.

Table 20.3

Where The New Travellers Come From
(Transatlantic Trips Per Thousand Families)

Income	Under $5,000	£5,000– $10,000	$10,000– $25,000	Over $25,000
Increase 1963 to 1966	45%	35%	25%	2%

The virtual stagnation in the richest market (0·6 per cent growth per year) is remarkable and has some very important implications.

It is a very profitable market but not one from which our future growth will come on a per capita basis. This growth will increasingly come from the middle and low income families as the above percentages clearly indicate.

To summarize: most gains will come from rising incomes as the bulk of the population graduates into higher income brackets and acquires the travel habits of that new income group. All other factors, however, especially lower fares, will exert their stimulating influence primarily on the lower and middle income groups. Consequently, increases in the number of trips by the higher income groups will be largely due to the increased number of families in that income group, whereas gains among the lower and middle income families will be, in part, also due to their increasing propensity to travel, apart from their rising income. Income is, of course, not the only determinant of international travel. Looking at some of the others, we find that virtually every economic and social trend that in the past has contributed to the exceptionally fast growth of the industry will continue to stimulate demand and will help maintain its rise at a virtually undiminished rate through 1980 at least, possibly even longer. Even if we look beyond the next decade, there is no indication of a reversal of these trends or their favourable effect on travel and tourism. Let us briefly review some of these trends.

Factors Stimulating Travel Growth

INCREASING LEISURE TIME
Money is only one of the major restraints on travel. Time is another, and on this signs are rather encouraging. Kahn and Wiener in their book *The Year 2000* list among their 'surprise-free' projections for the post-industrial society (i.e. those that are based on the continuation of present trends) the four-day work week and paid annual vacations up to 13 weeks. By today's standards, these mean four vacations and 52 'long weekends' (42 three-day and 10 four-day ones). The work year would shrink to 40 per cent of the calendar days. Along with the shorter work year will come greater freedom in choosing how the increased leisure time is taken. Current surveys show strong preference for shorter work week and longer vacations, the kinds of leisure that stimulate travel, rather than

a reduction in the work day. Coupled with these are earlier retirement and, through progress in medicine and science, longer active life, expanding the already very important 'retirement travel' in both directions.

All this will not happen overnight, of course; it will be a slow and gradual process, but US Steel employees, for example, already have a 13-week vacation every 5 years and almost every new labour contract brings us a step closer to this Utopia. (This is not to imply that labour contracts in this instance are any more than conveniently observable bench-marks rather than the cause of the movement.) Ours is one of the few industries that benefit no matter how the increased productivity is divided between more income and more leisure.

POPULATION

The average of the projected growth rates, 1·5 per cent per annum, was used. The age distribution will change quite radically, in that while the total population will be up by more than 15 per cent in 1980, the 35 to 50 group will grow by only 1 per cent in the same period. Since the participation of this group in foreign travel for pleasure is, surprisingly, only average, this shift does not affect our growth rate.

LOWER FARES

Fares have gone down over the last twenty years, both in current and constant dollars. This cycle seems to be coming to an end. It is not unreasonable to expect, however, that productivity gains, primarily through new aircraft types, will keep fare increases below the level of inflation, i.e. that fares will continue a moderate downward trend in constant dollars. As long as this is true, fares will remain on the plus side of the scale, although undoubtedly they will provide a less powerful stimulus than in the past.

The 'fare effect' is again the composite of two factors: changes in the level of fares in constant dollar and 'fare elasticity'. The latter is the multiplier, showing the per cent change in the number of trips resulting from a 1 per cent change in the fare. With the multiplicity of fares even on one route, the question arises: which fare? Ideally, only change in the lowest fare should be considered as only this changes the total size of the market; changes in other (premium) fares affect only the mix. (This is why declining fares should have their full effect even after introduction of SST service at premium fares, as long as subsonic service is available at the lower rate.) With the availability of the lowest fare restricted in so many ways, however, we are forced to use the average yield (excluding first class) to measure changes.

Fare elasticity, the sensitivity of volume to price, varies by destination, for the fare as a per cent of the total cost of the trip varies by destination. To distant points (Orient, South Pacific) the fare is a relatively large part of the travel budget so changes in it have a great effect. To off-shore islands fare is a relatively small part of the travel budget and changes affect volume to a lesser degree. (The length of the trip is involved in this, of course, and of weekend trips to off-shore islands, for instance, the opposite is true.)

Fare elasticity has been assumed to be 1·7 and 1·4 for the two periods; slightly higher for the long-haul markets and a little less for the short-haul markets. This is a rather high value, even as luxuries go, if we consider that about 50 per cent of the total cost is ground expenses which are not affected; a 2 per cent reduction in fare is only a 1 per cent reduction on the total cost of the trip and thus the real price elasticity for a trip is twice as high: 3·4 and 2·8. Fare elasticity is declining as the fare becomes an increasingly smaller proportion of people's income.

OTHER POSITIVE FACTORS

To mention a few more influences, without trying to do justice to any of them, we can start by *education*. The level of education affects the frequency of foreign trips, even apart from its effect on income. The growing proportion of the population receiving higher education thus gives a stimulus to foreign travel, especially to areas of cultural interest (Europe, Middle East, Orient), less so to resort areas (on the theory that it does not take a college degree to lie in the sun).

Another is what, for the lack of a better term, could be called *internationalism* – closer political, economic, social, and cultural ties among nations.

To the extent that *status seeking* is responsible for foreign trips (which is probably small) the effect is not likely to diminish. The incentive to be the first in the block to have been to Europe is likely to be exceeded, if anything, by the social pressure to avoid being the last one *not* to have been there.

The mere fact that people will tend to travel *further* from their home than before, will increase both volume (revenue passenger miles) and revenue for the transportation industry.

The spread of 747 and the introduction of SST *service* should provide some stimulus to pleasure travel. In the case of the 747, if the effect is not direct, it may be the result of the big advertising campaigns and promotions that accompany it or of the intensified efforts of the carriers to fill the seats. By the time the novelty wears off (and, coincidentally, demand catches up with capacity), pressure will build up to increase the number of seats, passing some of the saving on to the travelling public. So in this period, say 1972 to 1975, '747 stimulation' might manifest itself through fare reductions, at least in constant dollars. SST will provide a very mild stimulation to pleasure travel because of the anticipated surcharge and the much lower value pleasure travellers place on their time as opposed to business travellers. New or improved service to an area, with its attendant publicity and promotion, also stimulates travel to the area.

While it is hazardous to predict specific *destinations* that will gain or lose in popularity, we can speculate about some general trends. First and foremost, pleasure travel to secondary and new tourist areas is bound to grow faster than to the primary, old tourist spots. There are two reasons for this. First, the proportion of repeaters, who have already 'done' the traditional tourist circuit, will seek new destinations. Secondly, unique tourist attractions do not have unlimited capacity. It is hard to see how the number of tourists to Venice can quadruple by 1980, with not a square foot of land on which to build new hotels (and a laudable distaste for tearing down old ones). The Louvre and St Peter's Cathedral are not any bigger than they were a hundred years ago, nor can the Scala Opera in Milan and the Viennese Riding School seat more people. Tickets and rooms for major Festivals are booked a year ahead. Europe, however, is a big enough area for these shifts to take place within – shifts from England and France to Spain, Greece, Turkey, Russia, Yugoslavia; and even within those countries – from London and Paris to the countryside. While this trend is clearly discernible, its influence should not be exaggerated. New generations (and new generations of foreign travellers) continue to grow up who have not been to Europe and whose first (and even first few) targets will be the old warhorses on the Grand Tour circuit, so the decrease in their popularity is small and relative.

Some Negative Influences

Again to serve as nothing more than an incomplete checklist, we might enumerate a few trends that may retard the growth of international travel.

Restrictions of any kind, from outright bans to currency regulations, do not help.

Political *instability*, local wars, civil wars, unrest, revolutions, hijackings can temporarily disrupt or divert the flow of tourists.

Traffic related to *military* activity will, hopefully, subside.

Congestion of all kinds, from airport access roads, terminals, runways, and airways to museums, sites, beaches, shops, and even streets at popular destinations can discourage tourism.

Travel motivated by *ethnic ties* is very significant. Foreign born US residents, representing 5 per cent of the US population, account for 25 per cent of the transatlantic trips. The receding tide of immigration should have an adverse effect on this kind of movement.

Is Saturation Approaching?

A student of air travel forecasts, looking back to the '50s and '60s finds a curious phenomenon. Virtually all long-term forecasts start out by a high growth rate for the first half of the period covered (usually ten years), to be followed by a significantly slower growth rate.

What is remarkable is that while the growth rates for the first five years are reasonable enough and increasingly accurate with the passage of time, the second periods are invariably way off. The most unchanging fixture of these forecasts has been the drop five years from 'now', whenever that 'now' was. (*See* Figures 20.1 and 20.2.)

The underlying assumption has probably been that with the industry maturing a levelling-off in its growth is inevitable – although the consistency in these errors and the failure to learn from them would lead a cynic to conclude that behind these high sounding explanations is the forecaster's simple notion that 'this is too good to last'. Some forecasters may even have believed, rightly, that

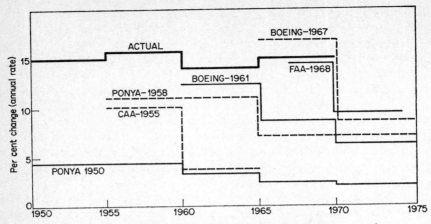

Figure 20.1 International traffic growth – forecasts *v.* actual

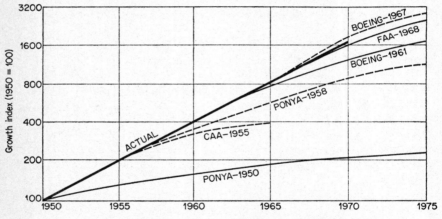

Figure 20.2 International traffic – forecasts *v.* actual

if they keep predicting the approaching saturation point, sooner or later they are bound to be right.

And here we have come to the crux of the matter. There is no doubt that the travel market, just as any other market, will, in time, become saturated. The question is whether this will happen over the next 10 years, 25 years or 75 years. (It may be noted that while these comments primarily apply to international air travel for pleasure, some are also valid for pleasure travel by other modes – but not for business travel.)

Will the 'Pull' Be There?

As we have seen, with more income, more leisure time, and relatively cheaper fares, the prerequisites of a continued rapid growth in travel are present. This 'push' alone, however, is not enough; increasing demand for travel also requires a 'pull' – people's desire to travel. If this is not there, the additional income and free time will be spent on other things.

Specifically, what we have to examine is whether what the forecast growth rates imply in terms of the size of the travel market and the frequency of trips is reasonable. A growth rate that would require five international trips a year by every man, woman, and child in the United States by 1980 is clearly excessive, no matter how justified by income and the other variables creating the 'push'.

First, we have to distinguish between products and services that have general appeal, such as automobile, radio, photographic equipment, and those that have only specialized appeal, such as Esperanto lessons, antique guns or Greek drama. (The fact that there is no clear line of demarcation and products generally start out in the 'nuts' market, partly because of their high price, and then some, usually by the painstaking effort of their promoters, shift to the 'general' market, is not relevant in this context.) The distinction is important as it determines the upper limit of the market size. International travel is clearly in the former category – most people who have the time and money engage in it. Accordingly the potential is almost the entire population. Let us subtract 30 per cent for the very old, the very young, the sick, and the poor who will always be with us. Another 15 per cent might be classified as 'hard core non-travellers', leaving 55 per cent.

Presently about 2·5 per cent of the population participates in foreign travel for pleasure and it will be the end of the century before 22 per cent and several more decades before the 55 per cent is reached (*see* Table 20.4).

Another contributor to the development of international air travel is the increasing frequency of trips by those who do travel. The purchase of most products, especially consumer durables, satisfies demand for a relatively long time. Once the market for, say, colour TV is fully penetrated, new sales can only come from replacement, new household formation or multiple-set-per-family demand. This is not so with services in general and travel in particular. Once a trip is over there is nothing left but the memories, mementoes, and a home movie. The desire for another trip is already present, although, because of the limitations of time and money, this desire may not become 'demand' for some time. The important thing is that travel is habit forming and thus it feeds upon itself. With the conversion of non-travellers there is an ever-widening pool from which repeaters will come. The very act of satisfying today's demand creates tomorrow's demand.

Presently the frequency is 0·5 or one trip every two years. This is an average, of course, including both the occasional or one-time traveller and the affluent 'jet set'. It will continue to increase with split vacations and weekend trips and will probably double between 1970 and 2000 to one trip per year and double again to two by 2050.

The overall growth rates these trends imply are fairly reassuring (*see* Table 20.5). Penetrating the 'non-traveller' market will inevitably slow down but this will not prevent traffic increases in excess of 10 per cent for the next 25 years and

Table 20.4

Participation in and Frequency of Travel

A Growth Model for International Pleasure Travel

Year	1950	1960	1970	1980	1990	2000	2010	2020	2030	2040	2050
Percent of population travelling	0·3	1·1	3·0	7·0	13·3	22·5	33·6	44·3	51·7	53·4	53·5
Average annual frequency	0·3	0·4	0·5	0·6	0·8	1·0	1·2	1·4	1·6	1·8	2·0
Trips as percent of population	0·1	0·5	1·6	4·6	10·9	22·5	40·3	62·5	83·8	97·2	106·9

some fairly respectable rates even thereafter, mostly coming from attracting to the travel market that sector of the population that has not travelled before (*see* Figure 20.3).

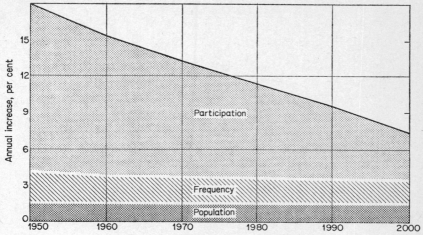

Figure 20.3 Growth rates by component

Table 20.5

Growth Rates by Component

Increase in travel due to increase in:	Annual percent increase				
	1950– 1960	1960– 1970	1970– 1980	1980– 1990	1990– 2000
Population	1·5	1·5	1·5	1·5	1·5
Participation in travel	12·0	10·5	8·6	6·6	5·4
Frequency	2·4	2·2	2·2	2·2	2·0
Total*	16·5	14·5	12·5	10·5	9·0

*Factors multiplied, i.e. $101·5 \times 112·0 \times 102·4 = 116·5\%$

These assumed rates (the rates of participation and the rate of frequency) do not seem unreasonable; therefore, we hope the forecast based on them is also attainable and possibly even conservative.

We have been talking primarily about travel by US residents abroad. Part of our international carriers' business comes, however, from foreign residents visiting the US and, to a lesser degree, foreign residents travelling to third countries.

For many decades after the saturation of the US market, growing demand for pleasure travel by foreign residents will, at least in part, take up the slack. In countries representing two-thirds of the world's population foreign air travel for pleasure is virtually non-existent (*see* Table 20.6).

Table 20.6

Foreign pleasure trips by air

Country or Area	Total No. of Trips Per Thousand Population In 1968	No. of Overseas Trips Per Thousand Population In 1968	No. of Intra-Continental Trips/Thousand Population In 1968
United States	13	11	2
Western Europe	14	4	10
Canada	11	9	2
Australia	7	7	–
Japan	3	3	–
South America	2	1	1
Rest of the World	1	0·3	0·7

It might be another 100 years before the rest of the world will reach what will be then the participation rate in the US. Only then will the uptrend for the industry level off and traffic grow no faster than the Gross National Product.

Travel Versus Automobiles

While our industry is unique, a comparison with the development of another industry holds some interesting clues. The automobile industry was chosen as the private automobile is the only other non-essential item in the household budget on which the annual expenditure is comparable to that of a foreign trip. (We will make due allowance for the differences in the degree to which they are 'essential'.)

The basic fact that emerges from a comparison of automobile ownership and participation in international travel is that the automobile has penetrated its market three times faster (*see* Figure 20.4). In other words, it takes air transportation three times longer from its beginnings to reach the same level of penetra-

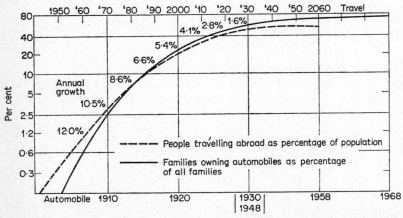

Figure 20.4 Growth cycles – automobile ownership *v.* foreign travel

tion as the automobile. This is perfectly understandable, if we consider that the private automobile is regarded almost as a necessity (and to many it is) while foreign pleasure travel is a luxury.

The similarity in the shape of the two growth curves is evident. The small divergence in the early years is due to the fact that commercial aviation was better and longer established in the somewhat arbitrarily chosen initial year, 1940, than the automobile industry in 1900. The higher ultimate penetration of automobile stems partly from the more essential nature of the product and partly from the fact that automobile ownership is per family while foreign trips are divided by the entire population that includes non-travelling children and old people.

Two interesting and significant facts are revealed by the figure. The first is that we are now where the automobile industry was in 1910. The other is that the maturing of an industry is a slow and gradual process that has already begun in our case but will not be completed for another half century. (Analysing the figure, a few things should be noted. First, a logarithmic scale is used so a straight line would represent the same per cent growth rather than the same absolute growth. Therefore, a declining per cent growth is not necessarily inconsistent with increasing increments in absolute terms. In fact, it is only in the year 2020 that the annual growth decreases even in absolute numbers. Secondly, two time scales are superimposed on one another to facilitate visual comparison. Thirdly, the years 1930 to 1948 for automobiles were skipped as there was no growth in this period. Lastly and obviously, while the automobile line is actual, most of the air travel line is projection.)

Having sold most people who could be expected to buy it on foreign travel or most families on automobile is not the end of the growth cycle. The second or third air trip in a year, just as the second or third car in the family, can sustain growth for decades past the 'primary saturation' (*see* Figure 20.5). The

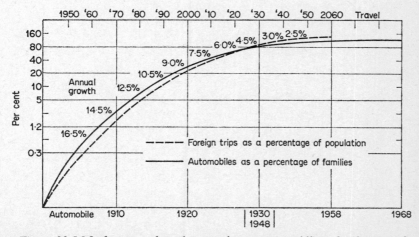

Figure 20.5 Market growth and saturation – automobile *v.* foreign travel

closeness of the fit is even more remarkable than in the previous figure. Here, however, the airline industry lags slightly in the early period, but exceeds the growth rate of the automobile industry in maturity. The reason for this is that while the number of cars per owner family has only gone from 1·0 to 1·7, the annual frequency of trips moves from 0·3 to 2·0 and need not stop even there. The nature of our service is such that the 'replacement cycle' that limits the growth of most mature goods producing industries, is singularly elastic. The ultimate in 'planned obsolescence' is inherent in our service.

Summary

Our forecasting starts with an examination of the relationship between, on the one hand, a number of economic, social, and demographic variables and various aspects of the product the airline industry offers (price, speed, comfort, schedule, etc.) and, on the other, international air travel. Next, we project these economic and social trends, or, rather, use projections published by authoritative sources. If the relationship is not expected to change, the two produce a trend forecast for travel. All this is done in three parts: pleasure travel by US residents, pleasure travel by foreign residents, and business travel. (We have concentrated only on the first in this paper.) Short term or one-time influences, such as Expo, Olympics, or US bi-centennial celebrations, are superimposed on these trends.

As a check on the reasonableness of the result, we then looked at foreign travel from another point of view: what per cent of the population participates and how frequently and what do projected growth rates imply for these two key elements. If we are approaching the saturation point, the abrupt drop in growth rates, found in most other long range forecasts, is justified. This was not the case; rather, saturation in travel and the 'maturing' of the industry is seen as a slow and gradual process, to take place over a hundred-year period, of which only twenty have passed.

For yet another check, the growth model for international travel is compared with the growth cycles of other industries and with that of the automobile industry in particular.

The forecast based on the growth model thus represents three independent projections in one, all three mutually supporting and re-enforcing one another. One is based on conventional correlations, one on an analysis of the demand by its components, and one on typical product life cycles.

Growth rates will be, as they always have been, uneven, both in time, from year to year, and in place, from area to area. There will be important shifts both among the originating countries and, especially, among the destinations.

Finally, the industry is beset by problems that have to be solved if this tremendous potential is to be realized. Besides the obvious one of profit squeeze due to rising costs, we have mentioned some of them earlier, especially the congestion associated with all phases of travel. But I am not here today to talk about our problems or my pet solution to them, much as I find it hard to resist the temptation to do just that.

Instead, my purpose was to put these ills and difficulties in the proper perspective, and warn you against allowing them to obscure the basic health of the industry and the uniquely durable nature of its good fortunes, assuring it a very bright future indeed.

Index

ABCs, *see* Advance Booking Charters
APEX, 116
Abrams, M., 80–5
Accommmodation
  investment, 211–12
  requirements of overseas tourists, 187
Advance Booking Charters, 114
African States
  tourist expenditure, 41
Air cargo, 112
Air Ministry, 18
Air transport, 17–19, 207
  airline offices, 144
  charter flights, 122–3
  competition, 141, 143
  forecasting, 215–29
  frequency related to income, 216–18
  national airline potential, 44
Aircraft Transport and Travel Ltd, 18
Alliance Internationale de Tourisme, 16
Amenity budget, 168–71
American tourists, 6, 17, 21–2
Amsterdam, 193
  hotel development, 194
Apseridis, G., 198
Argentina, 208
  expenditure on foreign travel, 31
Armstrong, C. W. G., 183, 201
Artus, J. R., 48
Associated Hotels, 106
Atelier Parisien d'Urbanisme, 201
Australia, 22
  expenditure on foreign travel, 31
Austria, 21, 22, 184, 205
  growth rate, 37
  tourist expenditure, 39

Bahamas, 40
Balance of Payments, 37, 38

Balearic Islands, 120
Bali, 211
Bank Holidays, 16
Basel, 19
Bath, 5
Beckerman, W., 50
Beeching Report, 77
Belgium, 205
  self-catering holidays, 65
Belgrade, 21
Berlage, 194
Bermuda, 134
  tourist expenditure, 40
Binder, Hamlyn, Fry & Co., 188, 201
Blue Train, 20
Bonne Chaine, 107
Bonsor, N. R. P., 17
Boyd-Carpenter, Lord, 111–19
Brand, Thomas, 8
Brazil, 208
  expenditure on foreign travel, 31
Brighton, 6, 7, 12
  restaurateurs' co-operation, 100
British European Airways, 140–3
British Hotels and Restaurants Association, 104
British Motel Federation, 101
British Rail, 77
  co-operative activities with hoteliers, 99
British Tourist Authority, 61–8, 182, 185, 201
  nationality surveys, 185
Brochures, 125
Brunner, Elizabeth, 23, 24
Brussels, 19
Buchanan, Colin, 164
Buckingham Palace, 188
Burkart, A. J., 120–7, 140–8
Buses, 20

Business travel, 34
Business visitors, 189
  see also Conference tourism
Butlin's Ltd, 23
Buxton, 5
Byrd, William, 151

CAA, *see* Civil Aviation Authority
Calais, 20
Camping Club of Great Britain, 23
Canada, 22, 205
  self-catering holidays, 68
Cannes, 13
Caribbean, 206, 207
Cars
  influence on tourism, 20, 33
  ownership by class, 80–1
  ownership by life-cycle stage, 81–3
  ownership trends, 80–5
  ownership *v.* foreign travel, 226–8
  use for leisure, 84–6
Cash and carry warehouses, 104
Caterers Association, 104
Central Bureau voor de Statistiek, 193,
  201
Central reservation systems, 102
Ceylon, 42
Changing of the Guard, 188
Cheltenham, 5, 7
Chile, 208
China, 208
Civil Aviation, 111–19
  profitable growth, 113
  see also Air transport
Civil Aviation Authority, 117, 118
Clements, H. G., 41
Coaches, 20
Colley, G., 35
Collier, Price, 15
Cologne, 19
Colonial Williamsburg Foundation, 153,
  155
Commissariat du Tourisme, 196, 198
Committee on Holidays with Pay, 23
Concorde, 115
Conference tourism, 189
  in France, 197–8
  in the Netherlands, 195
Congestion, 188–9, 221

Conservation, 151–74
Continental travel, 12–14, 19
Cook, Hartley Kemball, 16
Cook, Thomas, 11
  cross-Channel traffic, 14
Co-operation in hotels and catering,
  99–108
Co-operative Holidays Association, 16,
  23, 24
Cosgrave, I., 182, 201
Côte d'Azur, 20
Coxe, William, 8
Credit facilities, 96
Crete, 199
Crew utilization, 76
Cross-Channel traffic, 14, 19
Crusades, 3
Customs and Excise, 7
Cyclists' Touring Club, 16
Cyprus, 120

Dallington, Sir R., 4
Davis, H. D., 35, 43
Davison, Sir Ronald, 24
de Beer, Sir Gavin, 8
de Clifford, Lady, 9
Defert, Pierre-P., 13, 16
Deflation, 46
Demand elasticity, 74–5
Demography, 32
Denmark, 205
  self-catering holidays, 62, 66
Derby, 11
Design, 140–8
Devaluation of sterling, 47–8, 185
Developing countries, 40–4, 205–14
  tourist facilities, 210–11
Development areas, 179
Development Boards, 179
Development of resources, 160–74
  options, 167–8
Development of Tourism Act (1969),
  179, 187, 190
Diamond, P., 43
Domestic tourism, 28
Dominican Republic, 31
Donegal, 162–73
Dower, M., 160–74
Duchemin Agencies, 16

East African Tourist Travel Association, 43
Economic factors, 27–50
Economic significance, 27
Eden, Sir John, 177–81
Education, 220
   effects on tourism, 32
English Tourist Board, 62, 179, 190, 201–2
Environmental pollution, 113–14
Erdi, Louis, 183, 202
Ethnic factors, 221
Europe, 205
   balance on travel account, 36
European Economic Community, 189
Excelsior Hotel, 95
Exchange rates, 48
Expansion of tourism, 34
Expenditure
   on domestic tourism, 28
   on international tourism, 28–32

Fares
   anomalies in air transport, 117
   co-operation to reduce costs, 77–9
   elasticity, 219–20
   international regulation, 115
   levels, 114
   see also Advance Booking Charters; Transport costs
Fiji, 208
Finland, 37
Flanders, 20
Food preferences, 91–3
Foreign exchange, 212–13
Foreign holidays, 120–2
Frames' Tours Ltd, 16
France, 6, 20, 184, 195–8, 205
   destination of foreign tourists, 196
   self-catering holidays, 62
Franchises, 101
Fraser, Drummond, 23
Friendship Inns, 107

Galeotti, I. E., 44
Gerakis, A. S., 48
Germany, 20, 205
   self-catering holidays, 62
   travel account deficit, 37, 39

Gibraltar, 20
Giffen, Sir Robert, 73
Glasgow, 11
Goldstrom, J., 18
Government policy, 177–81
Grand Tour, 4
Gray, H. P., 42
Great Exhibition, 11
Great Western, 14
Greater London Council, 188, 202
Greece, 120, 184, 198–200
   growth rates, 37, 39
   tourist expenditure, 39
Gross National Product, 206
Gross travel propensity, 53–8
Guernsey, 19
Gulati, I., 41
Guneratue, D. P., 42

Hague, The, 195
Hall, J., 4
Hamilton, J. G., 35
Handley Page Ltd, 18
Harrogate, 5
Harrop, J., 34–50
Hawaii, 41
Henry, Patrick, 151
Historic Hotels of Britain, 101
Holiday camps, 23
Holland, 20
Homburg, 13
Hong Kong, 209
Hoorn, 193
Horizon Holidays Ltd, 124, 125
Hotel and Catering Economic Development Committee, 185, 202
Hotel and catering industry, 99–108
Hotel Development Incentives Scheme, 138, 177, 187, 190
Hotels, 187
   French provision, 196–8
   group marketing, 105–7
   in Greece, 199
   in London, 190
   international co-operation, 107
   lists, 12
Hurd, Bishop, 4

IATA, *see* International Air Transport Association

IT, 116, 117, 126
Imperial Airways, 19
Inclusive tours, 122
  mail order marketing, 125
  marketing, 124–6
  see also IT
Income
  expenditure on holidays, 72–4
  elasticity, 217
India, 19
Indonesia, 208
Industrial Revolution, 7
  influence on tourism, 9
Information centres, 154, 155
Inter Hotels, 101, 105–7
  France, 107
Interchange Hotels, 101, 105–7
International Air Transport Association,
  115, 116, 215
International Labour Organization, 212
International Monetary Fund, 185
International Passenger Survey, 185
International tourism, 182–201
  factors affecting growth, 183
  types, 184
International Union of Official Organ-
  izations for Tourist Propaganda, 22
International Union of Official Travel
  Organizations, 27–33, 34, 222
Ireland, 161–73
  tourist expenditure, 39
Israel, 213
  tourist expenditure, 40
Istanbul, 20
Italy, 20, 21, 184, 205
  Adriatic coast, 120
  expenditure on foreign travel, 31
  self-catering holidays, 62, 65
  tourist expenditure, 39
  travel surplus, 37

Jacks, L. P., 153
Jackson, R., 182, 201
Japan, 205
  expenditure on foreign travel, 31
Jefferson, Thomas, 151
Jugoslavia, *see* Yugoslavia

Kenya, 213
  tourist expenditure, 40, 41

Kerkira, 199
Kershaw, A. G., 3–24, 35
Koch, A., 55
Korea, 208
Kotler, P. H., 134
Krippendorf, J., 131

Labour – intensity, 42
Lake District, 167
Laker, Freddie, 118
Lakes Travel Association, 101
League of Nations, 21
Lebanon, 31
Leisure, 84–5
  effects on tourism, 32–3
  spent in travel, 218–19
Leningrad, 21
Lennard, R., 5
Le Roux, Pierre, 57
Lesbos, 199
Lesotho, 208
Levitt, K., 41
Libya, 31
Lickorish, L. J., 3–24, 35, 49, 183, 202
Liverpool & Manchester Railway, 10
Local Authorities, 100
Local Employment Act, 179
Locke, John, 4
London, 184, 185
London Tourist Board, 185, 202
Longden, J. P., 89–98
Loughborough, 11
Lunn, Sir Henry, 16, 24

McCarthy, P. E., 160–74
McGaskey, T. G., 151–9
Maddison, A., 39, 41
Maison, P., 182–201
Malagasy, 208
Malawi, 208
Margate, 7, 9
Marken, 193
Market research, 135
  in Williamsburg, 156
Marketing, 131–9
  co-operative, 100–3
Mauritius, 208
Mediterranean, 196, 206, 207
Medlik, S., 131–9

Meister, Leonard, 8
Merigo, E., 49
Mexico, 206, 213
   tourist expenditure, 40
Middle Ages, 3
Middleton, V. T. C., 131–9
Milton, John, 4
Mishan, E. J., 50
Mitchell, F., 41, 43, 50
Monaco, 13
Mont Blanc, 8
Morison, Fynes, 3
Morocco, 40, 41
Moscow, 21
Murray, Ian, 200, 202

Nash, (Richard) Beau, 5
National Cyclists' Union, 16
National Institute for Physical Planning
   & Construction Research, 162
National Parks, 160
Net travel prospensity, 53–8
Netherlands, 184, 193–5, 205
   self-catering holidays, 62
   travel account deficit, 39
New Caledonia, 208
Newman, G., 215–29
Nice, 6, 13, 20
Noise pollution, 113–14
North Africa, 20
Norval, A. J., 3, 17, 22
Nottingham, 100–1
Norway, 66

Oliver, F. R., 46
Opportunity costs, 43
Organization for Economic Co-operation
   and Development, 182, 185, 202
Ostend, 19
Oxford, 185

Package tours, *see* Inclusive tours
Paid holidays, 15, 23
Paint, H. M., 35
Pakistan, 41
Palmer, T., 4
Pan-American Airways, 19, 215–29
Panic, M., 49
Paraguay, 208

Paris, 196
   air routes, 19
   hotels, 197
Peace Conference, Paris (1919), 18
Peladan, R., 127
Peters, M., 41
Pickering, J. F., 99–108
Pilgrimages, 3
Pimlott, J. A. R., 4, 5, 6, 7, 10, 12
Political instability, 221
Polytechnic Touring Association, 16
Polytechnic Tours, 24
Population, 219
Population concentration, 9–10
Portugal
   growth rate, 37
   tourist expenditure, 39
Potter, S., 49
Prebisch thesis, 40
Prestige Hotels, 101, 105–7
Puerto Rico, 209

Quaedvlieg, A. H. W., 195, 202
Quality of service, 75

Racine, P., 202
Railways, 10
   cheap fares, 15–16
   excursion trains, 11–12
   termini hotels, 12
Ramsgate, 7
Randolph, Peyton, 151
Raynaud, P., 202
Restaurants
   co-operative marketing, 103
Rhodes, 199
Rhodesia, 31
Richmond, 151
Rockefeller, John D., Jr., 151, 153
Roman civilization, 3
Romantic Movement, 8
Rotterdam, 195
Route traffic density, 76–7
Royal Albert Hall, 189
Royal Festival Hall, 189
The Royal Hotel Guide, 12
Russell, Richard, 6

Safavi, F., 202

St Katharine Docks redevelopment, 190
St Moritz, 8
Saturation point, 221
Sauer, W., 54
Scarborough, 7
Schmidhauser, H., 53–60
Scotland, 185, 187
Scottish Tourist Board, 62, 202
Seaside resorts, 5–6
  population increases, 12
Seasonality, 209–10
Selective Employment Tax, 180
Self-catering holidays, 61–8
  definition, 61
Services for tourists, 89–98
Shaftesbury, Lord, 4
Singapore, 208, 209
Sixteenth century travel, 3–4
Skytrain, 118
Socio-economic classes, 80
Somalia, 31
Souchon, M.-F., 202
Southampton, 19
Spain, 20, 120, 184, 213
  as cheap holiday area, 33
  growth rates, 39
  self-catering holidays, 62, 66
  tourist expenditure, 39
  travel surplus, 37
  UK tourists, 47–8
Spas, 5
Statistiek Vreemdelingenverkeer, 193
Steamships, 14–15
Stratford-upon-Avon, 185
Sunair Holidays Ltd, 125
Supersonic transport aircraft, 215
Sussex Resorts and Hotels Association, 100
Swaziland, 208
Sweden, 205
  self-catering holidays, 66
  travel account deficit, 37, 39
Switzerland, 6, 8–9, 21, 205
  growth rate, 37
  introduction of skiing and tobogganing, 16
  self-catering holidays, 7, 65
  travel behaviour of population, 56

TGC, 118
Tahiti, 208
Taylor, E. L., 20
Terminal facilities, 76
Thailand, 208
Torquay Leisure Hotels, 100
Tour operators, 122
Touring Club de France, 16
Tourism
  as a product, 132–3
  marketing, 131–9
Tourist authorities, 126–7
Tourist Boards, 179
Tourist expenditure, 208
Tourist offices, 22
Traffic congestion, 188
Transatlantic shipping, 14, 17
Transport costs, 71–2
  demand elasticity, 74–5
  factors influencing, 75–7
  see also Fares
Travel frequency, 54
Travel propensity, 53–60
Travel restrictions, 46, 221
Travel time, 72
Tulip Inns, 107
Tunbridge Wells, 5
Turkey, 40
Turler, J., 4
Twain, Mark, 14

Uganda, 43
United Kingdom, 184–7, 205
  balance of payments on travel account, 45
  catering for tourists, 93–4
  destination of overseas visitors, 185, 187
  self-catering holidays, 65–6
  tourist economics, 44–9
  visitors taking self-catering holidays, 66, 68
United Nations Conference on Trade & Development, 213
United Nations Development Programme, 212
United States of America, 14–15, 205
  expenditure on foreign travel, 31
  self-catering holidays, 68

United States of America–*cont.*
  tourist offices, 22
  travel deficit, 40
University accommodation, 189
Uruguay, 208

Vanhove, N., 57
Vehicle load factor, 76
Vehicle size, 76
Vehicle utilization, 76
Virgin Islands, 209

Wales, 187
Wales Tourist Board, 62
Walpole, Horace, 8
Washington, George, 151
Weesperzidje, 194
West Germany, 184
West Indies, 40
West Midlands Tourist Board, 62
Westminster Abbey, 188

Weymouth, 6
Wheatcroft, S., 71–9, 215
Wiesbaden, 13
Williamsburg, 151–9
  restoration, 152
Wimperis, H. E., 18–19
Workers' Travel Association, 24
Working conditions, 32
World Bank, 205–14
World War I, 21

Young, Sir George, 185, 202
Young Tourism Study Group (1972), 188, 202
Youth Hostels Association, 23
Yugoslavia, 213
  growth rate, 37, 39
  tourist expenditure, 39

Zinder, H., 41
Zurich, 19